Health of Women with Intellectual Disabilities

Edited by

Patricia Noonan Walsh

National University of Ireland, Dublin

and

Tamar Heller

University of Illinois at Chicago

Blackwell
Science

© 2002 by Blackwell Publishing Company
Editorial Offices:
Osney Mead, Oxford OX2 0EL, UK
  Tel: +44 (0)1865 206206
108 Cowley Road, Oxford OX4 1JF, UK
  Tel: +44 (0) 1865 791100
Blackwell Publishing USA, 350 Main Street,
Malden, MA 02148-5018, USA
  Tel: +1 781 388 8250
Iowa State Press, a Blackwell Publishing Company,
2121 State Avenue, Ames, Iowa 50014-8300, USA
  Tel: +1 515 292 0140
Blackwell Munksgaard, Nørre Søgade
35, PO Box 2148, Copenhagen, DK-1016, Denmark
  Tel: +45 77 33 33 33
Blackwell Publishing Asia, 54
University Street, Carlton, Victoria 3053, Australia
  Tel: +61 (0)3 9347 0300
Blackwell Verlag, Kurfürstendamm 57, 10707
Berlin, Germany
  Tel: +49 (0)30 32 79 060

The right of the Author to be identified as
the Author of this Work has been asserted
in accordance with the Copyright, Designs and
Patents Act 1988.

First published 2002

A catalogue record for this title is available from the
British Library

ISBN 1-4051-0103-2

Library of Congress
Cataloging-in-Publication Data
is available

Set in 10/13 Palatino
by DP Photosetting, Aylesbury, Bucks
Printed and bound in Great Britain by
MPG Books Ltd, Bodmin, Cornwall

For further information on
Blackwell Publishing, visit our website:
www.blackwellpublishing.com

Dedication

To
Brendan, Colm, Nessa and Ben
and
Uri, Talya and Natalie

Contents

Contributors

Deborah J. Anderson PhD
Institute on Community Integration, University of Minnesota, Minneapolis, USA

Christine Bigby BA (Hons), MSocWk, PhD
Senior Lecturer, School of Social Work and Social Policy, LaTrobe University, Melbourne, Australia

Pamela Block PhD
Centre for Alcohol and Addiction Studies, Brown University, Providence, Rhode Island, USA

Allison A. Brown BA
Rehabilitation Research and Training Center on Aging with Developmental Disabilities, University of Illinois at Chicago, USA

Margaret Flynn BA (Hons), CQSW, PhD
Senior Lecturer, Department of Psychiatry of Disability, St George's Hospital Medical School, London, UK

Carol J. Gill PhD
Department of Disability and Human Development, University of Illinois at Chicago, USA

Susan M. Havercamp PhD, Licensed Clinical Psychologist
Clinical Assistant Professor, Center for Development and Learning, University of North Carolina at Chapel Hill, USA

Tamar Heller PhD
Professor and Interim Head, Department of Disability and Human Development, University of Illinois at Chicago, USA

Sheila Hollins MBBS, FRCPsych, FRCPCH
Professor and Head of Department of Psychiatry of Disability, St George's Hospital Medical School, London, UK; Consultant Psychiatrist in Learning Disabilities and Senior Policy Advisor, Department of Health (England)

Mike Kerr MBChB, MSc, MRCGP, MRCPsych
Senior Lecturer in Neuropsychiatry, Welsh Centre for Learning Disabilities, University of Wales College of Medicine, Cardiff, UK

Henny M.J. Van Schrojenstein Lantman-de Valk MD, PhD
Physician for people with learning disabilities, Echt, Netherlands; Researcher, Department of General Practice, Maastricht, Netherlands

Yona Lunsky PhD
Assistant Professor, Department of Psychiatry, University of Toronto, Canada; Psychologist, Centre for Addiction and Mental Health, Toronto, Canada

Beth Marks RN, PhD
Assistant Director, Rehabilitation Research and Training Center on Aging with Developmental Disabilities, University of Illinois at Chicago, USA

Mary McCarron RNMH, RGN, BNS (Hons)
PhD student in the School of Nursing and Midwifery Studies, University of Dublin, Trinity College, Ireland

Michelle McCarthy BA (Hons), BPhil/CQSW, MA, PhD
Senior Lecturer in Learning Disability, Tizard Centre, University of Kent, Canterbury, UK

Glynis Murphy BA, MSc, PhD, CPsychol, FBPsS
Professor of Clinical Psychology of Learning Disability, Tizard Centre, University of Kent, Canterbury, UK

Susan L. Parish PhD
Postdoctoral Fellow, Waisman Center, University of Wisconsin, Madison, USA

Kristiina Patja MD PhD
Tobacco and Health Co-ordinator, Public Health Institute, Helsinki, Finland

Nicole Schupf PhD, MPH, DrPH
Laboratory of Epidemiology, New York State Institute for Basic Research in Developmental Disabilities, Staten Island, New York, USA; Gertrude H. Sergievsky Center, Columbia University College of Physicians and Surgeons, New York, USA

Kathryn Pekala Service MS, RNC/NP, CDDN
Nurse Practitioner, Franklin-Hampshire Area Office, Massachusetts, USA; Department of Mental Retardation, Northampton, Massachusetts, USA

Patricia Noonan Walsh PhD
NDA Professor of Disability Studies, National University of Ireland, Dublin, Ireland

Series Foreword

Health of Women with Intellectual Disabilities introduces a new series of publications associated with the International Association for the Scientific Study of Intellectual Disabilities (IASSID). These publications are designed to address the issue of health, adult development, and aging among persons with intellectual disabilities. Originally a health policy initiative undertaken by the IASSID at the behest of the World Health Organization, this initiative has grown to become a major effort, undertaken by the members of IASSID, to explore a number of topics related to health and aging. It has also evolved into worldwide effort to promote research and practice designed to improve longevity and promote healthy aging of people with lifelong disabilities among the world's nations.

This compilation of chapters from many of the world's leading researchers and practitioners in the area of women's health and disability, is the first in this series. The editors and contributing authors of this text recognized that the inequities in national health policies and services as they affect women with lifelong disabilities seriously impair good health and successful aging. Because of this, they decided to compile a text that would begin to examine a host of issues and facts related to service access and health promotion for women with disabilities. The editors have chosen wisely and the number of topics that are explored show the range of concerns confronting women as they age. It is anticipated that these papers will enable health services administrators and practitioners to become more aware of the barriers faced by women with disabilities, and provide for more accessible and available services.

It is hoped that as the IASSID, as a non-governmental organization, continues to contribute to the worldwide interest and better understanding of the circumstances of people with intellectual disabilities and their conditions, this series will, in part, serve as a catalyst and contributor to the improvement of life conditions and our understanding of adult development and aging as related to lifelong disability.

Matthew P. Janicki, PhD
Series Editor
University of Illinois at Chicago
Department of Disability and Human Development
College of Health and Human Development Sciences
Chicago, Illinois, USA

Foreword

The ideal of equality is the touchstone on which the guarantees of international human rights law have been built. Its corollary is the principle of non-discrimination. The story of the international human rights movement, which covers the last half of the twentieth century, has largely been about the struggle to advance the ideal of equality through the elimination of all forms of discrimination. It is neither an easy struggle nor one that produces immediate results.

In the early years discrimination and disability – including the particular vulnerability and needs of persons with intellectual disabilities – was a neglected subject as compared to other forms of discrimination. That neglect has gradually been reversed. The treatment of the disabled has come to be recognised as involving questions of rights rather than exclusively social, humanitarian or welfare considerations.

Change can be dated from the influences that flowed from the UN International Year of Disabled Persons, 1981. From that Year we got the widespread adoption of full participation and equality as the overall goal in the disability field. The World Programme of Action concerning Disabled Persons, adopted by the General Assembly in 1982, spelled out what should happen if that goal was to be realised. Not much did happen, in fact, to change attitudes towards disability.

However, using this foundation, standard rules were elaborated and unanimously adopted by the General Assembly in its resolution 58/96 of 20 December 1993. The standard rules represented progress in that they were more concentrated and concrete in form. They also addressed more directly the issue of member states' responsibility. Most significant was the establishment of an independent and active monitoring mechanism on implementation of the rules – a special rapporteur within the framework of the Commission for Social Development.

The culmination of these developments came with the Declaration of the Vienna World Conference on Human Rights in 1993. That placed disabled persons, and their active participation in all aspects of society, explicitly in a human rights context: 'all human rights and fundamental freedoms are universal and thus unreservedly include persons with disabilities'.

It is against this backdrop, of standard setting and inclusion of disability perspectives in the human rights agenda, that this text on health of women with intellectual disabilities has been produced. I welcome its publication, as indeed I welcome the repeated opportunities I am granted, as UN High Commissioner for Human Rights, to reaffirm the importance of placing the issue of disability, and in particular the issue of intellectual disabilities, in a human rights context. For, in practice, it is unfortunately still the case that many people, and in particular those with intellectual disabilities, are unable to live full lives in equality and free from suffering. Whether such experiences are purposely inflicted or arise from neglect does not matter – we must continue to remind authorities and society that persons with intellectual disabilities are entitled to the same basic human rights as all others, and strive to ensure their attainment.

Persons with intellectual disabilities belong to the most vulnerable sections of society, and as such, are owed special care and attention by governments. It is regrettable that the mentally ill often do not receive that attention. The particular difficulties faced by women, and particularly older women, in this context must also be recognised. This important book will help that recognition. As life expectancy increases, health and quality of life are becoming an ever more pressing concern. The challenge is to ensure that these lives are lived out in the dignity to which we are all equally entitled.

Mary Robinson
United Nations High Commissioner for Human Rights

Acknowledgements

Preparation of the chapters and writings by Anderson, by Gill and Brown and by Heller and Marks was supported in part by the Rehabilitation Research and Training Center on Aging with Developmental Disabilities, Department of Disability and Human Development, University of Illinois at Chicago through the US Department of Education National Institute on Disability and Rehabilitation Research, Grant No. H133B980046. The Heller and Marks chapter was also funded by the Roybal Center on Health Maintenance through a grant from the National Institute on Aging, Grant No. AG15890-12.

In respect of the chapter by McCarron and Pekala Service, Mary McCarron acknowledges the financial support of the Health Research Board, Dublin, Ireland, by way of a Clinical Fellowship in Nursing and Midwifery Studies which was awarded to her.

Partial support for the preparation of the 1999 10th International Roundtable on Aging and Intellectual Disblilities held in Geneva was provided by grant 1R13 AG15754-01 from the National Institute on Aging, Bethesda, Maryland USA to M. Janicki (PI).

Patricia Noonan Walsh thanks her colleagues in the Centre for the Study of Developmental Disabilities, and her fellow psychologists at the National University of Ireland, Dublin – especially Alan Carr – for their instrumental and affective support.

Editorial assistance from Leslie Chapital in Chicago and Richard Molloy in Dublin is gratefully acknowledged.

Introduction
Women's Health

People alive at the start of the twenty-first century may expect to live longer lives than previous generations. While those born in wealthier, more industrialized countries may live longer, life expectancy is also on the increase in countries still developing. What is less certain is whether more opportunities will translate into richer life accomplishments – health, productivity, self-determination, and satisfying relationships with family members and friends. Health is increasingly viewed as a human right expressed in each society so that all citizens have equal opportunities to healthy living throughout their lives. A vast array of regions and political and cultural environments exerts constraints and presents diverse opportunities for health outcomes. But individuals are not merely silent partners governed by overwhelming environmental forces: they do and must contribute to their own health.

Gender has specific influences on health across the life course, as does the socioeconomic climate of people's lives. Thus, the magnitude and explanations of gender differences in socioeconomic status (SES) inequalities in health are likely to vary according to life stage as well as to the measures used (Matthews *et al.*, 1999). But these lenses of health and socioeconomic status have rarely focused on women with intellectual disability. As a consequence, detail about their lives as young, middle-aged or older adults is blurred. The first aim of this book is to cast light on the place where these domains intersect, to consider the needs and opportunities for women with intellectual disabilities as they emerge over the course of their adult lives in their homes and communities. A further aim is to gather evidence to inform women themselves, their family members and advocates, professional workers and policy-makers so that each can act in concert to promote healthy aging for this distinctive group of women.

Various terms are used to define the target population at the heart of this book. While in the United Kingdom 'learning disabilities' is preferred, this term has an entirely different meaning in the rest of the world, where it refers to individuals who have disorders of memory, auditory or visual perception of language and thinking. Mindful of cross-cultural differences in tradition and usage, the editors of this book have used 'intellectual disability' to express a state of functioning manifested before adulthood characterized by substantial limitations in the individual's present cognitive and adaptive functioning. While the editors acknowledge the use of 'disabled people' in the advocacy and research communities in some countries, they have adopted 'people first' language throughout the book – 'people with disabilities'. In addition, some contributors refer to the influence of ethnicity on the experiences of women with intellectual disabilities – for example, among those of African heritage.

This book addresses the health of women with intellectual disabilities from multiple disciplinary perspectives – medicine, psychology, education, public health, sociology, anthropology and nursing. It elaborates on and extends a program of collaborative research carried out by the WHO and the Special Interest Research Group on Aging within the International Association on the Scientific Study of Intellectual Disability (IASSID) culminating in a set of reports presented at the 11th World Congress of IASSID in Seattle in August 2000 (WHO, 2001).

Some chapters in this book explore the context of health to identify the cultural, economic and social factors that may thwart or enhance women's health. Others chart the terrain of health status and trends relating to women with intellectual disabilities. Finally, others propose best practices and public policies that promote health – either by changing the environment or by supporting individuals to enhance personal competencies and performance.

The context of health

The widest research lens encompasses the set of controls in the political, cultural and socioeconomic environments helping to determine health outcomes of women with intellectual disabilities. If gender determines health, it does so within the specific environments where women live. In Chapter 1 Walsh adopts a global perspective on the economic, cultural and social contexts of lifelong health for women with intellectual disabilities as they mature into middle and older adulthood.

Women with intellectual disabilities have specific health risks in comparison with men with intellectual disabilities and in comparison with other women. In Chapter 2 van Schrojenstein Lantman-de Valk and her colleagues lay the foundation of the book by documenting what is known about the physical and reproductive health of women with intellectual disability. The comprehensive chapter combines clinical data from experienced clinicians and epidemiological research to provide a look at the unique aspects of health among these women with disabilities.

In Chapter 3 Anderson delineates the health risks for women with intellectual disabilities using data gleaned from a national representative sample, the US National Health Interview Survey Disabilities Supplement. She examines how age, gender, disability and poverty combine to compound health risks.

Health status and trends

In Chapter 4 Lunsky and Havercamp critically apply the findings of available research literature related to the mental health of women in general to women with intellectual disabilities, generating a timely and challenging research agenda.

Yesterday's experiences also fuel today's ethical dilemmas. In Chapter 5, Block analyzes cultural historical evidence from Brazil and raises perplexing issues related to contemporary debates about genetics, bioethics and eugenics as these impact on the lives of women with intellectual disabilities.

In Chapter 6, McCarthy explores incisively yet with sensitivity some aspects of women's sexuality – at the core of personal identity and yet often denied to women in this group.

What happens when human rights expressed in personal preferences – to become a parent, for instance – encounter social controls and cultural biases? In Chapter 7 Parish focuses on the sociopolitical context and challenges of parenting among women with intellectual disabilities.

To extend the context of health in terms of social relationships, in Chapter 8 Bigby explores the social realm of women with intellectual disabilities, defining the social roles they play and the various social supports, both personal and instrumental, within their grasp.

Promoting health

Given the complex environmental factors governing their lives, what measures can best promote health among women with intellectual disabilities? A key theme is for women themselves to be personally engaged in efforts to reflect on and to promote their own health throughout their adult lives. In Chapter 9 Gill and Brown give a voice to women with intellectual disabilities by examining their perspectives regarding their health care needs, experiences and concerns. They point to the pressing need for more education of adults with intellectual disabilities, their carers, and health professionals regarding the specific health of women with intellectual disabilities.

Greater self-direction, no matter how desirable, may also expose women with intellectual disabilities to deleterious experiences such as abuse in the community. In Chapter 10 Walsh and Murphy raise issues to be resolved and suggest strategies to balance autonomy and risk.

In Chapter 11 Heller and Marks give an account of the evidence building to suggest that interventions aimed at enhancing women's physical health through nutrition and exercise programs and improved health care practices also yield benefits for their sense of mastery and self-direction and health outcomes.

In a chapter with a nursing perspective, Chapter 12, McCarron and Pekala Service acknowledge the traditional caring role of nurses who are often the mainstay of formal support for women with intellectual disabilities. The authors identify a host of practical considerations essential to promoting women's health based on current research evidence.

Effective health education for women must be targetted at their distinctive requirements. In chapter 13 Flynn and Hollins chart strategies for effective guidance and education linked to recent health policy directives in the UK. These authors focus on a key theme – that successful initiatives will recognize more similarities than differences in the health needs of people with intellectual disabilities.

Women's health is interwoven with that of the men with whom they share their everyday lives. Where women do not participate fully in political and social life, both the men and the women in that region are more likely to experience disadvantages leading to poorer health (Matthews *et al.*, 1999). While focused on the health of women with intellectual disabilities, the tone of this book does not diminish the importance of attending to that of men. On the contrary, Kerr's chapter on men's health, Chapter 14, is welcomed not as a full stop, but rather as a bridge to future exploration of the health status and needs of both men and women with intellectual disabilities.

References

Matthews, S., Manor, O. & Power, C. (1999) Social inequalities in health: are there gender differences? *Social Science & Medicine*, **48**, 49–60.

WHO (2001) Healthy Ageing – Adults with Intellectual Disabilities: Summative Report. *Journal of Applied Research in Intellectual Disabilities*, **14**, 256–275.

Part 1
The Context of Health

Coffee break at the Senior Centre – Holland.

1 Women's Health: A Contextual Approach

Patricia Noonan Walsh

Introduction

'By 2025 there will be more than 800 million older people in the world, two-thirds of them in developing countries, and a majority of them will be women.'

(WHO, 1998: 101)

Older women will emerge during the present generation as standard bearers of the third age in rich and poor countries alike. Understanding how best to promote their healthy aging will reap benefits for them and for all citizens. Dramatic increases in life expectancy during the twentieth century have been due chiefly to tremendous advances in medicine, public health, science and technology. Yet inequalities are rife: the poorest, least educated people live shorter lives with greater ill health. Only 4.6% of people in the developing world are elderly, in contrast with 12.6% of the population of the more developed countries (WHO, 1995: 2). However, the quality of human life is as important as its length – perhaps even more important. Today, individuals are also concerned about their health expectancy, that is, the years they can expect to live in good health (WHO, 1997). To meet these expectations, governments must advance the health gain of all citizens: increase life expectancy, improve health during life and minimize disability. Living in good health means more than the absence of disease; it means that men and women are supported so as to adjust to their environments, to prosper and to make a contribution to the lives of others.

Global strategies for achieving healthy aging must take gender, as well as regional, differences into account (WHO, 1997). The human rights of women and girl children are an integral part of universal human rights, according to the United Nations Vienna Declaration. Ensuring their full and equal participation in all aspects of life in society, without discrimination of any kind, is a priority objective for the international community. Suitable medical and health care are essential prerequisites if people with disabilities are to enjoy equal opportunities in the societies where they live (UN, 1994). The WHO's Global Strategy on the promotion of women's health falls within this rights-based framework, recognizing that gender helps to determine health. A gender approach to health includes an analysis of how different social roles, decision-making power and access to resources affect health status and access to health care. The right of all women to the best attainable standard of health, as well as their right of access to adequate health services, are primary considerations worldwide (UN-OFCHR, 1997: 10).

This chapter adopts a global perspective on the economic, cultural and social contexts of lifelong health for women with intellectual disabilities as they mature into middle and older adulthood. It suggests that, first, health care providers must be mindful that women's social roles are related to their access to health resources, in order to respond effectively to the needs of women with intellectual disabilities as they age. Second, it is important to create a greater understanding of the distinctive health needs they experience across the lifespan as girls, and as young, middle-aged and older women. Third, as self-determination gathers force as a principle to guide interventions on behalf of people with intellectual disabilities, carers and providers seek effective ways to support women in shaping their own good health within their families and communities. Finally, strategies for practice, policy and research related to healthy aging for this population are proposed.

Cultural contexts

Health outcomes across cultures tell a complex story, albeit one with a familiar beginning: in most countries women outlive men. However, women can expect more years of living with disabilities. A larger group of older women live on to experience more years of life with lowered quality, often alone, because of their longer survival after the development of disability or handicap (Robine *et al.*, 1999). As women live longer than men the quality of their longer life becomes a matter of central importance. Women with intellectual disabilities also strive today for longer, healthier lives. Increased longevity and improved services of all kinds have led to an unprecedented growth in the population of persons with intellectual disabilities. It is estimated that as many as 60 million persons in the world may have some level of intellectual disability (WHO, 1997: Table 3). Today's older people with intellectual disabilities may emerge as survivors but nonetheless they have significant physical health needs throughout their adult lives (Cooper, 1998; van Schrojenstein Lantman-de Valk, 1998).

Gender and health

The links between gender and health are forged in the interactions between women's experiences and needs at each stage of the life span with their social, economic and cultural environments. Outcomes for women with intellectual disabilities may be especially at risk when compared with the fortunes of their peers or family members:

'It is in situations of dire poverty that household members are subjected to neglect, and people with disabilities are particularly vulnerable.'

(Whyte & Ingstad, 1998: 43)

Gender is also a determinant of health across the life span for the general population, at times exerting a lethal influence on health. Social conditions and cultural practices in some countries may compromise the greater longevity women might otherwise expect – if all things were indeed equal. But negative practices in infancy and less investment in the education and nutrition of girls and young women take their toll. Extreme disadvantage occurs in countries where tradition dictates that women may not attend male health professionals at all, or that a male family member must accompany them in order to access any health care, or where further education of any sort is denied to women. Inevitably these women lose in the competition for greater health gain.

Gender roles are expressed in particular social and economic settings. Traditionally, women with intellectual disabilities living in cultures where gender inequality prevailed were especially at risk of being excluded from full participation in everyday life. In addition, they missed the defining moments typically available in their cultures to young, middle-aged and older women. Today, in countries with well-established service systems, being a 'service-user' or 'consumer' may blunt the distinctive experiences at rites of passage across life span developmental stages typically experienced by other women (Walsh, 2000). In Ireland, for example, only a handful of women with intellectual disabilities may become parents, home owners or full-time employees. Gender roles co-exist with other social roles within the family and workplace. Gender roles emerge from the productive work of the sexes. Traditionally, men engage in wage labor and women in domestic labor. The characteristics that are required to perform sex-typical tasks become stereotypic of women or men - *communal* tasks are construed as feminine, and *agentic* tasks as masculine behaviors (Eagly & Wood, 1999). Throughout Europe, sheltered work remains the most typical employment option for men and women with intellectual disabilities, and many engage merely in group day activity programs without any work option. The fact that men and women with intellectual disabilities might not assume stereotypic roles is less a sign of enlightened management within sheltered workshops than an expression of the belief that they have incomplete gender identity relative to their peers.

Equal opportunities

Healthy aging does not flourish in a vacuum. Efforts to promote women's health and well-being are embedded in a complex interplay between individuals and their physical and social environments. The quality of daily life experienced by individuals reflects and contributes to the texture of the society in which they live. Providing political environments which foster healthy social relationships, trust, economic security, sustainable development and other factors related to advancing the health and well-being of citizens has been identified as a priority for governments. The quality of social relationships in a society has been documented as part of health outcomes. Healthier, cohesive communities are likely to have a beneficial impact on their citizens. These and other factors make up a country's social capital, an essential element if states are to achieve the priorities for effective health promotion which are listed in the Jakarta Declaration, such as increased investment in health development, particularly for needy groups (Cox, 1997: 3).

Contentious issues arise when financial resources for health care are rationed. These may fuel dilemmas for health care providers. For example, will people with Down syndrome who require heart and lung transplants find ready access to sophisticated medical treatments funded by government health insurance systems? Grappling with such complex and costly health care decisions is a luxury in most countries. Global health promotion means improved training of health professionals, continued research into new drugs and vaccines and the genetic determinants of chronic diseases and strategies for healthy living (WHO, 1997: 136). Priority areas for international action in health range from comprehensive efforts to diagnose and control disease to long-term treatment, palliative care and rehabilitation. Each of these investments can potentially advance the healthy aging of women with intellectual disabilities.

Success in gaining a good age depends on gender, relative prosperity and active policies of health promotion. But healthy aging also depends on equity in the delivery of health care – whether health and social systems are attuned to people's needs and whether all citizens can expect equal access to health care. To address the special needs of women, global priorities today target:

- Advocacy for women's health and gender-sensitive approaches to health care and delivery and development of practical tools to achieve this
- Promotion of women's health and prevention of ill-health
- Making health systems more responsive to women's needs
- Policies for improving gender equality
- Ensuring that women take part in the design, implementation and monitoring of health policies and programs

(WHO, 1997: 83)

Inequity in women's health

'Disadvantage may also arise when health resources are rationed so as to discriminate against women with disabilities, even in the more developed countries. In the US, the Center for Research on Women with Disabilities in Houston, Texas, highlighted these challenges in a national study. Of the 506 women with physical disabilities surveyed, 31% said a doctor had refused to see them because of their disability. In addition, 50% of women with spinal cord injuries said the hospital could not accommodate their disabilities during child-birth, and 23% reported that it was impossible to position mammography equipment for them. "We're written off because we have a disability," said Margaret Nosek, principal investigator of the study.'

(Abelson, 2000)

Human rights and policy

Human rights have supplanted welfare-based policies as the basis for actions related to the lives of persons with disabilities. In Western Europe, for example, social policy promoted by the European Union of 15 member countries endorses a rights-based model of disability to replace a traditional model based on providing enough care to compensate people whose impairments left them at a disadvantage. Today, human rights are expressed as equal opportunities for all citizens, particularly those with disabilities, to take part fully in all aspects of everyday life in their own societies (Commission of the European Communities, 1998). Accordingly, respect for human diversity should inform all aspects of social planning in each country.

Cultures are diverse in their treatment of women and of older people. It is to be expected that they will also vary in how well they perform in achieving outcomes related to the specific health needs of women with intellectual disabilities. Some common threads are revealed in all countries:

> 'Simply put, no country on this planet treats women as well as it does men. The best we can say is that some countries are not as bad as others.'

(Alvarez, 1999)

Against this ominous global setting, women must enact healthy lives using a script written to take account of their individual characteristics and needs. The next section introduces the risks to health incurred by women with intellectual disabilities at different stages of their lives.

Promoting health: the social context

The differential impact of gender on health is dynamic, expressed as an individual grows and develops throughout his or her life span. Some gender differences are apparent for particular groups of people with intellectual disabilities. Among those with a mild level of intellectual disability, a male bias is widely reported. But mild intellectual disability may itself be socially constructed in different ways as social adaptation is defined variously across cultures, with distinctive expectations for each gender. Not surprisingly, socioeconomic status and mild intellectual disability are complex interlocking factors (Slone et al., 1998). Gender differences are less apparent in the prevalence of severe intellectual disabilities. People in the latter group – both males and females – are likely to have associated disorders or biomedical conditions. Individuals in this group display greater diversity in their social and economic backgrounds (Hatton, 1998).

Women's health in Ireland

Policy-makers may embed the distinctive health needs of women throughout the life span in national health strategies. In Ireland, the Department of Health shaped a plan for women's health in consultation with many women and groups throughout the country. It rests on the premise that women with disabilities face particular challenges to their health – a dearth of information, limited access to services and special difficulties related to advice about sexual and reproductive health. This policy document recommends direct consultation with women who have disabilities in order to develop health services on their behalf.

(Government of Ireland, 1997: 63)

Many risks to health are age-related. Men die earlier, while women experience greater burdens of morbidity and disability. Women constitute the majority of both the carers and the older clients in the health sector. In many countries with greater life expectancy and formal service systems, households comprising a middle-aged adult who has intellectual disability and a mother in her seventies or eighties are commonplace (Walsh *et al.*, 1993). A timely challenge for health policy-makers is to find sustainable ways to support an enlarging cohort of female carers (WHO, 1995: 6.1.5).

Women's roles

At all ages, women with intellectual disabilities carry the developmental baggage of exaggerated dependency. As they move from childhood and adolescence into young adulthood, women in the general population reach for independence, deepen intimate attachments and find productive work in the family home and labor force. Gender identity may be dampened or overlooked entirely (Brown, 1996), even if the particular risks related to their sexuality are apparent (McCarthy & Thompson, 1998). The average age of a group of women in the US with intellectual disabilities who had been victims of sexual abuse – 72% of the sample surveyed – was 30 years.

Special health issues are important to women at different stages of their lives, no less so if they have an intellectual disability. Eating disorders have serious consequences for younger women. Adult women confront health problems related to sexually transmitted diseases, HIV and AIDS. And the rising incidence of osteoporosis among elderly women has become a chief concern for women in Europe (Commission of the European Communities, 1997). But while European women live on average up to about 80 years, many die prematurely before the age of 65 because of accidents or diseases that could largely be avoided by healthier living or early detection.

Friendships and social networks mitigate some of these risks, enhancing the health and well-being of women in the general population. As yet, the nature of this contribution in the lives of women with intellectual disabilities is less well understood. Adults with intellectual disabilities tend to name significantly fewer individuals and to have more dense social networks than other adults. Those who receive formal services describe networks filled largely by members of staff. In addition, their networks include rather more family members than friends – although men with intellectual disabilities are likely to include fewer friends. When asked to name their own friends, adults tend to name individuals who are friends of their parents or other family members. Krauss *et al.* (1992) studied the social support networks available to men and women aged 15–66 years with intellectual disabilities living with their parents. While both men and women had large, active and diverse networks with family members predominant, women were less at risk for social isolation.

Women with intellectual disabilities are not likely to marry, at least as documented in the more developed countries, or to enact gender roles that are typical in their cultural settings (see Chapter 3). Few bear children. As a consequence, they lack key sources of informal support and care in later life. While brothers and sisters play an important part in the development and well-being of adults with intellectual disabilities across the life span, little is known about the extent and function of such relationships; empirical studies are not widespread. Women with intellectual disabilities are also less likely to become primary family carers. Yet as populations age, those women who become middle-aged may be called on to care for an elderly or frail parent who has up to then provided care for them. Some questions are unresolved. For example, can respite care – an important element in formal care – help to maintain or promote health and well-being among women with intellectual disabilities, either directly or through its impact on family members? While empirical evidence suggests that adopting multiple social roles may help to protect women from threats to their well-being, women with intellectual disabilities are much less likely to have such varied life opportunities.

Women, work and health

Women's level of income, employment status and family circumstances reflect the socioeconomic context in which they live, and help to determine health outcomes. Differences in life expectancy, income and access to health care are conspicuous when outcomes for women in developing countries are compared to those in the less developed countries – where the majority of all persons with developmental disabilities live. While these topics have been explored among the general population to some extent, little empirical research is available concerning women with intellectual disabilities.

Being employed can have a favorable impact on employees' income, personal satisfaction, esteem, friendships and health. These benefits have been documented consistently in the more developed countries. While less is known about the impact of employment status on the health and well-being of adults with intellectual disabilities, this has been identified as an important area for continued research (WHO, 2000). In addition, health conditions may impede access to employment. Women with intellectual disabilities are likely to be obese and this may act as a barrier to successful employment (see Chapter 11). It has been reported in Australian and North American studies that women with intellectual disabilities in community employment are more likely to experience loneliness at work than men do. Outcome data gathered in the US indicates that women with disabilities earn less income than men and are likely to be employed in stereotypically feminine jobs (Olson *et al.*, 2000). Issues related to the wider impact of employment on the personal and social experiences of women with intellectual disabilities have not been investigated systematically and across cultures. More evidence, too, is required about the impact on women of entry to the labor force, and their career prospects, patterns of employment and uptake of social benefits and other income transfers.

Some employment outcomes are less benign. While employment may bring benefits in terms of income, self-esteem and community participation, it may not be without hazard. People with intellectual disabilities may be likely to perform unskilled work, and to do so in environments where risks to health arise from exposure to toxic substances used in industry. Many occupational diseases can be prevented through improvements to the work environment and reduction of harmful exposure to toxins and other substances. For example, silicosis is common in many dust-generating activities such as ceramics, prompting a joint ILO-WHO initiative planned to eliminate this disease. It is not known whether, over time, occupational hazards will have a deleterious impact on the health of women with disabilities in the labor force.

It may be that in developing countries women with intellectual disabilities share in the feminization trend apparent in the more industrialized countries, notably among women with disabilities. The levels at which women have achieved gender equality and visible participation in political and economic life vary widely from region to region around the globe (UNDP, 1997). Regional differences in employment opportunities for women with intellectual disabilities are also conspicuous. Less is known about the employment experiences of women in developing countries, where a priority is to acquire skills so as to contribute to family – and thus, their own – livelihood. In these circumstances, women work to sustain themselves and their families.

It is difficult to disentangle women's livelihood from the measures sustaining their health. In developing countries, families are often the sole source of support for people with intellectual disabilities. Thus women's health is intertwined with that of their family members. Women with disabilities have typically found work in fields where women in general have made progress (Epstein, 1997). Many become self-employed and perform unskilled work in the informal sector, perhaps in traditional

agriculture or production, in an effort to contribute to their own livelihood and that of their family.

In the more prosperous countries employment is a priority for all citizens, endorsed as a central part of the European Community Disability
Strategy (European Commission, 1998). It is likely that women with
intellectual disabilities who have achieved employment in the regular
labor force will subsequently take a more active part in society. But
whether they will attain valuable outcomes in terms of greater social
inclusion – a core policy enacted by the European Community – has yet to
be determined. Accordingly, there is little evidence to indicate how
women's health and well-being may be promoted by virtue of their wider
participation in society.

Gender differences favoring women are apparent in the changing texture of the labor force. While still outnumbered by men, women in the
European Union accounted for most of the overall increase in the labor
force between 1994 and 1996 (Commission of the European Communities,
1997: 39). With less haste, women with intellectual disabilities nonetheless
seek and find employment. As residents in yesterday's institutions,
women with intellectual disabilities scrubbed, cooked and laundered.
They carried out domestic labors traditionally assumed by women but
had little chance of embracing the more valued social roles available to
other women of the day – neighbor, spouse, mother or paid employee.
The doors of institutions have closed throughout Europe, North America
and in many other countries in the wake of government policies favoring
community living for people with intellectual disabilities. But the supply
of employment opportunities for former residents has not always kept
pace with the demand for ordinary work in the community.

Satisfying employment promotes friendships, with further potential to
enhance individual well-being. A confiding relationship with a friend
was associated with better health among the group of Canadian women
studied by Walters et al. (1998). For people with intellectual disabilities,
ordinary employment generates more diverse, regular social interactions
with co-workers and other people who do not have disabilities (Kilsby &
Beyer, 1996). In a more varied array of social contacts, lasting friendships
may take root. Friendships at work may thus offer women a greater
chance of psychological well-being (Ohtake & Chadsey, 1999). But a
feminist critique of disability cautions against equating paid employment
status – worthy as it may be – with citizenship (Fawcett, 2000). While
women with intellectual disabilities have a right to employment, those
who do not work are nonetheless citizens with a right and responsibility
to play a part in society. In the next section, factors related to the capacity
of women to exercise their rights and to determine their own health
outcomes are considered.

Self-determination

Self-determination is expressed in self-regulation, psychological empowerment, self-realization and autonomy. This characteristic emerges over time as individuals become competent at directing their own lives (Wehmeyer, 1996). How women with intellectual disabilities make choices at different stages of their lives and what health-related outcomes they achieve for themselves are issues not fully understood. Stalker and Harris reviewed a host of empirical studies and concluded that 'people with intellectual disabilities often lack the opportunity to make choices for themselves' (1998: 70).

The context of choice-making shifts across an individual's life span. Homes, residential centers and hospitals where people with intellectual disabilities live vary markedly in the opportunities for choice they make available, even in the same country. A study of older adults living in the UK revealed that many had little control over their day-to-day lives. For those of retirement age, new experiences of leisure and further education frequently pursued by their peers in the general population were rare (Fitzgerald, 1998).

Informed choice

Access to information is not only a prerequisite for promoting healthy aging. It is a key element in making choices and thus shaping self-determined behavior. Women with intellectual disabilities have distinctive health-related information needs at different stages of the life span. For example, they are more likely than men with intellectual disabilities and than adults in the general population, to be obese and to exhibit lower levels of physical exercise. Primary health prevention programs aimed at promoting healthy eating and exercise behaviors have been shown to be cost-effective in terms of promoting quality of life measured by additional Quality of Life Years or QALYs (Kaplan, 2000). Strategies that support individuals to identify personal health promotion goals and to achieve these goals by changing their behavior, focus on autonomy and self-determination (Turner & Hatton, 1998). Applying this model, interventions targeting women with intellectual disabilities can engage them in helping to determine healthy outcomes in their own lives (see Chapter 11).

Supports for healthy lives

Family members, friends and professional workers in formal service systems make up the scaffolding to support women with intellectual disabilities. Inevitably they are in the front line of any primary health promotion on behalf of the people for whom they provide care. To promote well-being, family carers must be involved:

'Adults with intellectual disabilities, and their carers, need to receive appropriate and ongoing education regarding healthy living practices in areas such as nutrition, exercise, oral hygiene, safety practices, and the avoidance of risky behaviors such as tobacco use and substance abuse.'

(WHO 2000: 16)

Most often, women family members are the carers for women and men with intellectual disabilities. In Wales, mothers were found to provide nearly all personal care to their adult offspring living in the family home (Grant & Wenger, 1993). Evidence from the US, Ireland and Northern Ireland also identified mothers as the family members most assiduously providing care for co-resident adult children with intellectual disabilities (Seltzer *et al.*, 1995). The central importance of their role is reflected in the priority given by the WHO to the health of carers together with their family members with intellectual disabilities (Walsh *et al.*, 2001).

Priorities

How might scientific evidence contribute to equitable and gender-sensitive allocation of scarce health resources? Overall, to date there have been few empirical studies investigating the impact of the employment status or levels of social inclusion of women with intellectual disabilities on their health and well-being at different stages in the life span, and across different cultural settings. Women with intellectual disabilities are often of low socioeconomic status. No research has been conducted on how to integrate women's health issues into the medical practice of nations where women have a devalued status. Research needs to be undertaken to determine their needs in order for them to achieve a level of physical and subjective well-being equivalent to those of women and men without disabilities living in similar circumstances. Each of these important, if often complex, areas is ripe for rigorous investigation. At best, understanding what promotes health among this population will build expertise in devising and evaluating effective health care practices for women with intellectual disabilities, their families and the wider community.

Promoting women's health across the life span advances a laudable strategy aimed at equity of access to health care in pursuit of enhanced quality of life outcomes. In particular, addressing the distinctive health care needs and low socioeconomic status of women with intellectual disabilities will inform the allocation or reallocation of finite health resources. Self-determination is a guiding principle for involving women directly in shaping and evaluating health interventions on their behalf. While cultural differences should be respected in shaping health policies, many traditions are untenable. Not all cultural traditions nurture self-determination or equal opportunities for women whether or not they have disabilities. Such diversity potentially can enrich life experiences for women but challenges those charged with providing care and support.

Summary

People with intellectual disabilities will chart new territory during this century in every country. Most of those in this expanding cohort will be women likely to outlive their male peers. Gender and socioeconomic status will help to determine their health. Women with intellectual disabilities have distinctive health needs across cultures and across the life span. At the very least, these should not diminish their status or well-being. Even within cultures, individual women express distinctive needs and they will – if supported appropriately – make singular contributions to their own healthy lives, their families and communities. Global health policy is expressed by supporting women to become full partners in the formation of health strategies and interventions, thus crafting their own well-being.

References

Abelson, J. (2000) *Newsday* 12 September, p. 5.

Alvarez, J.T. (1999) Reflections on *Agequake* (Selected quotations from the speeches of Julia Tavares Alvarez, Alternate Permanent Representative of the Domincan Republic Mission to the United Nations). NGO Committee on Aging, New York.

Brown, H. (1996) Ordinary women: Issues for women with learning disabilities: a keynote review. *British Journal of Learning Disabilities*, **24** (2), 47–51.

Commission of the European Communities (1997) European women's health can still improve. *Prevention – Progress in Community Public Health*. No. 4/11-97. DG-V, Employment & Social Affairs, Brussels.

Commission of the European Communities (1998) *A New European Community Disability Strategy*. Document 98/0216 (CNS). CEC, Brussels.

Cooper, S-A. (1998) Clinical study of the effects of age on the physical health of adults with mental retardation. *American Journal on Mental Retardation*, **102**, 582–589.

Cox, E. (1997) Building social capital. *Health Promotion Matters 4*, (September), pp. 1–4. VicHealth, PO Box 154, Carlton, South Victoria, 3053, Australia.

Eagly, A.H. & Wood, W. (1999) The origins of sex differences in human behavior: evolved dispositions versus social roles. *American Psychologist*, **54**, 408–423.

Epstein, S. (1997) *We Can Make It*. Stories of disabled women in developing countries. International Labor Organization, Geneva.

European Commission (1998) From Guidelines to Action: the National Action Plans for Employment. European Commission, Employment & Social Affairs, D-G for Employment, Industrial Relations and Social Affairs, Directorate V/A. Office for Official Publications of the European Communities, Luxembourg.

Fawcett, B. (2000) *Feminist Perspectives on Disability*. Pearson Education Limited, Harlow, UK.

Fitzgerald, J. (1998) *Services for Older People with Learning Difficulties*. Joseph Rowntree Foundation, York.

Government of Ireland (1997) *A Plan for Women's Health*. The Stationery Office, Dublin.

Grant, G. & Wenger, C. (1993) Dynamics of support networks. *Irish Journal of Psychology*, **14**, 79–98.

Hatton, C. (1998) Intellectual disabilities – epidemiology and causes. In: *Clinical Psychology and People with Intellectual Disabilities* (eds E. Emerson, C. Hatton, J. Bromley & A. Caine), pp. 20–38. John Wiley & Sons Ltd, Chichester.

Kaplan, R. (2000) Two pathways to prevention. *American Psychologist*, **55**, 382–396.

Kilsby, M. & Beyer, S. (1996) Engagement and interaction: a comparison between supported employment and day service provision. *Journal of Intellectual Disability Research*, **40**, 348–357.

Krauss, M.W., Seltzer, M.M. & Goodman, S.J. (1992) Social support networks of adults with mental retardation who live at home. *American Journal on Mental Retardation*, **96**, 432–441.

McCarthy, M. & Thompson, D. (1998) *Sex and the 3R's: Rights, Responsibilities and Risks*, 2nd edition. Pavilion, Brighton.

Ohtake, Y. & Chadsey, J. (1999) Social disclosure among co-workers without disabilities in Supported Employment Settings. *Mental Retardation*, **37**, 25–36.

Olson, D., Cioffi, A., Yovanoff, P. & Mank, D. (2000) Gender differences in supported employment. *Mental Retardation*, **38**, 89–96.

Robine, J-M, Romieu, I. & Cambois, E. (1999) Health expectancy indicators. *Bulletin of the World Health Organization*, **77**, 181–185.

van Schrojenstein Lantman-de Valk, H. J. A. (1998) *Health Problems in People with Intellectual Disability*. Unigraphic, Maastricht.

Seltzer, M.M., Krauss, M.K., Walsh, P.N., Conliffe, C., Larson, B., Birkbeck, G., Hong, J. and Choi, S.C. (1995) Cross-national comparisons of aging mothers of adults with intellectual disability. *Journal of Intellectual Disability Research*, **39**, 408–18.

Slone, M., Durrheim, K., Lachman, P. & Kaminer, D. (1998) Association between the diagnosis of mental retardation and socioeconomic factors. *American Journal on Mental Retardation*, **102**, 535–546.

Stalker, K. & Harris, P. (1998) The exercise of choice by adults with intellectual disabilities: a selected literature review. *Journal of Applied Research in Intellectual Disabilities*, **11**, 60–76.

Turner, S. & Hatton, C. (1998) Working with communities: health promotion. In: *Clinical Psychology and People with Intellectual Disabilities* (eds E. Emerson, C. Hatton, J. Bromley & A. Caine), pp. 80–297. John Wiley & Sons, Chichester.

UN (1994) *Standard Rules on the Equalization of Opportunities for People with Disabilities*. United Nations, New York.

UNDP (1997) *Human Development Report 1997*. United Nations Development Program. Oxford University Press, New York.

UN-OFCHR (1997) *Women's Rights the Responsibility of All.* Basic Information Kit No. 2. United Nations Office of the High Commissioner for Human Rights, United Nations, New York and Geneva.

Walsh, P.N. (2000) Rights of passage: Life course transitions for women with intellectual disabilities. In: *Transition and Change in the Lives of People with Intellectual Disabilities* (ed. D. May), pp. 135–156. Jessica Kingsley, London.

Walsh, P.N., Conliffe, C. & Birkbeck, G. (1993) Permanency planning and maternal well-being: a study of caregivers of people with intellectual disability in Ireland and Northern Ireland. *Irish Journal of Psychology*, **14**, 176–88.

Walsh, P.N., Heller, T., Schupf, N. & van Schrojenstein Lantman-de Valk, H.J.A. (2001) Healthy aging – adults with intellectual disability: women's health and related issues. *Journal of Applied Research in Intellectual Disabilities*, **14**, 195–217.

Walters, V., Eyles, J., Lenton, R., French, S. & Beardwood, B. (1998) Work and health: a study of the occupational and domestic roles of women registered nurses and registered practical nurses in Ontario, Canada. *Gender, Work and Organization*, **5**, 230–244.

Wehmeyer, Michael (1996) Essential characteristics of self-determined behavior of individuals with mental retardation. *American Journal on Mental Retardation*, **100**, 632–42.

Whyte, S.R. & Ingstad, B. (1998) Help for people with disabilities: do cultural differences matter? *World Health Forum*, **19**, 42–46.

WHO (1995) *Aging and Health.* A Programme Perspective. World Health Organization, Geneva.

WHO (1997) *The World Health Report 1997*, p. 83. World Health Organization, Geneva.

WHO (1998) *The World Health Report 1998*. Life in the 21st century – a vision for all. World Health Organization, Geneva.

WHO (2000) *Aging and Intellectual Disabilities – Improving Longevity and Promoting Healthy Aging: Summative Report*. World Health Organization, Geneva.

2 Reproductive and Physical Health

Henny M.J. van Schrojenstein Lantman-de Valk, Nicole Schupf and Kristiina Patja

Introduction

This chapter will review information on reproductive and physical health, health practices and medical care for women with intellectual disabilities (ID). It will focus on reproductive health status throughout adulthood and on barriers to effective prevention and/or treatment of health conditions. Topics include menstruation, fertility and contraception, menopause and postmenopausal disorders, endocrine and neuroendocrine abnormalities, sexual health, sexually transmitted disease, sexual abuse, sterilization, and the impact of psychotropic and anti-epileptic medication on reproductive health. Barriers to effective screening and access to quality medical care will be discussed.

Compared with women in the general population, women with intellectual disabilities have several characteristics that increase their risk for reproductive and physical health conditions. These include higher rates of hypogonadism and failure to menstruate, early menopause, high levels of co-morbid conditions such as epilepsy and hypothyroidism and obesity, a high frequency of psychiatric illness, epilepsy and behavioral problems, high frequency of psychotropic medication and anti-epileptic drug use, and a relatively sedentary lifestyle. The various risks and protective factors for the most important diseases are summarized in Table 2.1.

Reproductive and physical health

Menstruation

Among women with intellectual disabilities, the average age at onset of menarche is similar to that of women in the general population. Most appear to have regular menstrual cycles. A study of maturational rate of children with and without intellectual disabilities in Japan showed that children with intellectual disabilities did not differ in age at pubertal height spurt or at menarche (Lindgren & Katoda, 1993). Studies of gonadal function in women with Down syndrome (DS) living in the community have found distributions of age at menarche and frequencies

Table 2.1 Protective and risk factors of health of women with ID.

Protective	Disease group	Risk
Low blood pressure Low use of alcohol	Cardiac disease	Low physical activity Use of depot progestagens as contraception
Low occupational risk Low smoking frequency	Chronic obstructive pulmonary disease	Passive smoking by care staff Medication by inhaler requires adequate technique
Low smoking frequency Low occupational risk	Lung cancer	Passive smoking by care staff
Low estrogen protects from certain types of breast cancer	Breast cancer	Hypogonadism Being childless
No sexual intercourse Short menstrual life Low estrogen level	Cervical cancer	Poor hygiene Insufficient education on sexually transmitted diseases Obesity
	Osteoporosis	Hypogonadism Anticonvulsants – *phenytoin* and *phenobarbitone* Sedentary lifestyle or low physical activity
	Fractures	Same as osteoporosis Epilepsy Low physical activity
	Amenorrhea and fertility problems	Neuroleptic drug use
Higher endogenous estrogen levels	Alzheimer's disease	Down syndrome

of women with regular menses that are much closer to those found in the general population than had been presumed from earlier studies of institutionalized women (Goldstein, 1988). Oster (1953) and Scola & Pueschel (1992) found that between 65% and 80% of women with Down syndrome have regular menstrual cycles, while 15–20% have never menstruated.

More precise information could be obtained from studies of hormone status providing documentation of ovulation. Methodological problems in studies of hormonal status during menstrual cycles in women with intellectual disabilities include small sample sizes, sampling of only a few cycles and lack of control for the stage of menstrual cycle at which the blood sample was drawn. Nonetheless, the studies have generally supported the conclusion that many cycles show evidence of ovulation and formation of a corpus luteum, suggesting that gonadal endocrine function is within normal ranges in many women with intellectual disabilities despite the higher rates of gonadal dysfunction in this population. There is little information on how hormone levels and gonadal function change with age. Both men and women show elevations of follicle stimulating hormone (FSH) and luteinizing hormone (LH) at puberty. This indicates primary gonadal dysfunction, which appears to progress with age and to be more frequent in men (Campbell et al., 1982; Hsiang et al., 1987; Hasen et al., 1980; Hestnes et al., 1991).

Fertility and contraception

While little research has addressed fertility in women with intellectual disabilities, it is reasonable to assume that adults are fertile unless they have a disorder that affects genital organs or brain regions responsible for hormones that regulate ovarian function. However, fertility is likely to be reduced in women with gonadal dysfunction, low hormone levels and early menopause. For example, only a few births in women with Down syndrome have been documented. Further, in some countries most women with intellectual disabilities use contraception. Oral contraception is preferred, with low dose combinations of progestins and estrogens. Depot progesterones are also widely used as contraceptives. Their advantage stems from the fact that they need to be administered only four times a year. However, irregular vaginal bleeding or spotting and effects on cholesterol metabolism that might increase risk for coronary heart disease need to be considered. Developments in this field are the introduction of progesterone implants and progesterone producing intra-uterine devices (IUDs) which are reliable contraceptives and may diminish or stop the monthly vaginal bleeding.

Therapeutic amenorrhea

Therapeutic amenorrhea may be used in women with intellectual disabilities who are unable to manage menstrual hygiene effectively, or in women who show self-injurious behavior related to menstruation. The most common form of therapeutic amenorrhea is suppression of menstrual cycles with *lynestrenol*. Huovinen (1993) reports that 66% of his patients with intellectual disability had been prescribed *lynestrenol* at some time in their life. Alternatively, endometrial ablation – abrasion of the inner layer of the uterus – may be used to suppress menstruation and establish therapeutic amenorrhea (Wingfield et al., 1994). Hysterectomy, removal of the uterus, may also be used to prevent pregnancy. Endometrial ablation, hysterectomy and sterilization, while effective, are irreversible, raising legal and ethical concerns about these procedures. It is important to determine that the perceived problems surrounding management of menstruation and/or fertility are medically documented and are undertaken as much for the information of the woman herself as for the convenience of the carer. In the past, sterilization was widely used to prevent pregnancy, often without the consent of the person with intellectual disability. In more developed countries, guidelines for sterilization now require extensive documentation of the medical rationale for the treatment, including documentation of informed consent procedures (Servais *et al.*, 1999; McLachlan & Peppin, 1986).

Menopause

Very little is known about menopause in women with intellectual disabilities. Only two studies have reported on the median age at menopause and none has systematically tracked changes in hormones and ovarian function with age in a large group of women with intellectual disabilities. Thus, we have very little information on how decreases in hormones after menopause may affect health and cognitive ability. The two studies of menopause both found that the median age at menopause was three to five years earlier in women with intellectual disabilities compared with women in the general population. Carr & Hollins (1995) surveyed the menstrual histories of 45 women with DS and 126 women with other forms of intellectual disability who were between 36 and 61 years of age. They found that 66% of the women with DS were experiencing regular menstruation between 31 and 40 years of age. By age 46, 87% of women with DS and 69% of women with other forms of intellectual disability had stopped menstruating. No woman with DS aged over 51, or aged over 54 with other causes of intellectual disability, was still menstruating.

These results are consistent with the hypothesis that women with intellectual disabilities have an earlier age at onset of menopause, particularly so for women with DS. Schupf *et al.* (1997) have confirmed and extended this finding in a sample of 344 women with and without DS. Among women with DS, they found that 6.4% between 40 and 44 years, 52% between 45 and 49 years and 91% aged over 50 years of age were no longer menstruating, compared with 10.3%, 31.4% and 91% of age-matched women with other forms of intellectual disability. The estimated median age at menopause was significantly lower – 47.1 years – for women with DS than for women without DS (49.3 years); for women in the general population, median age was 51.6 years. The age-adjusted likelihood of menopause was 2.3 times greater in women with DS (odds ratio = 2.3, 95% confidence interval 1.1, 4.9). The earlier median age at menopause of women with DS is consistent with the hypothesis that persons with DS show premature aging in a number of organ systems.

Menopause in women with FRAXA

Women with the fragile-X (FRAXA) premutation, a partially expanded variant of the fragile-X gene (FMR-1), are another group of women at high risk of premature ovarian failure (POF) and early menopause. Women who carry the premutation experience cessation of menses before age 40 at a significantly higher rate than women in the general population and are over represented among women with idiopathic premature ovarian failure (Schwartz *et al.*, 1994; Marozzi *et al.*, 2000). Conway *et al.* (1995) have proposed that alleles in the premutation range in FRAXA interfere with the fragile-X gene transcription in fetal ovary, leading to a reduced number of oocytes at birth, earlier depletion of the oocyte pool and hence earlier onset of menopause. Women who carry the FRAXA premutation have high levels of follicle stimulating hormone or FSH (Murray *et al.*, 1999), and premature menopause, although estradiol and inhibin levels were reported to be within normal range (Murray *et al.*, 2000).

Medications and reproductive health

Many women with intellectual disabilities are treated with psychotropic medications and/or anti-epileptic drugs (AEDs) and the prevalence of psychotropic drug use increases with age (Aman & Singh, 1988; Anderson *et al.*, 1987; Intagliata & Rink, 1985). Although estimates of psychotropic medication use vary, approximately 20–40% of the elderly with intellectual disabilities are likely to be taking one or more psychoactive medications, primarily antipsychotic, anti-anxiety and antidepressant medications (Aman *et al.*, 1985; Intagliata & Rinck, 1985; Pary, 1993). Of these, antipsychotic medications are the most frequently used, followed by anxiolytics and antidepressants (Intagliata & Rinck, 1985).

Changes in drug potency, toxicity and duration of effect with age have been well documented and raise issues of appropriate dosage, increased side effects and adverse drug reactions, effects on other age-related medical conditions and in drug interactions (see Aman, 1990). These changes include increases in the level of drug in the blood available for acting on tissues, decreased drug metabolism, and decreased rate of drug clearance; the net effect may be a more potent or longer lasting response to psychotropic drugs (Aman, 1990). A common finding is hyperprolactinemia in association with neuroleptic drug use. Prolonged elevations in prolactin can lead to declines in follicular (FSH) and luteinizing hormone (LH) release, leading to declines in ovarian function. Reduced gonadal function may lead, in turn, to menstrual disturbances, including amenorrhea or infertility and reduced estrogen release which may increase the risk of disorders associated with reduced estrogen levels (Baldessarini et al., 1988). Elevated levels of sex-hormone binding globulin, FSH and LH have been described and long-term AED therapy has been associated with primary gonadal dysfunction and increased risk of polycystic ovarian syndrome. Other endocrine effects of neuroleptics include inhibition of the release of growth hormone and the hormonal response to stress (Baumeister et al., 1993).

Sexual health

People with intellectual disabilities have the same sexual needs and the same rights and responsibilities as all other people. They too want to enjoy physical contact and sexual activity, and they have the right to be given opportunities to do so. They have the right to be free from abuse, not to be forced to participate in activities against their wishes, nor to be restricted in activities they want to experience. They have the responsibility not to offend or inflict harm on others. It may be difficult for parents to recognize the fact that their son or daughter with intellectual disability has an adult body and adult sexual feelings. Some parents tend to ignore the issue, while others wish to protect their child against possible sexual abuse and harm. Parents are often not aware whether their child with intellectual disability is engaging in sexual activity, or of the level of sexual activity. Direct care workers are not always adequately educated on this issue. Often, discussion of menstrual function and of sexuality is not a regular part of adaptive or independence training. Similarly, education about the signs and symptoms of the onset of menopause is often not available to women with ID, especially those with more severe disabilities. As a result, they may not be prepared for the changes that accompany menopause, and are unable to correctly interpret or understand these changes. In addition, parents and staff may seek ways to limit opportunities for sexual activity (McCarthy, 1999).

In many societies, general attitudes toward persons with intellectual disabilities, and toward women in particular, may result in denial or trivialization of sexual health concerns. Such attitudes limit access to health services related to gynecological concerns and function. There are only a few health professionals who are willing *and* trained to address sexual health issues for people with intellectual disabilities. People who are sexually active are prone to sexually transmitted diseases (STDs). Education on symptoms and early treatment is necessary to avoid further transmission and the development of late-stage complications of the infection. Some STDs are characterized by chronic pelvic pain, vaginal discharge or abdominal pain. The symptoms may be interpreted as vague complaints. Other STDs may be present without any clinical manifestations (e.g. 65% of the Chlamydia infections).

However, even symptom-free women may transmit their infections and, if untreated, may develop severe complications. Therefore preventative health care, such as Pap smear testing, is essential to find women with intellectual disabilities who may be asymptomatic carriers of STDs. It is important that women understand what may happen to them if they have unprotected sexual intercourse. Most women with intellectual disabilities may have limited verbal skills and low self-esteem: optimal teaching strategies will take into account their distinctive learning requirements. (The British Institute of Learning Disabilities has a catalogue with useful materials: bild@bild.demon.co.uk)

Research in the UK indicates that among adults with intellectual disabilities, HIV is mainly spread by males with ID having paid sex with male partners without a disability. As many men with ID have low incomes, the prospect of payment for having unprotected sexual intercourse with other men, possibly HIV carriers, may be irresistible. These men often have sexual relations with female partners with ID as well (Cambridge & Brown, 1997). Although no data could be found about the prevalence of STDs in women with ID, a study among people with ID registered in general practices in the Netherlands revealed a prevalence of STD in males with ID of 2.4%. This was seven times higher than in males in the general population (van Schrojenstein Lantman et al., 2000).

Even if they are well informed about the risks of STDs and are familiar with using condoms, women with intellectual disabilities with low self-esteem may be persuaded not to use such protection if the male partner insists. Focus groups have formed, often initiated in service agencies in English-speaking countries, for women to meet and explore their experiences and sexuality and to share knowledge. Reports indicate that these groups meet women's long-existing needs (Walsh et al., 2000).

Age-related health problems

Cardiac and respiratory diseases

The frequency of heart disease is lower in menstruating women than in men of the same age, but after menopause the frequency of heart disease is the same in women as in men. Studies have shown that the risk of a coronary event is reduced by about 50% in postmenopausal women who take oral estrogen compared with women who do not (Stampfer *et al.*, 1991). It is thought that this decrease in coronary heart disease is related to the ability of estrogen to prevent coronary artery disease and prevent the build-up of some types of cholesterol in the bloodstream. Yet it should be noted that hormone replacement therapy (HRT) may heighten the risk of breast cancer in some women. Compared with their peers in the general population, women with Down syndrome are six times as likely to have mitral valve prolapse, heart murmurs and other forms of non-ischemic heart disease, while their risk for ischemic heart disease is similar to that of women in the general population. A similar, although less extreme, pattern is seen in women with other forms of ID, who are approximately twice as likely to have any form of heart disease as women in the general population. By contrast, risk of hypertension is significantly lower among women with Down syndrome, but similar among women with other forms of ID, when compared with women in the general population (Kapell *et al.*, 1998). Children with ID have more cardiac diseases because of more frequent cardiac malformations (Grech & Gatt, 1999) and many syndromes carry an increased risk of cardiac malformations.

Cardiac diseases are responsible for 42% of deaths of women with ID over 40 years of age (Table 2.2), although low prevalence rates are often cited. Cardiac disease was reported in 14–26% of adults older than 50 years (Janicki & Jacobson, 1986; Hand, 1994). Compared to the general population, women with ID seem to have a similar risk of ischemic heart disease (Table 2.2). It has been suggested that minimal use of alcohol and cigarettes reduce cardiac mortality markedly. However, risk factors for cardiac diseases are low physical activity (Center *et al.*, 1994) and overweight, which is reported even as high as 59% of women with ID (Rimmer *et al.*, 1994). Nutritional management – essential in cardiac disease prevention – is often too complicated or inaccessible for women with ID, who may depend on others to plan and prepare their meals.

Respiratory diseases, especially pneumonia, are common among people with ID. Rates of chronic obstructive pulmonary disease (COPD) and lung cancer are low, perhaps reflecting less exposure to smoking and occupational risks. But women with ID have a high risk of death from respiratory disease throughout their lives: among older age groups, the risk is three times higher than in the general population. Best practice in preventing or treating pneumonia should be more accessible to this population.

Table 2.2 Observed (O) and expected (E) deaths of Finnish women age over 20 years with intellectual disability with age-standardized relative mortality (RR) with their 95% confidence intervals (CI), compared with the general population (n = 546).

Age group		% of deaths within age group	O	E	RR	95% CI
20–39	Infectious diseases	8.6	6	1.5	4.1	0.6–9.5
	Cancer	2.9	2	22.4	0.1	0–0.3
	Vascular diseases	21.4	15	12.8	1.2	0.6–1.9
	Respiratory diseases	15.7	11	3.5	3.2	1.1–5.1
	Digestive system	8.6	6	1.9	3.1	0.4–6.1
	External causes	11.4	8	27.1	0.3	0–0.3
	Other causes	31.4	22	19.8	1.1	0.5–1.2
40–59	Infectious diseases	1.9	3	2.0	1.5	0–3.8
	Cancer	10.8	17	64.3	0.3	0–0.8
	Vascular diseases	31.2	49	48.4	1.0	0.7–1.3
	Respiratory diseases	22.9	36	5.8	6.2	4.1–8.2
	Digestive system	7.6	12	3.8	3.1	1.7–7.1
	External causes	6.4	10	19.5	0.5	0.1–0.6
	Other causes	19.2	30	19.5	1.5	0.9–2.1
60+	Infectious diseases	1.9	6	2.9	2.1	0.3–4.9
	Cancer	13.6	43	71.3	0.6	0.5–0.9
	Vascular diseases	47.5	150	168.3	0.9	0.8–1.2
	Respiratory diseases	17.4	55	16.8	3.3	1.7–3.0
	Digestive system	6.3	20	9.4	2.1	1.9–5.2
	External causes	5.1	16	10.2	1.6	0.6–2.0
	Other causes	8.2	26	31.3	0.8	0.5–1.2

Osteoporosis

Osteoporosis is considered to be characteristic of disorders that increase after menopause and are related to estrogen loss. This condition leads to a heightened burden of disease, not only through fractures, but also through pain. Long-term use of anticonvulsant medication is a further risk factor for osteoporosis, as are small body size, sedentary lifestyle, poor nutrition, smoking, excessive alcohol use, hyperthyroidism, lack of postmenopausal estrogen replacement therapy, high phosphate levels, and low dietary calcium intake (Scott & Hochberg, 1993). In women with osteoporosis, bone mass slowly declines over the years to produce thinner, more porous and thus weaker bones. Postmenopausal bone loss is associated with wrist fractures in about 15% of women and with spine fractures in 25–40%. The most serious complication of osteopenia is hip fracture, which occurs in 15% of older fair-skinned women and causes high rates of morbidity and mortality.

Clinical trials of effects of estrogen on bone density have consistently shown that estrogen prevents or delays bone loss when taken within five years of surgical or natural menopause. In one study, the prevalence of osteoporosis among adults with intellectual disabilities of 40–60 years of age was 21%, and 34% for osteopenia. Bone mineral density was significantly lower in adults with Down syndrome, those with poor mobility, and those of Caucasian race. Smaller effects were noted for those with seizure disorders and anti-epileptic drugs (Tyler *et al.*, 2000). Osteoporosis and an increased risk for fractures were also found in younger women with intellectual disabilities (mean age: 36 years) who had hypogonadism, small body size, high phosphate levels or Down syndrome (Center *et al.*, 1998). These authors found that 37% of the women had experienced fractures: they had lower bone mineral density and higher serum phosphate than those who did not have fractures.

Cancer

The incidence of cancer in people with ID is uncertain. Many studies based on death rates report lower prevalence of different types of cancer than in the general population (Jancar & Jancar, 1977; Achterberg *et al.*, 1978; Jancar *et al.*, 1984; Uno, 1996). In most studies, overall cancer prevalence has been reported as lower (from 4.6–17.5%) in different populations of persons with ID compared with a higher rate (20%) prevailing in the general population (Carter & Jancar 1983; Jancar, 1990; Cooke, 1997).

In one population-based sample, the incidence of cancer among persons with intellectual disabilities was found to be similar to that in the general population (Patja *et al.*, 2001). The level of ID is not significantly correlated with overall cancer incidence. However, persons with ID seem to have a higher risk of cancers with an indefinite location of pain, such as cancer of the gallbladder (Patja *et al.* 2001). Assessing pain may be difficult (Brandt & Rosen, 1998; Martinez-Cue *et al.*, 1999). Poor cognitive functioning impedes the person's ability to express pain complaints. Determining the source of pain in persons with profound or severe ID who have no verbal ability depends on the carer's interpretation (McGrath *et al.*, 1998). The indefinite nature of gastric pains may therefore increase the risk of neoplasms in the gallbladder and esophagus remaining undetected.

Breast cancer

Women with ID and women in the general population have a similar risk of breast cancer (Table 2.3). Additional risk factors for breast cancer in the

Table 2.3 Observed (O) and expected (E) numbers of gynecological cancers and standardized incidence ratios (SIR) with their 95% confidence intervals (CI) among women with ID in 1967 to 1997 (n = 1083).

	O	E	SIR	95% CI
Breast cancer	22	25.7	0.8	0.5–1.3
Genitals (all)	17	15.7	1.0	0.6–1.7
Cervical	0	2.9	0	0–1.3
Uterine	8	5.9	1.4	0.6–2.7
Ovarian	7	5.7	1.2	0.5–2.5
Undefined	2	0.9	2.2	0.3–7.8

general population are high dietary fat, alcohol consumption, low physical activity and estrogen-only hormone replacement therapy (Cooper *et al.*, 1999). Women with ID have both protective factors – low estrogen levels (Carlson & Wilson, 1996) and lower use of alcohol and tobacco – and predisposing factors such as being childless, obesity, low physical activity and low frequency of breast screening (Cowie & Fletcher, 1998).

Screening programs for both breast and cervical cancers are available in most western countries, but less so for women with ID. To improve their health care, the causes of the low participation rates need to be identified so that adequate screening rates and early treatment of affected women can be achieved (see panel on screening for breast cancer in the Netherlands).

In the UK, invitations for breast screening are sent out by the local primary care center. It appears that women with ID are more easily overlooked, since health care staff may not be convinced of the benefits of screening for this group of women (Jones & Kerr, 1997). In countries with a predominantly private health insurance system, women must be referred for screening by their primary health care physician or must initiate the request for screening themselves. As many women with ID are not employed, they remain invisible to health authorities in countries where only women on payrolls are invited for screening.

Gynecological cancers

Women with ID have a distinctive risk profile for genital cancer compared with women in the general population, due to differences in the prevalence of both biological and behavioral factors – for example, smoking, diet and occupational risks – associated with level of ID. Nonetheless, the overall risk of genital cancer is similar among women with ID and women

Screening for breast cancer in the Netherlands

In some developed countries, screening for breast cancer includes mammography every two years for women aged over 50, where the prevalence is highest. Women aged over 50 in the Netherlands are invited by mail to participate in breast cancer screening, with addresses selected by postal code and provided by the local council. However, not all women respond, especially women of lower socioeconomic status and/or women with intellectual or physical disabilities. Literacy also influences uptake: women or their carers may not understand written reminders to make an appointment for screening. In some countries, screening is carried out in a mobile unit, reducing travel difficulties for participants. For people who use wheelchairs or who otherwise have reduced mobility, access to the X-ray unit may be the next problem, surmounted by contacting the nearest hospital to arrange for screening. Other difficulties may arise if the woman cannot use the telephone, is unable to deal with hospital staff effectively or finds the time allotted to each session – 10 minutes – too short. The schedule assumes that each woman is able to undress quickly, has no fear of the equipment and is fully cooperative. One regional screening center in Maastricht has a policy which recognizes the special needs of people with ID. On request, a more ample time schedule can be drawn up for groups of women with ID, and a wheelchair-accessible unit can be sent to a location where such a group of women has to be examined. Organizing this requires alert medical staff, but is effective in providing critical support for women who need more training and time for the screening procedures.

in the general population (Patja *et al.*, 2001). The risk of cervical cancer is reduced in women with ID, but the risk of cancers of the corpus uteri and ovaries is increased, and there is an increased prevalence of undefined genital cancers, which include those of external and internal female genital organs (Table 2.4).

Cervical and uterine cancers are most prevalent among women aged between 35 and 55 years. Screening systems for cervical cancer reflect each country or region's capacities and policies in extending preventative health measures. Thus, women who are not literate or who cannot comply fully with examination procedures may fail to take part in screening. For example, full cooperation is essential to undergo a Pap smear test for cervical cancer. Effective collection of material for examination requires the woman to lie down on a rather uncomfortable table with legs spread wide open – a difficult position to adopt for women with additional motor or musculoskeletal problems. Highly skilled health care staff can, with time and patience, support many women with ID and physical disabilities through the examination procedures. Nevertheless, the examination may prove difficult for many women with ID who do not understand what is happening and who are afraid. It is generally accepted that the risk for

Table 2.4 Observed (O) and expected (E) numbers of cancer cases and standardized incidence ratios (SIR) with their 95% confidential intervals (CI) among women with intellectual disability by age and level of intellectual disability (n = 1083).

	O	E	SIR	95% CI
Age		Women		
7–14	0	0.1	0	0–9.6
15–29	2	1.3	1.5	0.1–4.4
30–44	9	10.6	0.8	0.4–1.5
45–59	25	27.4	0.9	0.6–1.3
60+	56	53.5	1.0	0.8–1.3
Total	**92**	**93.0**	**1.0**	**0.8–1.2**
Level of ID				
Profound	8	6.2	1.3	0.6–2.5
Severe	8	8.0	1.0	0.4–2.0
Moderate	28	30.2	0.9	0.6–1.3
Mild	47	47.7	1.0	0.7–1.3

cervical cancer is reduced in women who are not sexually active, but more research is necessary to determine whether it is acceptable to omit screening among some groups of women.

Other conditions

Other age-related conditions that appear to occur with increased frequency in women with intellectual disabilities are thyroid problems, sensory impairment, heart rhythm disorders and musculoskeletal disorders.

Alzheimer's disease

Ovarian hormones such as estrogen are also important to maintain brain function in regions of the brain affected by Alzheimer's disease (AD) (Simpkins *et al.*, 1994). Some evidence shows higher age-specific rates of AD in women compared with men (Bachman *et al.*, 1993) and lower risk of AD in women who have received estrogen replacement therapy (ERT) (Paganini-Hill & Henderson, 1994; Barrett-Conner & Kritz-Silverstein, 1993; Mortel & Meyer, 1995; Tang *et al.*, 1996). Such findings support the hypothesis that estrogen deficiency contributes to the etiology of AD. The relative risks for dementia in women on estrogen or hormone replacement therapy have ranged from 0.33 to 0.80. In contrast, randomized controlled clinical trials of ERT in women with AD have failed to show a beneficial effect, suggesting that the major effect of estrogen is to delay onset rather than prevent it (Mulnard et al., 2000; Henderson et al., 2000). Adults with Down syndrome are at increased risk of Alzheimer's disease (Burger & Vogel, 1973; Malamud, 1972; Ropper & Williams, 1980; Zigman et al., 1996).

Gender differences and the effects of estrogen on Alzheimer's disease in women with Down syndrome and other forms of intellectual disability have not been systematically investigated. More work is needed to clarify how hormonal risk factors may influence age of onset of dementia. Few studies have presented results separately for men and women. Studies that have compared women with men have found earlier (Raghavan et al., 1994; Lai et al., 1999), later (Farrer et al., 1997; Schupf et al., 1998) or no difference in (Visser et al., 1997; Lai & Williams, 1989) age at onset.

One study examined the influence of estrogen deficiency on age at onset of dementia in 143 women with DS (Cosgrave et al., 1999). Age at menopause was available for approximately half of this group, of whom 12 were postmenopausal and diagnosed with dementia. Although the sample size is small, results are consistent with the hypothesis that higher endogenous estrogen levels can lower risk of dementia. If the association between age at menopause and onset of dementia can be confirmed and supporting hormonal data provided, estrogen replacement therapy could prove to be an important intervention to delay the onset of dementia.

Summary

In general, patterns of menstruation and fertility are similar for women with and without ID, although a significant minority of women with ID is infertile. Contraception is advised for those women who may be sexually active. Psychoactive and anti-epileptic medication can interfere with hormonal and metabolic functions. Evidence suggests that menopause is some years earlier in women with ID, especially if they have DS or fragile-X premutations.

People with ID have the same sexual needs and rights as all other people. Education on sexual activity, pregnancy and sexually transmitted disease should be developed and extended.

The risk for ischemic heart disease appears to be similar to that experienced by the general population, but more data on older women is necessary to confirm this finding. The risk for osteoporosis in women with ID is higher than in the general population, due to several factors such as the use of anticonvulsants, poor nutrition, a sedentary lifestyle and early onset of menopause. Screening programs for breast and cervical cancer should specifically reach out to target women with ID. Risk of age-related dementia, such as Alzheimer's disease, is elevated in adults with Down syndrome.

References

Achterberg J., Collerrain I. & Craig P. (1978) A possible relationship between cancer, mental retardation and mental disorders. *Social Science & Medicine*, **12** (3), 135.

Aman, M.G. (1990) Considerations in the use of psychotropic drugs in elderly mentally retarded persons. *Journal of Mental Deficiency Research*, **34**, 1–10.

Aman, M.G. & Singh, N.N. (1988) Patterns of drug use, methodological considerations, measurement techniques, and future trends. In: *Psychopharmacology of the Developmental Disabilities* (eds M.G. Aman & N.N. Singh), pp. 1–28. Springer-Verlag, Berlin.

Aman, M.G., Field, C.J. & Bridgeman, G.D. (1985) Citywide survey of drug patterns among non-institutionalized retarded persons. *Applied Research in Mental Retardation*, **5**, 159–171.

Anderson, D.J., Lakin, K.C., Bruiniks, R.H. & Hill, B.K. (1987) *A National Study of Residential and Support Services for Elderly Persons with Mental Retardation. Report # 22*. Department of Educational Psychology, University of Minnesota, Minneapolis, Minn.

Bachman, D.L., Wolf, P.A., Linn, R.T., Knoefel, J.E., Conn, J.L., Belanger, A.J., White, L.R. & D'Agostino, R.B. (1993) Incidence of dementia and probable Alzheimer's disease in a general population: the Framingham Study. *Neurology*, **43**, 515–519.

Baldessarini, R.J., Coyne, B.M. & Teicher, M.H. (1988) Significance of neuroleptic dose and plasma levels in the pharmacological treatment of psychosis. *Archives of General Psychiatry*, **45**, 79–91.

Barrett-Conner, E. & Kritz-Silverstein, D. (1993) Estrogen replacement therapy and cognitive function in older women. *JAMA*, **269**, 2637–2641.

Baumeister, A.A., Todd, M.E. & Selvin, J.A. (1993) Efficacy and specificity of pharmacological therapies for behavioral disorders in persons with mental retardation. *Clinical Neuropharmacology*, **16**, 271–294.

Brandt, B.R. & Rosen, I. (1998) Impaired peripheral somatosensory function in children with Prader-Willi syndrome. *Neuropediatrics*, **29** (3), 124.

Burger, P.C. & Vogel, F. (1973) The development of pathologic changes of Alzheimer's disease and senile dementia in patients with Down's syndrome. *American Journal of Pathology*, **73**, 457–468.

Cambridge, P. & Brown, H. (eds) (1997) *HIV and Learning Disability*. BILD, Kidderminster.

Campbell, W.A., Lowther, J., McKenzie, I. & Price, W.H. (1982) Serum gonadotrophins in Down's syndrome. *Journal of Medical Genetics*, **19**, 98–99.

Carlson, G. & Wilson, J. (1996) Menstrual management and women who have intellectual disabilities: service providers and decision-making. *Journal of Intellectual and Developmental Disability*, **21**, 39–57.

Carr, J. & Hollins, S. (1995) Menopause in women with learning disabilities. *Journal of Intellectual Disability Research*, **39**, 137–139.

Carter, G. & Jancar, J. (1983) Mortality in the mentally handicapped: a 50 year survey at the Stoke Park group of hospitals (1930–1980). *Journal of Mental Deficiency Research*, **27** (2), 143.

Center, J.R., McElduff, A. & Beange, H. (1994) Osteoporosis in groups with intellectual disability. *Australian and New Zealand Journal of Developmental Disability*, **19**, 251–258.

Center, J., Beange, H. & McElduff, A. (1998) People with mental retardation have an increased prevalence of osteoporosis: a population study. *American Journal on Mental Retardation*, **103**, 19–28.

Conway, G.S., Hettiarachchi, S., Murray, A. & Jacobs, P.A. (1995) FrX pre-mutations in familial premature ovarian failure. *Lancet*, **346**, 309–310.

Cooke, L.B. (1997) Cancer and learning disability. *Journal of Intellectual Disability Research*, **41** (4), 312–316.

Cooper, D.A., Eldridge, A.L. & Peters, J.C. (1999) Dietary carotenoids and certain cancers, heart disease, and age-related macular degeneration: a review of recent research. *Nutrition Reviews*, **57** (7), 201.

Cosgrave, M.P., Tyrrell, J., McCarron, M., Gill, M. & Lawlor, B.A. (1999) Age at onset of dementia and age of menopause in women with Down's syndrome. *Journal of Intellectual Disability Research*, **43**, 461–465.

Cowie, M. & Fletcher, J. (1998) Breast awareness project for women with a learning disability. *British Journal of Nursing*, **7**, 774.

Ellis, W.G., McCulloch, J.R. & Corley, C.L. (1974) Pre-senile dementia in Down's syndrome. *Neurology*, **24**, 101–106.

Farrer, M.J., Crayton, L., Davies, G.E., Oliver, C., Powell J., Holland, A.J. & Kessing, A.M. (1997) Allelic variability in D21S11, but not in APP or APOE, is associated with cognitive decline in Down's syndrome. *Neuroreport*, **8**, 1645–1649.

Goldstein, H. (1988) Menarche, menstruation, sexual relations and contraception of adolescent females with Down's syndrome. *European Journal of Obstetric Gynecology and Reproductive Biology*, **27**, 343–349.

Grech, V. & Gatt, M. (1999) Syndromes and malformations associated with congenital heart disease in a population-based study. *International Journal of Cardiology*, **68**, 151–56.

Hand, J.E. (1994) Report of a national survey of older people with lifelong intellectual handicap in New Zealand. *Journal of Intellectual Disability Research*, **34**, 275–287.

Hasen, J., Boyar, R.M. & Shapiro, L.R. (1980) Gonadal function in trisomy 21. *Hormone Research*, **12**, 345–350.

Henderson, V.W., Paganini-Hill, A., Miller, B.K., Eible, R.J., Reyes, P.F., Shoupe, D., McCleary, C.A., Klein, R.A., Hake, A.M. & Farlow M.R. (2000) Estrogen for Alzheimer's disease in women: randomized, double-blind placebo-controlled trial. *Neurology*, **54**, 295–301.

Hestnes, A., Stovener, L.J., Husoy, O., Folling, A., Fougner, K.J. & Sjaastad, O. (1991) Hormonal and biochemical disturbances in Down's syndrome. *Journal of Mental Deficiency Research*, **35**, 179–193.

Hsiang, Y-H.H., Berkovitz, G.D., Bland, G.L., Migeon, C.J. & Warren, A.C. (1987) Gonadal function in patients with Down's syndrome. *American Journal of Medical Genetics*, **27**, 449–458.

Huovinen, K.J.L. (1993) Gynecological problems of mentally retarded women. *Acta Obstetrica Gynecologica Scandinavia*, **72**, 475–480.

Intagliata, J. & Rinck, C. (1985) Psychoactive drug use in public and community residential facilities for mentally retarded persons. *Psychopharmacological Bulletin*, **21**, 268–278.

Jancar, J. (1990) Cancer and mental handicap: a further study (1976–85). *British Journal of Psychiatry*, **156**, 531.

Jancar, M.P. & Jancar, J. (1977) Cancer and mental retardation. *Bristol Medico-Chirurgical Journal*, **92**, 341–342.

Jancar, J., Eastham, R.D. & Carter, G. (1984) Hypocholesterolaemia in cancer and other causes of death in the mentally handicapped. *British Journal of Psychiatry*, **145**, 59.

Janicki, M.P. & Jacobson, J.W. (1986) Generational trends in sensory, physical, and behavioral abilities among older mentally retarded persons. *American Journal of Mental Deficiency*, **90**, 490–500.

Jones, R.G. & Kerr, M.P. (1997) A randomized control trial of an opportunistic health screening tool in primary care for people with intellectual disability. *Journal of Intellectual Disability Research*, **41**, 409–415.

Kapell, D., Nightingale, B., Rodriguez, A., Lee, J.H., Zigman, W.B. & Schupf, N. (1998) Prevalence of chronic medical conditions in adults with mental retardation: comparison with the general population. *Mental Retardation*, **36**, 269–279.

Lai, F. & Williams, R.S. (1989) A prospective study of Alzheimer disease in Down's syndrome. *Archives of Neurology*, **46**, 849–853.

Lai, F., Kammann, E., Rebeck, G.W., Anderson, A., Chen, Y. & Nixon, R.A. (1999) APOE genotype and gender effects on Alzheimer disease in 100 adults with Down's syndrome. *Neurology*, **53**, 331–336.

Lindgren, G.E. & Katoda H. (1993) Maturational rate of Tokyo children with and without mental retardation. *American Journal on Mental Retardation*, **98**, 1228–1234.

Malamud, N. (1972) Neuropathology of organic brain syndromes associated with aging. In: *Aging and the Brain* (ed. C.M. Gaitz) pp. 63–77. Plenum, New York.

Marozzi, A., Vegetti, W., Manfredinji, E., Tibiletti, M.G., Testa, G., Crosignani, P.G., Gineeli, E., Meneveri, R. & Dalpra, L. (2000) Association between idiopathic premature ovarian failure and fragile X pre-mutation. *Human Reproduction*, **15**, 197–202.

Martinez-Cue, C., Baamonde, C., Lumbreras, M.A., Vallina, I.F., Dierssen, M. & Florez, J. (1999) A murine model for Down's syndrome shows reduced responsiveness to pain. *Neuroreport*, **10** (5), 1119.

McCarthy, M. (1999) *Sexuality and Women with Learning Disabilities*. Jessica Kingsley, London.

McGrath, P.J., Rosmus, C., Canfield, C., Campbell, M.A. & Hennigar, A. (1998)

Behaviors caregivers use to determine pain in non-verbal, cognitively impaired individuals. *Developmental Medicine & Child Neurology*, **40** (5), 340.

McLachlan, R. & Peppin, P. (1986) Sexuality and Contraception for Developmentally Handicapped Persons. *Canadian Family Physician*, **32**, 1631–7.

Mortel, K.F. & Meyer, J.S. (1995) Lack of postmenopausal estrogen therapy and risk of dementia. *Journal of Neuropsychiatry and Clinical Neuroscience*, **14**, 332–337.

Mulnard, R.A., Cotman, C.W. & Kawas, C.W. (2000) Estrogen replacement therapy for treatment of mild to moderate Alzheimer disease: a randomized controlled trial. Alzheimer's Disease Cooperative Study. *Journal of the American Medical Association*, **283**, 1007–1015.

Murray A., Webb, J., MacSwiney, F., Shipley, E., Morton, N.E. & Conway, G.S. (1999) Serum concentrations of follicle stimulating hormone may predict premature ovarian failure in FRAXA pre-mutation women. *Human Reproduction*, **14**, 1217–1218.

Murray, A., Enis, S., MacSwiney, F., Webb, J. & Morton, N.E. (2000) Reproductive and menstrual history of females with fragile X expansions. *European Journal of Human Genetics*, **8**, 247–252.

Oster, J. (1953) *Mongolism*. Danish Science Press Ltd, Copenhagen.

Paganini-Hill, A. & Henderson, V.W. (1994) Estrogen deficiency and risk of Alzheimer's disease in women. *American Journal of Epidemiology*, **140**, 256–261.

Pary, R. (1993) Psychoactive drugs used with adults and elderly adults who have mental retardation. *American Journal on Mental Retardation*, **98**, 121–127.

Patja, K., Molsa, P., Iivanainen, M. & Vesala, H. (2001) Cause-specific mortality of people with intellectual disability in a population-based, 35-year follow-up study. *Journal of Intellectual Disability Research*, **45**, 30–40.

Raghavan, R., Khin-Nu, C., Brown, A.G., Day, K.A., Tyrer, S.P., Ince, P.G., Perry, E.K. & Perry, R.H. (1994) Gender differences in the phenotypic expression of Alzheimer's disease in Down's syndrome (trisomy 21). *Neuroreport*, **5**, 1393–1396.

Rimmer, J.H., Braddock, D. & Fujiura, G. (1994) Cardiovascular risk factor levels in adults with mental retardation. *American Journal on Mental Retardation*, **98**, 510–518.

Ropper, A.H. & Williams, R.S. (1980) Relationship between plaques, tangles, and dementia in Down's syndrome. *Neurology*, **30**, 639–644.

van Schrojenstein Lantman-de Valk, H.M.J., Metsemakers, J.F.M., Haveman, M.J. & Crebolder, H.F.J.M. (2000) Health problems in people with intellectual disability in general practice: a comparative study. *Family Practice*, **17**, 405–407.

Schupf, N., Zigman, W., Kapell, D., Lee, J.H., Kline, J. & Levin, B. (1997) Early menopause in women with Down's syndrome. *Journal of Intellectual Disability Research*, **41**, 264–7.

Schupf, N., Kapell, D., Nightingale, B., Rodrigyez, A., Tycko, B. & Mayeux, R. (1998) Earlier onset of Alzheimer's disease in men with Down's syndrome. *Neurology*, **50**, 991–995.

Schwartz, C.E., Dean, J., Howard-Peebles, P.N., Bugge, M., Mikkelsen, M., Tommerup, N., Hull, C., Hagerman, R., Holden, J.J.A. & Stevenson, R.E. (1994) Obstetrical and gynecological complications in Fragile X carriers: a multi-center study. *American Journal of Medical Genetics*, **51**, 400–402.

Scola, P.S. & Pueschel, S.M. (1992) Menstrual cycles and basal body temperature curves in women with Down's syndrome. *Obstetrics and Gynecology*, **79**, 91–94.

Scott, J.C. & Hochberg, M.C. (1993) Arthritis and other musculoskeletal diseases. In: *Chronic Disease Epidemiology and Control* (eds R.C. Brownson, P.L. Remington, & J.R. Davis). pp. 285–305. American Public Health Association, Washington DC.

Servais, L., Hoyois, P. & Rousseaux, J.P. (1999) Sterilizing People with Learning Disabilities: a problem belonging to the past? *European Journal of Mental Disability*, **6**, 4–14.

Simpkins, J., Meharvan, S. & Bishop, J. (1994) The potential role for estrogen replacement therapy in the treatment of the cognitive decline and neuro-degeneration associated with Alzheimer's disease. *Neurobiology of Aging*, **15**, Supplement 2, 5195–5197.

Stampfer, M.J., Colditz, G.A., Willet, M.C., Manson, J.E., Rosner, B., Speizer, F.E. & Hennekens, C.H. (1991) Postmenopausal estrogen therapy and cardiovascular disease: ten year follow-up from the Nurses Health Study. *New England Journal of Medicine*, **325**, 756–762.

Tang, M.X., Jacobs, D., Stern, Y., Marder, K., Schofield, P., Gurland, K.B., Andrews, H. & Mayeux, R. (1996) Effect of oestrogen during menopause on risk and age at onset of Alzheimer's disease. *Lancet*, **348**, 429–432.

Tyler, C.V., Synder, C.W. & Zyzanski, S. (2000) Screening for osteoporosis in community-dwelling adults with mental retardation. *Mental Retardation*, **38**, 316–321.

Uno, Y. (1996) Mental retardation and colorectal disease: colonoscopic mass screening to determine whether the risk of adenomatous polyposis syndrome is increased in the mentally retarded. *Journal of Gastroenterology & Hepatology*, **11** (3), 275.

Visser, F.E., Aldenkamp, A.P., van Huffelen, A.C., Kuilman, M., Overweg, J. & van Wijk, J. (1997) Prospective study of the prevalence of Alzheimer-type dementia in institutionalized individuals with Down's syndrome. *American Journal on Mental Retardation*, **101**, 400–412.

Walsh, P.N., Heller, T., Schupf, N. & van Schrojenstein Lantman-de Valk, H.M.J. (2000) *Healthy Aging – Adults with Intellectual Disabilities: Women's Health Issues.* World Health Organization, Geneva.

Wingfield, M., Healy, D.L. & Nicholson, A. (1994) Gynecological care for women with intellectual disability. *The Medical Journal of Australia*, **160**, 536–538.

Zigman, W., Silverman, W. & Wisniewski, H.M. (1996) Aging and Alzheimer disease in Down's syndrome: Clinical and pathological changes. *Mental Retardation and Developmental Disabilities Research Reviews*, **2**, 73–79.

3 Women Aging with Intellectual Disabilities: What are the Health Risks?

Deborah J. Anderson

Introduction

This chapter examines the health status of women aging with intellectual disabilities in the US, using data from the community-based National Health Interview Survey Disability Supplement, 1994 and 1995 (NHIS-D). The NHIS-D offers a relatively rare opportunity to draw direct comparisons between women with and without intellectual disabilities (ID), drawn from the same nationally representative population base.

Women with ID often have multiple risk factors that can exacerbate their physical condition. The combined effects of gender, age and disabilities alter the risks for different diseases and impairments, the health care opportunities and barriers, the informal support system, and even the pharmacological action of medications for these conditions. In addition, poverty, lifestyle (diet, smoking, exercise), mental health, particularly depression, race and long-term medication use may influence health risks and health care.

Findings from the general medical literature suggest that women's health problems may present themselves in ways different from men's, that women often have different risk factors, and that women's response to illness may also differ from that of men. Wizemann & Pardue (2001: 133) note that 'exposures, susceptibilities, responses to initiating agents, energy metabolism, genetic predisposition, and responses to therapeutic agents are important factors in understanding how each sex responds to insult, injury, disease progression, and treatment'. In addition, women's support structure for health care may differ from men's. Katz *et al.* (2000) found that elderly women with disabilities were much more likely to be living alone, and they also received much less care if they were married, reflecting sex role differences in caregiving.

Findings from younger adults cannot be assumed to be applicable to older adults, due to differences in pharmacokinetics, more frequent polypharmacy and comorbidity (Bugeja *et al.*, 1997; Anderson & Polister, 1993). Although older adults have the greatest medical needs, they are more likely to be excluded, even when their inclusion would be appropriate or even essential, from both clinical research studies and clinical trials (Bugeja *et al.*, 1997). A review of Medline over a 10 year period found only 50 articles about randomized, controlled, clinical trials that dealt specifically with elderly persons (Bene & Liston, 1998). This seriously limits our understanding of age-appropriate health care for older adults.

In addition, specific syndromes associated with ID (e.g. syndromes caused by toxins, metabolic/genetic disorders, injuries or infections, typically during fetal development), are in turn associated with higher risks for certain medical conditions (Evenhuis et al., 2000). Women with intellectual disabilities have made considerable gains in life expectancy (Janicki et al., 1999), with even more striking gains among individuals with Down syndrome (Friedman, 2001), but it is still less than the life expectancy for women in general, averaging 67 years for women with mild to moderate disabilities (Brown & Murphy, 1999), 57 years for women with Down syndrome and 79 years for women in general in the US. Down syndrome is a risk factor for congenital heart and other defects, as well as for later hypothyroidism, cardiac, vision and hearing disorders, and dementia. Severe disabilities are associated with shorter life expectancies. Age-related changes in mobility and sensory perception (hearing, vision) tend to occur earlier among people with ID than in the general population (Kapell et al., 1998), particularly in those with Down syndrome (Bagley & Mascia, 1999).

Two large-scale US studies have reported lifetime prevalence rates for depression of 5.2–17.1% (Kessler et al., 1994; Weissman et al., 1996). Rates varied considerably by culture, ranging from 1.5% (Taiwan) to 19.0% (Beirut), the latter reflecting postwar trauma (Weissman et al., 1996). Women and divorced or separated persons had significantly higher rates of psychological disorders than men and married persons, respectively, in all countries. A 40 year prospective Canadian study reported stable rates of about 5%, but also found a shift toward more younger and fewer older adults with depression (Murphy et al., 2000). In contrast, a study of adults age 65 and older with ID in the UK found higher rates of psychiatric illness among older than younger adults (Cooper, 1997).

Depression has been found to be predictive of several major health problems in recent studies of the general population. In the area of cardiovascular disease (CVD), three large, well-controlled prospective studies of elderly persons, depression and CVD, found that mortality rates varied directly with the number of depressive symptoms, with CVD, but not cancer, being a major cause (Whooley & Browner, 1998); that depression was a risk factor for CVD only for women, and primarily for relatively healthy women (Mendes de Leon et al., 1998); and that rates of stroke (but not high blood pressure) were substantially higher among those with high numbers of depressive symptoms (Simonsick et al., 1995). A Norwegian study found that the presence of severe depression among outpatients with congestive heart failure increased death rates fourfold over a two year period (Murberg *et al.*, 1999).

Depression has also been implicated in prospective studies of vertebral fractures, falls and osteoporosis among older women (Whooley *et al.*, 1999; Cizza *et al.*, 2001), in declining function (balance, walking and getting in and out of a chair) (Penninx *et al.*, 1998), and as a risk factor for physical disability (Cronin-Stubbs *et al.*, 2000). Higher levels of depression were inversely related to cognitive function and cognitive change scores among older women (Yaffe *et al.*, 1999), and to Alzheimer disease (AD) in twins discordant for AD (Wetherell *et al.*, 1999).

Anxiety and stress have also been linked to health outcomes. Cortisol has been implicated in the damaging effects of stress and hostility on cardiovascular function, has been shown experimentally to increase homocysteine, which has been associated with CVD, and has been linked to decrements in declarative memory (Newcomer *et al.*, 1999; Stoney, 1999). Orth-Gomer *et al.* (2000) found that marital, but not work stress, predicted additional coronary events in women who had been hospitalized for myocardial infarction or unstable angina. Traumatic life events and accumulated lifetime traumas have been linked to increased risk for psychological disorders, which in turn are strong predictors for poor physical function and high health care utilization (Turner & Lloyd, 2001; Holman *et al.*, 2000). Anxiety that fails to reach clinical proportions may still exert a major, negative impact on quality of life (Gurian & Miner, 1991), and psychological intimate partner violence may have health effects as strong as physical violence (Coker *et al.*, 2000). However, diagnosis of anxiety among older adults is more difficult, since a variety of medical conditions that are more common with age (e.g. hyperthyroidism, hypoglycemia and CVD) have symptoms which may be mistaken for anxiety (Fisher & Noll, 1996).

Analysis of the National Health Interview Survey: comparison of women with and without ID

Study method

The National Health Interview Survey (NHIS) is a household survey administered annually to elicit detailed health information about the US population. In 1994 and 1995, a two-stage Disability Supplement (NHIS-D) was added to the core survey to identify respondents with disabilities and to then elicit additional information about health perceptions, their health care experiences, service usage and other health-related concerns (National Center for Health Statistics, 1997, 1998).

The NHIS is administered annually by the US Census Bureau to a representative sample of over 40 000 households, and over 100 000 civilian, non-institutionalized adults in the US. The sampling design from 1985–1994 included 49 000 households and 132 000 individuals; from 1995–2004, this was changed to 41 000 households and 107 000 persons. Households of black people were oversampled in 1994; in 1995, households of black and Hispanic people were oversampled (Russell, 2000). A national probability sample is selected, using a multistage, stratified cluster design. The household was the sampling unit. Sampling was done in stages, with primary sampling units (PSUs) being selected from total PSUs, stratified by state (1995) or region (1994) and MSA/non-MSA (urban/rural); within each PSU, clusters of blocks were systematically selected; within each block, clusters of 4–12 households were selected. Details of the sampling design changed between 1994 and 1995.

The NHIS and NHIS-D samples did not include people in long-term care facilities, such as nursing homes, psychiatric facilities or congregate care/institutional settings of four or more residents, or people in the military or in prison. Interviews were conducted in two stages. In the first stage, the core survey and the NHIS-D, Phase I, were completed for all household members by any respondent familiar with the health of other household members. Several months later, interviewers returned to interview individuals identified in Phase I as having disabilities. In Phase I, women with ID were sole respondents 49% of the time, and another 14% were partial respondents. Phase II was very similar to Phase I. The data discussed in this chapter includes the sample of women aged 30 and older with intellectual disabilities, the majority (62%) of whom also had developmental disabilities (see next section for definitions).

Definitions

The definitions used in this study differ from typical usage in the US, in which 'developmental disabilities' is often used interchangeably with 'mental retardation'. These terms have definitions which are grounded in United States law and professional definitions respectively, and they can be considered to be separate entities, even though there is often a high degree of overlap. The definition of 'developmental disabilities' in the United States is determined by the Developmental Disabilities Assistance and Bill of Rights Act (PL 98-527) (DD Act), which indicates that the disability must occur prior to the age of 22, it must require extended care, treatment or other services, and it must cause substantial functional limitations in three or more major areas of life, including self-care, receptive or expressive language, learning, self-direction, capacity for independent living, and/or economic self-sufficiency. The definition of 'mental retardation' employed by the American Association on Mental Retardation (AAMR) requires 'significantly subaverage intellectual functioning ... with related limitations in two or more ... adaptive skill areas: communication, self-care, home living, social skills, community use, self-direction, health and safety, functional academics, leisure and work, with the limitations manifested prior to age 18' (AAMR, 1992: 1). Professional diagnostic practices are delineated by both AAMR (1992) and the American Psychological Association (Jacobson & Mulick, 1996).

An individual may have 'mental retardation' *in the absence of* a developmental disability, or a developmental disability but not mental retardation, or both. These definitions were delineated for the NHIS by Larson *et al.* (2000, 2001). Adults were considered to have 'mental retardation' if they reported having mental retardation, or had an ICD code of 'mental retardation' as a cause of work or other activities, or had an ICD code of mental retardation as a *reason for a limitation* in any of 24 items, clustered within seven categories of functional limitations, or reported both a 'learning disability' and a 'related condition' (28 conditions often associated with intellectual disabilities, such as Down syndrome), and a substantial decrement in learning.

In this chapter, intellectual disabilities, a term more consistent with international usage, is used instead of the term 'mental retardation'.

Population estimates were based on Phase I data, 1994–95 combined. Approximately 77 million women in the US were estimated to be age 30 and older and living in the community (the non-institutionalized, civilian US population) at the time of the 1994–1995 NHIS. The total US resident population in 1994 was 260 327 021, 133 277 846 of whom were female; in 1995, it was estimated to be 262 803 276, or 134 509 564 females (US Census Bureau, 2000). Women with ID comprised about 0.37% of the non-institutionalized, civilian population of women age 30 and older living in the community, or an estimated 434 330 women, 282 486 of whom had intellectual disabilities (see Table 3.1).

Demographics of women with ID

Some important demographic indicators which may bear upon women's health status or health care include their marital status, education, age, living situation, major activity (i.e. employed outside of the home, homemaker, etc.) and family income, as well as other developmental

Table 3.1 Estimated population, women age 30+ in the community by disability, NHIS-D 1994–1995.

Women 30+	Est. no.	RSE[†]	Sample	% Women 30+[b]
ID	106,201	10.41	89	0.14
ID/DD	176,285	10.07	137	0.23
Women in general[a]	76,571,324	0.90	60,649	99.44

Estimates based on Phase I sample, US non-institutionalized population.
ID = intellectual disability; ID/DD = an intellectual and a developmental disability.
[a] Women without an intellectual and/or developmental disability.
[b] Women with DD but not ID (0.19% of women 30+) are not included in these totals.
[†] RSE (Relative standard error) = Weighted SE/estimated population × 100.

disabilities. About four in ten (41%) of women age 30 and older with ID had married, but only one in six (17%) were still living with their spouse. Another 8% were widowed. Overall, 13% of participating women with ID had no formal education (or just kindergarten), but this obscures the fact that most of these women also had a developmental disability – 31% with such a disability had no formal education, but this was rare among women with ID who did *not* have a developmental disability (2%). Another 28% of women with ID had completed between one and eight years of education. One in ten women with ID (9.8%) also had Down syndrome, and 7.7% had cerebral palsy.

Women with ID tended to be clustered in the younger age groups, 37% being between the ages of 30 and 39 and 28% between 40 and 49 years. The age distribution of women with ID who did not have an associated developmental disability is similar to that of women in general, but women with a developmental disability were under represented in the older (sixties and seventies) age ranges (13% and 16% respectively for women with ID alone to just under 5% for women with both an intellectual and a developmental disability).

The most common living arrangement for women with ID was with their families (62%), but another 17% lived alone and a similar number lived with their spouses. Few lived with someone unrelated. One in five (21%) women with ID were working. About one-third of respondents with ID indicated that their major activity was keeping house. Reported family incomes were typically quite low, with 60% reporting 1994–95 family incomes of less than $20 000, and slightly over one-quarter reporting family incomes of less than $10 000. A similar proportion (26%) of women with ID lived below the poverty level, which was about 2.5 times the percentage of women in general in this age group living below the poverty threshold (10%).

Health indicators for women with ID

Women's perceptions of their health status, their Activities of Daily Living (ADL) and Instrumental Activities of Daily Living (IADL) status, health care services utilized in the prior year, activity limitations due to health problems, and indicators of psychological functioning were used to provide a broad picture of the health and health-related functioning of women with ID. Women with ID were more than twice as likely as women in general to report that their health was fair or poor (36% and 16% respectively) (see Fig. 3.1).

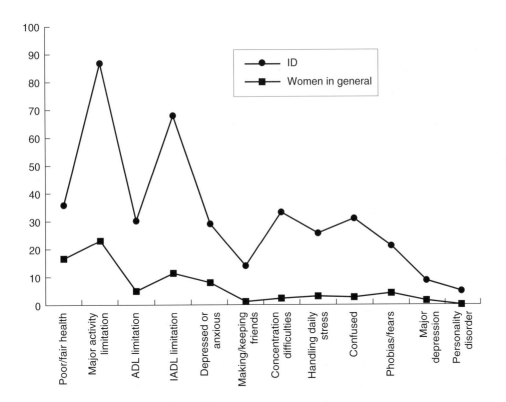

Fig. 3.1 Health indicators in women age 30+ with and without intellectual disabilities.

Most participants were independent in all ADLs, including bathing, dressing, eating, transferring in and out of a chair, using the toilet and/or getting around inside of the house. About two in three women with ID reported being independent in all ADLs (69%); women in the general population were almost always (96%) independent in ADLs. An examination of specific ADL areas found that 90% or more of women with ID reported that they had no problems eating, getting in and out of a chair, getting around inside, and using the toilet. The most difficult tasks were dressing and bathing, but two in three women with ID were independent in these tasks as well.

IADLs, which included preparing meals, shopping, managing money, using the telephone, doing heavy work around the house and doing light work, were problematic for many respondents, and group differences were much larger than for ADLs. Just over half (55%) of women with ID, but without a developmental disability, were independent in all IADL areas. Women with both ID and development disabilities were seldom independent in IADLs (17%); the areas in which they had the greatest difficulty were in 'managing money' and 'shopping'. Almost nine in ten women in general reported independence in all IADLs (89%).

Another health-related indicator is the extent to which individuals receive medical and allied health services. Almost nine in ten women with ID indicated that they had seen a doctor within the previous year. Very few received physical therapy (6%) or occupational therapy (2%). About one in three received case management services.

Activity limitations were common for women with ID (87%), in contrast with women in general of this age group (22%). For most respondents, 'activity limitations' meant being unable to perform a major activity (e.g. work, student, housewife), with slightly over half of women with ID, but only 6% of women in general, so indicating. About one-quarter of women with ID indicated that they were limited in the *kind or amount* of activity they engaged in; this was true of 8% of women without these disabilities.

Psychological distress was much more widespread among women with ID than among women in general (see Fig. 3.1). About 30% of women with ID, but only 8% of women in general, reported 'frequent feelings of depression or anxiety' (see Fig. 3.1). Some additional questions elicited more specific information about possible clinical conditions. About 10% of women with ID, and 2% of women without ID, reported having experienced major depression lasting two or more weeks in the previous year. The presence of 'phobias or unreasonable fears' was indicated by 22% of women with ID, but only 5% of women in general. Personality disorders (antisocial personality or obsessive compulsive disorder) were reported by 6% of women with ID.

A substantial minority (27%) of women with ID reported serious difficulty 'coping with day to day stresses'. Women in general were very unlikely to report such difficulty, only 3% so indicating. One in three participants with ID reported frequently feeling 'confused, disoriented or forgetful' and having 'a lot of trouble' concentrating enough to complete tasks, far exceeding the extent of concentration difficulties among women without such disabilities (2%). Women with ID had somewhat greater success in the social sphere, including making and keeping friends and getting along in social settings, but they still had a great deal more difficulty than women without such disabilities (15% of women with ID, compared with less than 1% of women in general indicated serious difficulties with friendships; 13% and 0.5% respectively had difficulty getting along socially).

The reported incidence of the most serious disorders in the previous year was lower than for other disorders. Schizophrenia was alleged by 3.5% of women with ID, 5% reported paranoid disorder, and 1.6% reported bipolar disorder. Alcohol abuse was infrequent (1.5%), and Alzheimer's disease was uncommon among community dwelling women (1.8%). Two thirds of women with ID reporting a mental health problem indicated that it had interfered with their lives over the prior year.

Implications for health care

Marital status

The findings about marital status differ considerably from findings from most samples of women with intellectual disabilities. This doubtless reflects some important differences between women who remain in the community, who are likely to have more freedom in their life (and health) choices, and women living in licensed residential facilities. Although marriage is often viewed as social support, which can be a buffer to stress and an aid in encouraging appropriate health care, it is less clear that this is the case with women, whose traditional caretaker role may extend to their spouse's health care, but who are less likely to be the recipients of such care. Even if a positive relationship exists between marriage and health status, the high rate of disrupted marriages among this group may suggest that there are considerable stresses on such relationships for women with ID.

Poverty

The high rate of poverty was one of the more troubling findings from this study. Extremely low incomes are likely to cause multiple strains that may affect health, including difficulty in paying for health care services that are not fully covered, in obtaining transportation to access medical care, and in having sufficient income for a healthful diet, supplements, medications, preventive care and medical devices that may be needed to enjoy a reasonably healthful life. Altman *et al.* (1999) noted that disabilities are disproportionately in the families with the lowest incomes, who have the fewest resources with which to deal with additional expenses and care needs.

Poverty may be a strong disincentive to living independently. It is notable that only one in six women with wheelchairs used an electric wheelchair, which raises the issue of the financial accessibility of available technologies. In addition, numerous research findings attest to the adverse health effects of poverty, although the aspects of poverty involved and how these effects are translated into health outcomes are unclear. In the general population, Kraus (1996) found adverse health effects associated with financial problems as well as with the most deteriorated environmental conditions among older adults. Fried *et al.* (1998) found poverty to be an independent predictor of mortality within a five-year period. Winkleby *et al.* (1998) found that lower socioeconomic status (SES) was associated with CVD *risk factors* among white, black and Hispanic people, including significantly higher rates of smoking and physical inactivity, higher body mass indices and higher non-HDL cholesterol levels. A longitudinal study of participants 45–64 years of age found residents of disadvantaged neighborhoods to be at substantially greater risk for cardiovascular disease, controlling for education, income and occupation (Diez Roux *et al.*, 2001).

Mortimer (1998) suggested that poverty might indirectly contribute to poor health by failing to provide the protection needed to prevent expression of a genetic propensity. For example, among persons with a family history of Alzheimer's disease, childhood poverty increased the risk of Alzheimer's five to eleven times, compared with the risk associated with the same history but without early poverty. Relative affluence may be protective in those with genetic risk factors by early nutritional enhancement of brain development. Poverty may also contribute to stress, which, if prolonged, is associated through corticosteroids with adverse health outcomes.

ADL and IADL

The *extent* of the difference between women with and without ID across most ADL and IADL areas was striking. There were dramatic differences in the percentage of women in general and women with ID with at least some degree of ADL and IADL limitation. The impact on major activity limitations was similarly large, and perceptions of health status followed accordingly.

Mental health

The extent of psychological and social difficulties reported by participants was unanticipated. This is an extraordinarily distressed group, in contrast to women without intellectual disabilities. Horwitz *et al.*'s (2000) review indicates that US studies find a higher prevalence of mental health disorders among individuals with mild ID, but European research finds individuals with more severe ID to have a higher prevalence of mental health disorders. The discrepancies are large and unresolved. One possibility is that the samples may not be representative of the population as a whole. The results of this survey cannot be compared with surveys using DSM (*Diagnostic and Statistical Manual*) criteria and expert opinion for assessing clinical disorders. However, the subjective views of the individuals themselves are valuable by definition, since only they can know the depth and breadth of their distress. The extent of mental health disorders among women in general was modest, and at times even lower than might be expected from national studies (perhaps because women in their twenties were not included). Fig. 3.1 illustrates the magnitude of difference for selected physical and mental health indicators.

In comparison with women in general, women with ID have considerable vulnerability – a combination of very poor financial resources, physical disability and limitations, and psychological distress, particularly depression and anxiety, but also marked confusion or forgetfulness, difficulty concentrating, difficulty coping with life's stresses, and social difficulties. These findings present a picture of women with few coping skills, whose sense of well-being and ability to plan and implement strategies to deal with challenges is often poor, and who may not have adequate financial, emotional and practical support. The majority had no case coordinator, many were not living with their families, and few worked. High levels of depression and stress have been shown in many studies to be a risk factor for disease and disability, including cardiovascular diseases, osteoporosis, cognitive decline and others. The markedly elevated rates of several risk factors for disease and disability strongly suggest that more attention needs to be paid to the social context, and in particular to psychological health.

Many risk factors, including untreated depression, nutritional deficiencies and smoking can be reduced. Findings from the US National Long-Term Care Survey found a decline in disability among the elderly which is accelerating, with particularly dramatic changes among elderly black people (Manton & Gu, 2001). The factors responsible for this include a major decline in smoking (one-third since the 1960s), improved medical treatment, including drugs and surgical techniques, a more educated populace and public health measures. It is not clear that women with ID will benefit from much of that trend. Cutler (2001) notes that more educated people have about half the disability rate of less educated people. Smeltzer (2000) notes that prevention of secondary disabilities is not a focal point in health care for women with disabilities, particularly older women and women with more severe disabilities. In 1995, Birenbaum pointed out that managed health care was potentially problematical for adults with ID, because primary care physicians generally are not trained in examining or treating adults with ID, and the tight time constraints for physician–patient contact are not adequate for patients with ID. In 2001, Kaiser Permanente, the largest health maintenance organization in the US, settled a class-action lawsuit alleging inferior care to patients with disabilities, with the admission that the entire health care system knew little about treating people with disabilities (Lewin, 2001). Problems included inaccessible equipment (examining tables, X-rays, mammograms, etc.), which resulted in physicians failing to examine people for pressure sores and other conditions, or Pap smear testing.

The findings from the US national sample of women are informative about future trends, since increasing numbers of individuals with ID are likely to continue integrating within their community following graduation from school, with a corresponding increase in the choices available to them, including lifestyle choices, marriage, health care and others. Their health care has lagged behind, and is likely to continue to do so unless advocacy efforts are made on their behalf. It is important to reduce existing risk factors, including psychological risks, to conduct research on the impact of health interventions with women with these disabilities, and to implement strategies to prevent further disability and to enhance independence within the community.

Acknowledgements

This project was developed in consultation with Carol Gill and Lisa Brown at the Rehabilitation Research and Training Center on Aging with Developmental Disabilities, University of Illinois at Chicago. Sheryl Larson, Charlie Lakin, Linda Anderson and Nohoon Kwak were instrumental in developing the definitions of disabilities used in this manuscript.

Project funding was provided by the National Institute on Disability and Rehabilitation Research (NIDRR), US Department of Education, through the Rehabilitation Research and Training Center on Aging with Developmental Disabilities under grant number H133B980046. The opinions expressed are those of the author and do not necessarily reflect the views of the Institute, Center, University or their funding sources.

References

AAMR (1992) *Mental Retardation: Definition, Classification, and Systems of Support* (9th edition). American Association on Mental Retardation, Washington DC.

Altman, B.M., Cooper, P.F. & Cunningham, P.J. (1999) The case of disability in the family: Impact on health care utilization and expenditures for nondisabled members. *Milbank Quarterly*, **77** (1), 39–75.

Anderson, D.J. & Polister, B. (1993) Psychotropic drug use among older adults with mental retardation. In: *Older Adults with Developmental Disabilities: Optimizing Choice and Change* (eds E. Sutton, A. Factor, B. Hawkins, T. Heller, & G. Seltzer), pp. 61–75. Paul H. Brookes, Baltimore.

Bagley, M. & Mascia, J. (1999) *Hearing Changes in Aging People with Mental Retardation*. The Arc of the United States and the Rehabilitation Research and Training Center (RRTC) on Aging with Mental Retardation, Chicago.

Bene, J. & Liston, R. (1998) Clinical trials should be designed to include elderly people. *British Medical Journal*, **316**, 1905.

Birenbaum, A. (1995) Managed care and the future of primary care for adults with mental retardation. *Mental Retardation*, **33** (5), 334–337.

Brown, A.A. & Murphy, L. (1999) *Aging with Developmental Disabilities: Women's Health Issues*, p. 522. The Arc, Silver Springs, MD.

Bugeja, G., Kumar, A. & Banerjee, A.K. (1997) Exclusion of elderly people from clinical research: a descriptive study of published reports. *British Medical Journal*, **315**, 1059.

Cizza, G., Ravn, P., Chrousos, G.P. & Gold, P.W. (2001) Depression: a major, unrecognized risk factor for osteoporosis? *Trends in Endocrinology Metabolism*, **12** (5), 198–203.

Coker, A.L., Smith, P.H., Bethea, L., King, M.R., & McKeown, R.E. (2000) Physical health consequences of physical and psychological intimate partner violence. *Archives of Family Medicine*, **9**, 451–457.

Cooper, S.A. (1997) Psychiatry of elderly compared to younger adults with intellectual disabilities. *Journal of Applied Research in Intellectual Disabilities*, **10** (4) 303–311.

Cronin-Stubbs, D., Mendes de Leon, C.F., Beckett, L.A., Field, T.S., Glynn, R.J. & Evans, D.A. (2000) Six-year effect of depressive symptoms on the course of physical disability in community-living older adults. *Archives of Internal Medicine*, **160**, 3074–3080.

Cutler, D.M. (2001) The reduction in disability among the elderly. *Proceedings of the National Academy of Sciences USA*, **98** (12), 6546–6547.

Diez Roux, A.V., Merkin, S.S., Arnett, D., Chambless, L., Massing, M., Nieto, J., Sorlie, P., Szklo, M., Tyroler, H.A. & Watson, R.L. (2001) Neighborhood of residence and incidence of coronary heart disease. *New England Journal of Medicine*, **345** (2), 99–106.

Evenhuis, H., Henderson, C.M., Beange, H., Lennox, N., Chicoine, B. & Working Group (2000) *Healthy Aging – Adults with Intellectual Disabilities: Physical Health Issues*, p. 5. World Health Organization, Geneva, Switzerland.

Fisher, J.E. & Noll, J.P. (1996) Anxiety disorders. In: *The Practical Handbook of*

Clinical Gerontology, (eds L. Carstensen, B.A. Edelstein & L. Dornbrand), pp. 304–323. Sage, Thousand Oaks.

Fried, L.P., Kronmal, R.A., Newman, A.B., Bild, D.E., Mittelmark, M.B., Polak, J.F., Robbins, J.A. & Gardin, J.M. (1998) Risk factors for 5-year mortality in older adults: the Cardiovascular Health Study. *Journal of the American Medical Association*, **279**, 585–592.

Friedman, J.M. (2001) Racial disparities in median age at death of persons with Down syndrome – United States, 1968–1997. *Morbidity and Mortality Weekly Report*, **50** (22), 463–465.

Gurian, B. & Miner, J.H. (1991) Clinical presentation of anxiety in the elderly. In: *Anxiety in the Elderly* (eds C. Salzman & B.D. Lebowitz). Springer, New York.

Holman, E.A., Silver, R.C. & Waitzkin, H. (2000) Traumatic life events in primary care patients: a study in an ethnically diverse sample. *Archives of Family Medicine*, **9**, 802–810.

Horwitz, S.M., Kerker, B.D., Owens, P.L. & Zigler, E. (2000) *The Health Status and Needs of Individuals with Mental Retardation*. Department of Epidemiology and Public Health, Yale University School of Medicine, Department of Psychology, Yale University, New Haven, CT.

Jacobson, J.W. & Mulick, J.A. (Eds) (1996) *Manual of Diagnosis and Professional Practice in Mental Retardation*. American Psychological Association, Washington DC.

Janicki, M.P., Dalton, A.J., Henderson, C.M. & Davidson, P.W. (1999) Mortality and morbidity among older adults with intellectual disability: health service considerations. *Disability Rehabilitation*, **21**, 284–294.

Kapell, D., Nightingale, B., Rodriguez, A., Lee, J.H., Zigman, W.B. & Schupf, N. (1998) Prevalence of chronic medical conditions in adults with mental retardation: comparison with the general population. *Mental Retardation*, **36** (4) 269–279.

Katz, S.J., Kabeto, M. & Langa, K.M. (2000) Gender disparities in the receipt of home care for elderly people with disability in the United States. *Journal of the American Medical Association*, **284**, 3022–3027.

Kessler, R.C., McGonagle, K.A., Ahao, S., Nelson, C.B., Hughes, M., Eshleman S., Wittchen H.U. & Kendler, K.S. (1994) Lifetime and 12 month prevalence rates of DSM-III-R psychiatric disorders in the United States: Results from the National Comorbidity Survey. *Archives of General Psychiatry*, **51**, 8–19.

Kraus, N. (1996) Neighborhood deterioration and self-rated health in later life. *Psychology and Aging*, **11** (2), 342–352.

Larson, S., Lakin, C., Anderson, L., Kwak, N., Lee, J. & Anderson, D. (2000) Prevalence of mental retardation and/or developmental disabilities: analysis of the 1994–1995 NHIS-D. *MR/DD Data Brief*, **2** (1), University of Minnesota, RRTC on Community Living, Institute on Community Integration, Minneapolis, MN.

Larson, S.A., Lakin, C.K., Anderson, L., Kwak, N., Lee, J.H. & Anderson, D. (2001) The prevalence of mental retardation and developmental disabilities: estimates from the 1994/1995 National Health Interview Survey Disability Supplements. *American Journal of Mental Retardation*, **106** (3), 231–252.

Lewin, T. (2001) Disabled patients win sweeping changes from HMO. *The New York Times*, 13 April 2001.

Manton, K.G. & Gu, X. (2001) Changes in the prevalence of chronic disability in the United States black and nonblack population above age 65 from 1982 to 1999. *Proceedings of the National Academy of Sciences USA*, **98** (11), 6354–6359.

Mendes de Leon, C.F., Krumholz, H.M., Seeman, T.S., Vaccarino, V., Williams, C.S., Kasl, S.V. & Berkman, L.F. (1998) Depression and risk of coronary heart disease in elderly men and women New Haven EPESE, 1982–1991. *Archives of Internal Medicine*, **158**, 2341–2348.

Mortimer, J. (1998) Poverty, poor education in childhood can greatly increase risk of Alzheimer's. *Doctor's Guide to the Internet*, http://www.docguide.com, retrieved 1 March 2000 from http://www.pslgroup.com/dg/8FCAE.htm.

Murberg, T.A., Bru, E., Svebak, S., Tveteras, R. & Aarsland, T. (1999) Depressed mood and subjective health symptoms as predictors of mortality in patients with congestive heart failure: a two-years follow-up study. *International Journal of Psychiatry in Medicine*, **29** (3), 311–326.

Murphy, J.M., Laird, N.M., Monson, R.R., Sobol, A.M. & Leighton, A.H. (2000) A 40-year perspective on the prevalence of depression: the Stirling County study. *Archives of General Psychiatry*, **57**, 209–215.

National Center for Health Statistics (1997, 1998) *1994, 1995 National Health Interview Survey* (database on CD-ROM). CD-ROM Series 10, Nos. 9 and 10c. SETS Version 1.21a. US Government Printing Office, Washington, DC.

Newcomer, J.W., Selke, G., Melson, A.K., Hershey, T., Craft, S., Richards, K. & Alderson, A.L. (1999) Decreased memory performance in healthy humans induced by stress-level cortisol treatment. *Archives of General Psychiatry*, **56**, 527–533.

Orth-Gomer, K., Wamala, S.P., Horsten, M., Schenck-Gustafsson, K., Schneiderman, N. & Mittleman, M.A. (2000) Marital stress worsens prognosis in women with coronary heart disease: the Stockholm female coronary risk study. *Journal of the American Medical Association*, **284**, 3008–3014.

Penninx, B.W., Guralnik, J.M., Ferrucci, L., Simonsick, E.M., Deeg, D.J. & Wallace, R.B. (1998) Depressive symptoms and physical decline in community-dwelling older persons. *Journal of the American Medical Association*, **279** (21), 1720–1726.

Russell, J.N. (2000) *Sample Design, Weighting, and Variance Estimation for the NHIS-D*. Paper presented at the Robert Woods Johnson National Health Interview Disability Supplement Users' Conference, University of Minnesota, RRTC on Community Living, Institute on Community Integration, Minneapolis, MN.

Simonsick, E.M., Wallace, R.B., Blazer, D.G. & Berkman, L.F. (1995) Depressive symptomatology and hypertension-associated morbidity and mortality in older adults. *Psychosomatic Medicine*, **57** (5), 427–435.

Smeltzer, S.C. (2000) Double jeopardy: the health care system slights women with disabilities. *American Journal of Nursing*, **100** (8), 11.

Stoney, C.M. (1999) Plasma homocysteine levels increase in women during psychological stress. *Life Sciences*, **64** (25), 2359–2565,

Turner, R.J. & Lloyd, D.A. (2001) Lifetime traumas and mental health: the significance of cumulative adversity. *Journal of Health and Social Behavior*, **36** (4), 360–376.

US Census Bureau (2000) *Resident Population of the United States, 1970 to 1999, by Sex*. Online, accessed at http://www.census.gov/population/estimates/

nation/e90s/e9494rmp.txt (1994 figures) and http://www.census.gov/population/estimates/nation/e90s/e9595rmp.txt (1995 figures).

Weissman, M.M., Bland, R.C., Canino, G.J., Faravelli, C., Greenwald, S., Hwu, H.G., Joyce, P.R., Karam, E.G., Lee, C.K., Lellouch, J., Lepine, J.P., Newman, S.C., Rubio-Stipec, M., Wells, J.E., Wickramaratne, P.J., Wittchen, H. & Yeh, E.K. (1996) Cross-national epidemiology of major depression and bipolar disorder. *Journal of the American Medical Association*, **276** (4), 293–299.

Wetherell, J.L., Gatz, M., Johansson, B. & Pedersen, N.L. (1999) History of depression and other psychiatric illness as risk factors for Alzheimer disease in a twin sample. *Alzheimer Disease and Associated Disorders*, **13** (1), 47–52.

Whooley, M.A. & Browner, W.S. (1998) Association between depressive symptoms and mortality in older women. *Archives of Internal Medicine*, **158**, 2129–2135.

Whooley, M.A., Kip, K.E., Cauley, J.A., Ensrud, K.E., Nevitt, M.C. & Browner, W.S. (1999) Depression, Falls, and Risk of Fracture in Older Women. *Archives of Internal Medicine*, **159**, 484–490.

Winkleby, M.A., Kraemer, H.C., Ahn, D.K. & Varady, A.N. (1998) Ethnic and socioeconomic differences in cardiovascular disease risk factors findings for women from the third National Health and Nutrition Examination Survey, 1988–1994. *Journal of the American Medical Association*, **280**, 356–362.

Wizemann, T.M. & Pardue, M. (eds) (2001) Exploring the biological contributions to human health: does sex matter? *Committee on Understanding the Biology of Sex and Gender Differences, Institute of Medicine*, p. 133. National Academy Press, Washington, DC.

Yaffe, K., Blackwell, T., Gore, R., Sands, L., Reus, V. & Browner, W.S. (1999) Depressive symptoms and cognitive decline in nondemented elderly women: a prospective study. *Archives of General Psychiatry*, **56**, 425–430.

Part 2
Health Status and Trends

Girl with intellectual disability in a crowd – Bangladesh.

4 Women's Mental Health

Yona Lunsky and Susan M. Havercamp

Introduction

Mental illness has long been treated as a genderless problem (Eichler & Parron, 1986). Both the social and physiological characteristics unique to women have been ignored in psychiatry research. As a result, women with mental health problems have suffered unnecessarily. The area of women's mental health has grown since the 1980s with the aim of better understanding of the social conditions in women's lives and their relationship to emotional distress as well as the influence of hormones and biology on women's brains and emotional lives (Rhodes & Goering, 1998). Women with intellectual disabilities, unfortunately, have been excluded from this important movement. This chapter will review what is known about the mental health of women with intellectual disabilities and will identify current gaps in research.

Gender and mental health

There are social, biological and epidemiological reasons for studying the mental health of women separately from men. The biological argument considers that the brains of women and men differ in terms of structure and function, as do men and women's endocrine systems. The social argument for considering women's mental health separately from men's is broader in scope. With a largely biomedical model of mental illness, the social causes and exacerbations that are specific to women are ignored (Johnson & Fee, 1997). Issues such as poverty, inequities in the workplace, societal expectations of women and gender differences in coping are particularly relevant to women's mental health and are under emphasized in the research literature (Astbury & Cabral, 2000). The epidemiological argument for studying men and women separately is simply that prevalence rates differ across gender by disorder. Research is needed to better understand this phenomenon.

Women with intellectual disability

Strong arguments, both biological and social, can be made on the importance of including women with ID in the women's mental health movement. Individuals with ID are at an increased risk for mental health problems. Prevalence estimates place the rate of 'dual diagnosis' or co-occurrence of intellectual disability and mental health problems at 39% (Reiss, 1990), generally higher than that of the general population (Maxmen & Ward, 1995). In the general population, it is recognized that women are more vulnerable to certain psychiatric disorders, such as depression (Culbertson, 1997). Conclusive research has not been completed to know if the same gender differences are found in persons with ID.

It is important to consider the social context of women with ID because they have arguably been more marginalized than women without intellectual disabilities (Baum & Burns, 2000). They are reinforced for passivity, they are at increased risk for suffering from abuse, and they are commonly unemployed and have limited access to proper mental health treatment because of poverty or low income (Traustadottir & Johnson, 2000). The limited research on psychiatric illness and women with ID has not examined the influence of such social factors.

Risk factors

Several risk factors for mental health problems have been identified in the women's mental health literature. They are reviewed here with consideration given to how these risk factors are relevant to women with intellectual disabilities.

Biological considerations

Important gender differences have been found in the development, organization and degeneration of the human brain. Such differences have been linked to the later onset and differing presentation of serious mental illness, such as schizophrenia, in women (Castle, 2000a). Biological differences between men and women with intellectual disabilities and their potential influence on mental health have not been studied.

Differences are also found in the endocrine system of women and men. Such differences have been linked to a higher frequency of mental health difficulties prior to, during or following reproductive events such as menstruation, pregnancy, childbirth, abortion and menopause (Kulkarni

& Fink, 2000). Syndrome specific research (e.g. Down syndrome, Prader–Willi syndrome) has also highlighted relevant hormonal differences between women with and without ID that could be relevant in terms of biological risk for mental health problems. How these women's endocrine abnormalities relate to mental illness has not yet been studied.

Psychosocial considerations

Stress has been identified as an important risk factor for mental health problems. Women experience stress differently than men and have been shown to use different coping strategies than men when faced with stress. Men are more likely to deal with stress actively, by engaging in athletics, for example. This coping strategy distracts them from their turmoil and ameliorates emotional duress. Women, in contrast, tend to focus attention on themselves and 'ruminate' when facing stress (Nolen-Hoeksema, 1987). There has been some research on stress and individuals with intellectual disabilities, including mild intellectual disability (Bramston *et al.*, 1999) and autism (Groden *et al.*, 1996). However, gender differences have not been reported. Preliminary findings suggest that women with ID, when faced with conflict or interpersonal stress, may internalize their frustration and cope poorly (Benson & Fuchs, 1999) but further research is warranted.

Social support has been identified as an important buffer of mental illness, such that its presence can prevent the onset of or minimize the severity of emotional distress (Cohen & Wills, 1985). Overall, women have been reported to have greater social support than men (Leavy, 1983) as well as stronger social skills, which are important in the recruitment and maintenance of relationships (Seeman & Fitzgerald, 2000). According to carers, women with ID may have relatively more social support than men with ID (Krauss *et al.*, 1992; Lunsky & Benson, 1999). However, men and women with ID suffer from significantly less social support than people without ID (Rosen & Burchard, 1990; Sands & Kozleski, 1994).

One unique risk factor for mental health problems faced by women is referred to as the 'cost of caring'. The fact that women tend to have more social resources than men helps to protect them from mental health problems. However, with social resources often comes distress because of women's involvement and sometimes enmeshment in the stressful events that happen to others around them (Eichler & Parron, 1986: Rhodes & Goering, 1998). Limited research on the cost of caring hypothesis has been done with women who have ID. Walmsley (1996) examined family relationships from the perspective of men and women with ID living with their parents. She reported that seven of fourteen women experienced stress because of their responsibilities to their parents; only one of eight men reported this situation.

Women face barriers to proper health care because of poverty, due in part to lower wages in the workplace, and difficulties balancing work with other responsibilities like child care. Although women with ID are less likely to be responsible for children, they face poverty because of their inability to obtain high paying employment and because of their dependency on financial aid from the government. They have limited access to medical care for their mental health problems and also suffer many stresses related to their lower socioeconomic status (Traustadottir & Johnson, 2000).

The relationship between the experience of abuse and psychiatric difficulties is strong in the general population. In one large study, 72% of female psychiatric patients reported a history of sexual abuse (Eichler & Parron, 1986). Women with ID are more likely to be abused physically and sexually than women in the general population; they are also at higher risk for abuse than men with ID (Furey, 1994). Furthermore, treatment for such problems is often unavailable, inaccessible or inappropriate (see Chapter 10).

Gender differences in prevalence

The two most widely cited epidemiological studies on psychiatric disorders are the Ecological Catchment Area (ECA) Study (Robins & Regier, 1991) and the National Comorbidity Study (NCS) (Kessler et al., 1994), both completed in the US. While no differences were found in the overall rate of psychiatric disturbance in men versus women, differences were noted in the prevalence of specific disorders across gender.

Research on the prevalence of mental health problems in individuals with intellectual disabilities has largely overlooked the question of gender differences. In fact, several recent reviews on dual diagnosis that outline directions for future research make no mention of gender differences or mental health concerns specific to women (Horwitz et al., 2000; Jacobson & Holland, 2000; Moss et al., 1997).

Research limitations in ID

Prevalence estimates for mental health problems in ID vary widely from 10% to 80% (Borthwick-Duffy, 1994; Crews et al., 1994). Such discrepant findings are partially the result of research design artifacts (for a detailed review, see Borthwick-Duffy, 1994). These artifacts also influence the results of gender difference studies. One artifact concerns sample selection. Studies that draw their sample from referrals to a mental health service may over represent certain types of mental health or behavioral problems. This is due to the fact that very few individuals with ID initiate the referral process themselves (Fletcher, 1993; Nezu & Nezu, 1994). As many individuals with ID have a limited ability to report verbally with accuracy, their referral for mental health services largely depends on the ability of family members and program/service staff to recognize the presence of behavioral and emotional disturbance (Borthwick-Duffy, 1994). Aggression and other acting-out behaviors attract notice (Charlot *et al.*, 1993; Edelstein & Glenwick, 1997; Ghaziuddin, 1988; Stack *et al.*, 1987). This finding has implications for women's mental health because men are more likely to display acting out behaviors while women are more likely to have depressive or anxious symptoms (Day, 1985; Benson, 1985). There is a tendency, then, for women's mental health problems to go unrecognized and untreated.

Another design artifact has to do with the assessment procedures used. Studies based exclusively on informant data may overlook certain symptoms. In research using the PAS-ADD (Psychiatric Assessment Schedule for Adults with Development Disabilities), for example, informants tended to overlook subjective symptoms, such as anxiety or sadness (Moss *et al.*, 1996). This tendency was attributed to the informants' being unaware of the symptoms and/or not recognizing the symptoms as potential mental health problems. Again, it is more likely that subjective or internalizing symptoms of women would be overlooked than the more outward difficulties of men. The solution to this methodological weakness is to include a self-report measure of mood and anxiety symptoms in the study whenever possible.

Overall prevalence in ID by gender

Few studies have examined gender differences in the rate of mental health problems in men and women with ID. The handful of studies that have been done have reported discrepant findings. Iverson & Fox (1989) and Borthwick-Duffy & Eyman (1990) reported no differences between men and women in overall rate of disturbance. This corresponds to the findings in the general population where overall rates of mental health problems are the same in men and women (Kessler *et al.*, 1994; Robins & Regier, 1991). However, Crews *et al.* (1994) reported that men had more symptoms overall than women in their study of case files in a large institution. Differences between studies may be explained by differences in sampling and assessment procedures; more research is needed.

Gender differences by disorder

Perhaps some researchers in the ID area have ignored issues of gender because of the apparent lack of difference discussed above. The NCS and ECA study highlight the importance of considering mental health problems and treatment response by disorder for men separately from women. The main finding from these epidemiological studies in the general population is that women are twice as likely to have mood and anxiety disorders, while men tend to have more difficulties with substance abuse and antisocial behaviors. Women are also more likely to report physical symptoms of distress such as headaches or fatigue, than men are. When gender differences are examined by disorder for adults with developmental disabilities, similar trends have been reported to those of the general population (e.g. Benson, 1985; Koller et al., 1983; Reiss, 1988). These findings will be explored in the following sections of this chapter.

Given the limitations outlined above, a brief discussion is presented here on relevant issues for women by disorder.

Depression and depressed mood

Depression has been found to occur twice as often in women than men (McGrath et al., 1990). This increased prevalence emerges in adolescence, which has led some researchers to believe that pubertal hormones combined with socialization differences at this time are the cause (Walsh, 1998). Studies involving adolescents with mild intellectual disability report similar findings, with girls reporting more depression symptoms than boys (Reynolds & Miller, 1985; Heiman & Margalit, 1998). This same pattern has been reported for adults with ID in the community (Lunsky & Benson, 2001; Meins, 1993; Reiss, 1988) and clinical samples (Benson, 1985; Reiss, 1982; Reiss & Trenn, 1984). However, not all community sample studies using self-report measures have found gender differences (Dagnan & Sandhu, 1999; Reynolds & Baker, 1988).

One of the greatest concerns in relation to depression is the risk of suicide. In the general population, it has been reported that men are three times more likely to succeed in killing themselves than women, in part because they tend to use more lethal and immediate means to do so – guns or hanging, for example (Skegg, 1998). There is very little research on suicidal behavior and ID and most papers on the topic ignore gender issues (e.g. Pary, 1996; Johnson et al., 1995; Walters et al., 1995). One exception was a study by Benson & Laman (1988), where they noted that those who repeatedly attempted suicide tended to be women.

Case study: Tammy

Tammy is a 38-year old African-American woman who has cerebral palsy and a mild intellectual disability. After her father's unexpected death, she began to have aggressive episodes at work, which resulted in her losing her job and then her independent living apartment. She was moved to a more supervised setting with an extremely aggressive housemate. Her access to community activities, including visiting her grieving mother, became limited because of her explosive behavior. House staff referred Tammy to a mental health clinic, reporting that she was agitated and irritable, always pacing and yelling at staff. Staff commented that her hygiene and personal habits had deteriorated, which they attributed to 'laziness'. When Tammy spoke privately with a psychologist, a different picture emerged. She reported that she cried and worried about her housemate attacking her all of the time. She also reported that she missed seeing her mother and worried about how her mother was managing alone. Tammy complained that her life was ruined because she lost her apartment and job. She asserted that she was worthless, her situation was hopeless, and that she had considered suicide.

A diagnosis of major depressive episode was made and Tammy began treatment with SSRI anti-depressants and individual cognitive-behavioral therapy. In addition, she began attending a women's mental health group, where she spoke with other women like herself about coping strategies and ways to improve their self-esteem. Tammy learned important skills from individual and group therapy and also developed some new friendships. After four months of treatment, Tammy reported that she was able to control her thoughts as well as her behavior. It had been weeks since she was forced to leave a public place because of her emotions. She returned to work, began visiting her mother again, and resumed various community activities independently.

Bipolar disorder

Bipolar disorder has been found to occur equally often in men and women in the general population (Walsh, 1998) and in persons with ID (Glue, 1989). In a small study of ten individuals with ID and rapid cycling bipolar disorder, Glue (1989) reported that men had an earlier onset of affective symptoms and an earlier onset of rapid cycling than did women. Research is needed to explore possible gender differences in the presentation and course of this disorder.

Anxiety disorders

In the general population, women have been reported to experience higher rates of panic disorder, agoraphobia, social phobia, specific phobias and general anxiety (Kessler *et al.*, 1994). Few studies have been published on specific anxiety disorders in persons with ID and even fewer have considered gender. One paper reported the diagnostic findings on 300 consecutive psychiatric referrals (Ryan, 1994). Fifty-one individuals (17%) met criteria for post traumatic stress disorder (PTSD); women made up two-thirds of the PTSD group. Other studies have reported on PTSD symptomatology in women who were sexually abused but did not diagnose it as such (e.g. Varley, 1984; Weinman *et al.*, 1990). A thorough study on fears in children with and without ID in Australia (Gullone *et al.*, 1996) noted that similar to children without ID, girls with ID reported more fears and more intense fears than boys.

Schizophrenia and/or psychotic disorders

In the general population, research suggests that males and females are affected with schizophrenia in roughly equal numbers. However, differences in the course of the disorder are noteworthy. Women tend to have a later onset, more prominent mood symptoms and a better prognosis (Castle, 2000b) but also tend to be diagnosed later and may first be misdiagnosed as having a mood disorder. There is limited research on schizophrenia and ID, and even less research that considers gender. This absence of research is in part due to the difficulty of making a diagnosis in someone with more limited verbal ability, particularly in terms of ascertaining the presence of positive symptoms such as delusions or hallucinations (Reiss, 1994). The few studies that have reported on gender differences have not found different prevalence rates in men and women (Benson, 1985). These studies did not consider differences in the course of disorder.

Eating disorders

Anorexia nervosa and bulimia nervosa occur much more frequently in women than men (10:1, Bulik, 1998). This dramatic gender difference has been attributed to the fact that, especially for females, being considered attractive is linked to being thin. Minimal research on eating disorders exists in individuals with ID. Studies that report behavior characteristic of anorexia nervosa do not report a fear of becoming fat but instead consider the starvation to be secondary to other problems such as depression (Raitasuo *et al.*, 1998; Reiss, 1994) or conversion disorder (Weinman *et al.*, 1990). Obesity has been a greater concern in the ID literature, with women having higher rates of obesity than men (Rimmer *et al.*, 1993). It is difficult to account for the relative absence of eating disorders in women with ID. We could hypothesize that women with ID are less concerned with body image than women without ID, hence the higher rates of obesity. Interestingly, anorexia nervosa and bulimia nervosa are almost unknown in developing countries, suggesting that the disorders are somewhat culture bound (Bulik, 1998). Perhaps eating disorders are less prevalent in women with ID because these individuals are, like those in developing countries, less attuned to western cultural pressures. Research is needed on how women with ID understand their weight and body shape issues, as well as research on what women with ID understand about nutrition and health.

Alcohol/substance abuse

In the general population, men have been found to have more substance abuse problems than women (Robins & Regier, 1991; Kessler *et al.*, 1994). However, these problems are on the rise for women, particularly young women (Eichler & Parron, 1986). There is limited research on substance abuse and ID (Delaney & Poling, 1990). One study (Westermeyer *et al.*, 1988) noted that the sex ratio of substance abusers was 2:1 men to women, similar to the general population, but pointed out that men are more likely to have ID (2:1), arguing that women with ID were therefore at greater risk. In their sample, they observed that women with ID were more likely to marry substance abusers, thus gaining entry into that community. Despite the relatively low prevalence in women with ID, substance abuse is an important disorder to consider for them. Women who abuse substances are at greater risk for sexually transmitted diseases, unwanted pregnancy, exploitation and abuse.

Treatment issues

There are several important findings on treatment issues for women with mental health problems in the general population. These findings have implications for women with ID. These are considered in turn.

Women who experience mental health problems are more likely than men to be treated by a primary care physician and with medication (Eichler & Parron, 1986). Non-specialists may not recognize subtle changes in symptoms and they may make incorrect diagnoses that can delay appropriate treatment, for example, treating schizophrenia as a mood disorder. Women make up 64% of patients prescribed psychotropic medications and receive 90% of prescriptions given by GPs (Eichler & Parron, 1986).

Whether this treatment issue applies to women with ID is uncertain. It is likely that women with ID have certain barriers to specialist care but these barriers may apply to men with ID as well. This question has not yet been pursued in research.

Research and development for new pharmaceutical products are restricted to men in the interest of obtaining a homogeneous sample and avoiding possible risk to a fetus (Romans, 1998). Researchers worry that women's menstrual cycle and related hormonal changes would confound the study's results. After the new products are tested and demonstrated to be safe with men, they are released to the population at large without adequate testing with women. This practice puts women at risk for unknown side effects, interactions and decreased medical efficacy. Women need to be included in pharmaceutical research *because* of anticipated variability in drug response (Johnson & Fee, 1997).

Fitzgerald and Seeman (2000) noted that women who take neuroleptics complain of weight gain, skin problems, menstrual problems, constipation and pseudopregnancy while on the drugs. There is little controlled research on the teratogenic effects of such medications on the fetus (Romans, 1998). Tardive dyskinesia occurs more frequently in women as well. It seems evident that the drug metabolism interacts with the woman's menstrual cycle or hormones but exactly how is uncertain. One unfortunate consequence of the lack of attention paid to these issues is that medication compliance can become a problem. More research is needed to understand the effects of psychotropic medication on women.

Pharmacological treatment is the most common form of treatment for mental health problems in persons with ID, but minimal attention has been paid to gender issues. Rinck (1998) reflected the general attitude of the field when she reported that gender is not an important variable in the epidemiology of psychotropic medication in ID. Unfortunately, an entire book devoted to the use of psychotropic medications in the ID population has little mention of women's issues or concerns (Reiss & Aman, 1998).

Qualitative research has suggested that women with ID may benefit from individual and group therapy for mental health issues (Prout & Nowak-Drabik, 1999). However, there is a need for controlled research to establish the effectiveness of psychotherapy with this population (Prout *et al.*, 2000).

Mental health promotion

The area of women's mental health is not just about women's struggles with mental illness but also about how women can lead healthy emotional lives. Mental health promotion is an important part of general health promotion for women with ID. Because women with ID are unlikely to self-report symptoms of emotional distress, physicians should consider these women's emotional state as part of their routine health check-up. Also, physicians should review current medications, possible interactions and side effects on a regular basis.

Preventing abuse and offering treatment if abuse has occurred is an important part of mental health promotion for women with ID. Women with ID are at a high risk of abuse, which is a known risk factor for mental health problems. Qualitative research has demonstrated the utility of individual and group therapy with other women regarding abuse issues (McCarthy, 1999).

Women with ID should be taught to advocate for their mental health needs. They should be taught how to recruit help from others and how to successfully manage stress and difficulties in their relationships. If women are indeed more passive in treatment, they could be taught assertiveness skills.

There is a need to address the self-esteem of women with ID (Walsh *et al.*, 2000). How can we help these women come to terms with what it means to be a woman with an intellectual disability? How can we help them better understand their difficulties, accept their limitations and sustain a positive self-image in the face of societal demands? Perhaps through education and support from other women with and without ID, women with ID could learn how to feel better about themselves and how to take care of themselves. Feminist therapy in the general population has succeeded in developing interventions that expose and challenge gender role messages for women in a supportive environment (Toner, 2001). Such an approach might be very positive for women with ID as well.

Thus far, discussion on mental health promotion has focused on what should be available to the woman with ID. Services and resources also need to be made available to carers who may be misinformed about women with ID and their mental health. Carers could be taught, for example, how to recognize mental health problems as well as how to encourage the women under their care to express mental health concerns. It would be helpful for carers to know, for example, about the major risk factors for mental health problems in women and about the tendency to underestimate mood and anxiety disorders. They could also learn how best to ask women with ID about their feelings and how to encourage them to get help without feeling stigmatized.

Future areas for research

We need to go beyond gender differences in overall rates of psycho-pathology. It is time to study gender differences in the prevalence, course and symptomatology of specific disorders. It could be that women and men with ID express depression differently, for example, with men displaying greater overlap between depression and aggression than women.

Research should combine self-report and informant measures. We should also combine quantitative and qualitative approaches to understanding women's mental health issues. Qualitative studies may help us understand women's subjective experience in the mental health system.

Treatment of mental health problems must be examined for women, including medication issues, therapy and social concerns. Empowerment of women, support for women's crises and specific risk factors should be the focus of research.

Finally, how can women with ID be part of the larger women's mental health movement? This question should drive future research. Just as women's mental health research has implications for women with ID, findings regarding women with ID should contribute to our understanding of issues for the general population.

References

Astbury, J. & Cabral, M. (2000) *Women's Mental Health: An Evidence Based Review.* World Health Organization, Geneva.

Baum, S. & Burns, J. (2000) Editorial. Waiting to be asked: women with learning disabilities. *Clinical Psychology Forum,* **137**, 4.

Benson, B.A. (1985) Behavior disorders and mental retardation: associations with age, sex, and level of functioning in an outpatient clinic sample. *Applied Research in Mental Retardation,* **6**, 79–95.

Benson, B.A. & Fuchs, C. (1999) Anger-arousing situations and coping responses of aggressive adults with intellectual disability. *Journal of Intellectual and Developmental Disability,* **24**, 207–214.

Benson, B.A. & Laman, D.S. (1988) Suicidal tendencies of mentally retarded adults in community settings. *Australia and New Zealand Journal of Developmental Disabilities,* **14**, 49–54.

Borthwick-Duffy, S. (1994) Epidemiology and prevalence of psychopathology in people with mental retardation. *Journal of Consulting and Clinical Psychology,* **62**, 17–27.

Borthwick-Duffy, S. & Eyman, R.K. (1990) Who are the dually diagnosed? *American Journal on Mental Retardation,* **94**, 586–595.

Bramston, P., Fogarty, G. & Cummins, R.A. (1999) The nature of stressors reported by people with an intellectual disability. *Journal of Applied Research in Intellectual Disabilities,* **12**, 1–10.

Bulik, C.M. (1998) Women and disordered eating. In: *Folding Back the Shadows: A Perspective on Women's Mental Health* (ed. S.E. Romans), pp. 177–192. University of Otago Press, New Zealand.

Castle, D.J. (2000a) Sex differences in brain development, organization and degeneration: are they relevant to sex differences in schizophrenia? In: *Women and Schizophrenia* (eds D.J. Castle, J. McGrath, & J. Kulkarni), pp. 5–18. University of Cambridge Press, Cambridge.

Castle, D.J. (2000b) Women and schizophrenia: an epidemiological perspective. In: *Women and Schizophrenia* (eds D.J. Castle, J. McGrath, & J. Kulkarni), pp. 19–34. University of Cambridge Press, Cambridge.

Charlot, L.R., Doucette, A.C. & Mezzacappa, E. (1993) Affective symptoms of institutionalized adults with mental retardation. *American Journal on Mental Retardation*, **98**, 408–416.

Cohen, S. & Wills, T.A. (1985) Stress, social support, and the buffering hypothesis. *Psychological Bulletin*, **98**, 310–357.

Crews, W.D., Bonaventura, S. & Rowe, F. (1994) Dual diagnosis: prevalence of psychiatric disorders in a large state residential facility for individuals with mental retardation. *American Journal on Mental Retardation*, **98**, 688–731.

Culbertson, F.M. (1997) Depression and gender: an international review. *American Psychologist*, **52**, 25–31.

Dagnan, D. & Sandhu, S. (1999) Social comparison, self-esteem and depression in people with intellectual disability. *Journal of Intellectual Disability Research*, **43** (5), 372–392.

Day, K. (1985) Psychiatric disorder in the middle-aged and elderly mentally handicapped. *British Journal of Psychiatry*, **147**, 660–667.

Delaney, D. & Poling, A. (1990) Drug abuse among mentally retarded people: an overlooked problem? *Journal of Alcohol and Drug Education*, **35**, 48–54.

Edelstein, T.M. & Glenwick, D.S. (1997) Referral reasons for psychological services for adults with mental retardation. *Research in Developmental Disabilities*, **18**, 45–59.

Eichler, A. & Parron, D.L. (1986) *Women's Mental Health: Agenda for Research.* National Institute of Mental Health, Rockville, MD.

Fitzgerald, P. & Seeman, M.V. (2000) Women and schizophrenia: treatment implications. In: *Women and Schizophrenia* (eds D.J. Castle, J. McGrath & J. Kulkarni), pp. 95–110. University of Cambridge Press, Cambridge.

Fletcher, R.J. (1993) Mental illness and mental retardation in the United States: policy and treatment challenges. *Journal of Intellectual Disability Research*, **37**, 25–33.

Furey, E.M. (1994) Sexual abuse of adults with mental retardation: who and where. *Mental Retardation*, **32**, 173–180.

Ghaziuddin, M. (1988) Referral of mentally handicapped patients to the psychiatrist: a community study. *Journal of Mental Deficiency Research*, **32**, 491–495.

Glue, P. (1989) Rapid cycling affective disorders in the mentally retarded. *Biological Psychiatry*, **26**, 250–256.

Groden, J., Cautela, J., Velicer, W., Diller, A. & Norman, G. (1996) A stress schedule for persons with autism and developmental disabilities. *Poster presented at the American Association on Mental Retardation Annual Meeting, 31 May 1996*, San Antonio, Texas.

Gullone, E., Cummins, R.A. & King, N.J. (1996) Self-reported fears: a comparison study of youths with and without intellectual disability. *Journal of Intellectual Disability Research*, **40**, 227–240.

Heiman, T. & Margalit, M. (1998) Loneliness, depression, and social skills among students with mild mental retardation in different educational settings. *The Journal of Special Education*, **32**, 154–163.

Horwitz, S.M., Kerker, B.D., Owens, P.L. & Zigler, E. (2000) *The health status and needs of individuals with mental retardation*. Report for Special Olympics, Inc, December.

Iverson, J.C. & Fox, R.A. (1989) Prevalence of psychopathology among mentally retarded adults. *Research in Developmental Disabilities*, **10**, 77–83.

Jacobson, J.W. & Holland, T. (2000) *Mental Health and Intellectual Disabilities: Addressing the Mental Health Needs of People with Intellectual Disabilities* (draft). Report by the Mental Health Special Interest Research Group of the IASSID to the World Health Organization, Villepinte, France.

Johnson, T.L. & Fee, E. (1997) Women's health research: an introduction. In: *Women's Health Research: A Medical and Policy Primer* (eds F.P. Haseltine & B.G. Jacobson), pp. 3–26. American Psychiatric Press, Washington, DC.

Johnson, C., Handen, B., Lubetsky, M. & Sacco, K. (1995) Affective disorders in hospitalized children and adolescents with mental retardation: a retrospective study. *Research in Developmental Disabilities*, **16**, 221–231.

Kessler, R.C., McGonagle, K.A. & Zhao, S. (1994) Lifetime and 12-month prevalence of DSM-III-R psychiatric disorders in the United States: results from the National Comorbidity Study. *Archives of General Psychiatry*, **51**, 8–19.

Koller, H., Richardson, S., Katz, M. & McLaren, J. (1983) Behavior disturbance since childhood among a 5-year birth cohort of all mentally retarded young adults in a city. *American Journal of Mental Deficiency*, **87**, 386–395.

Krauss, M., Seltzer, M. & Goodman, S. (1992) Social support networks of adults with mental retardation who live at home. *American Journal on Mental Retardation*, **96**, 432–441.

Kulkarni, J. & Fink, G. (2000) Hormones and psychosis. In: *Women and Schizophrenia* (eds D. J. Castle, J. McGrath & J. Kulkarni), pp. 51–60. University of Cambridge Press, Cambridge.

Leavy, R.L. (1983) Social support and psychological disorder: a review. *Journal of Community Psychology*, **11**, 3–21.

Lunsky, Y. & Benson, B. A. (1999) Social circles of adults with mental retardation as viewed by their caregivers. *Journal of Developmental and Physical Disabilities*, **11**, 115–129.

Lunsky, Y. & Benson, B.A. (2001) Association between perceived social support and strain, and positive and negative outcome for adults with mild intellectual disability. *Journal of Intellectual Disability Research*, **45**, 106–114.

Maxmen, J.S. & Ward, N.G. (1995) *Essential Psychopathology and its Treatment*, 2nd edition. Norton & Company, New York, NY.

McCarthy, M. (1999) *Sexuality and Women with Learning Disabilities*. Jessica Kingsley Publishers, London.

McGrath, E., Keita, G.P., Strickland, B. & Russo, N.F. (1990) *Women and depression: Risk factors and treatment issues*. American Psychological Association, Washington, DC.

Meins, W. (1993) Prevalence and risk factors for depressive disorders in adults with intellectual disability. *Australia and New Zealand Journal of Developmental Disabilities*, **18**, 147–156.

Moss, S., Prosser, H., Ibbotson, B., & Goldberg, D. (1996) Respondent and informant accounts of psychiatric symptoms in a sample of patients with learning disability. *Journal of Intellectual Disability Research*, **40**, 457–465.

Moss, S., Emerson, E., Bouras, N. & Holland, A. (1997) Mental disorders and problematic behaviours in people with intellectual disability: future directions for research. *Journal of Intellectual Disability Research*, **41**, 440–447.

Nezu, C.M. & Nezu, A.M. (1994) Outpatient psychotherapy for adults with mental retardation and concomitant psychopathology: research and clinical imperatives. *Journal of Consulting and Clinical Psychology*, **62**, 34–42.

Nolen-Hoeksema, S. (1987) Sex differences in unipolar depression: evidence and theory. *Psychological Bulletin*, **101**, 259–282.

Pary, R.J. (1996) Down syndrome update: does suicidal behavior occur in persons with Down syndrome? *The Habilitative Mental Healthcare Newsletter*, **15**, 59–62.

Prout, H.T. & Nowak-Drabik, K.M. (1999) *The effectiveness of psychotherapy with persons with mental retardation: status of the research*. Presentation at the 16th Annual Conference of the NADD, Niagara Falls, Ontario, Canada, 10–13 November 1999.

Prout, H.T., Chard, K.M., Nowak-Drabik, K.M. & Johnson, D.M. (2000) Determining the effectiveness of psychotherapy with persons with mental retardation: the need to move toward empirically based research. *NADD Bulletin*, **3**, 83–86.

Raitasuo, S., Virtanen, H. & Raitasuo, J. (1998) Anorexia nervosa, major depression, and obsessive-compulsive disorder in a Down syndrome patient. *International Journal of Eating Disorders*, **23**, 107–109.

Reiss, S. (1982) Psychopathology and mental retardation: survey of a developmental disabilities mental health program. *Mental Retardation*, **20**, 128–132.

Reiss, S. (1988) *The Reiss Screen for Maladaptive Behavior – Test Manual*. IDS Publishing Corporation, Worthington, OH.

Reiss, S. (1990) Prevalence of dual diagnosis in community-based day programs in the Chicago metropolitan area. *American Journal on Mental Retardation*, **94**, 578–585.

Reiss, S. (1994) *Handbook of Challenging Behavior: Mental Health Aspects of Mental Retardation*. IDS Publishing Corporation, Worthington, OH.

Reiss, S. & Aman, M. (1998) *Psychotropic Medication and Developmental Disabilities: The International Consensus Handbook*. The Ohio State University Nisonger Center, Columbus, OH.

Reiss, S. & Trenn, E. (1984) Consumer demand for outpatient mental health services for mentally retarded people. *Mental Retardation*, **22**, 112–115.

Reynolds, W.M. & Baker, J.A. (1988) Assessment of depression in persons with mental retardation. *American Journal on Mental Retardation*, **93**, 93–103.

Reynolds, W.M. & Miller, K.L. (1985) Depression and learned helplessness in mentally retarded and non-mentally retarded adolescents: an initial investigation. *Applied Research in Mental Retardation*, **6**, 295–306.

Rhodes, A. & Goering, P. (1998) Gender differences in the use of outpatient mental health services. In: *Women's Mental Health Services: A Public Health Perspective* (eds B.L. Levin, A.K. Blanch & A. Jennings), pp. 19–33. Sage Publications, Thousand Oaks, CA.

Rimmer, J.H., Braddock, D. & Fujiura, G. (1993) Prevalence of obesity in adults with mental retardation: implications for health promotion and disease prevention. *Mental Retardation*, **31**, 105–110.

Rinck, C. (1998) Epidemiology and psychoactive medication. In: *Psychotropic Medication and Developmental Disabilities: The International Consensus Handbook* (eds S. Reiss & M. Aman), pp. 31–44. The Ohio State University Nisonger Center, Columbus, OH.

Robins, L.N. & Regier, D.A. (1991) *Psychiatric Disorders in America: The Epidemiological Catchment Area Study*. Free Press, New York, NY.

Romans, S.E. (1998) Gender differences in psychiatric disorder. In: *Folding Back the Shadows: A Perspective on Women's Mental Health.* (ed. S.E. Romans), pp. 43–62. University of Otago Press, New Zealand.

Rosen, J. & Burchard, S. (1990) Community activities and social support networks: a social comparison. *Education and Training in Mental Retardation*, **25**, 193–204.

Ryan, R. (1994) Posttraumatic stress disorder in persons with developmental disabilities. *Community Mental Health Journal*, **30**, 45–54.

Sands, D.J. & Kozleski, E.B. (1994) Quality of life differences between adults with and without disabilities. *Education and Training in Mental Retardation and Developmental Disabilities*, **29**, 90–101.

Seeman, M.V. & Fitzgerald, P. (2000) Women and schizophrenia: clinical aspects. In: *Women and Schizophrenia* (eds D.J. Castle, J. McGrath & J. Kulkarni), pp. 35–50. University of Cambridge Press, Cambridge.

Skegg, K. (1998) Women and suicide. In: *Folding Back the Shadows: A Perspective on Women's Mental Health.* (ed. S.E. Romans), pp. 193–202. University of Otago Press, New Zealand.

Stack, L.S., Haldipur, C.V. & Thompson, M. (1987) Stressful life events and psychiatric hospitalization of mentally retarded patients. *American Journal of Psychiatry*, **144**, 661–663.

Toner, B. (2001) *Women's Mental Health: Challenges and Opportunities.* Invited professor's address, 30 May 2001. Department of Psychiatry, University of Toronto.

Traustadottir, R. & Johnson, K. (2000) *Women with Intellectual Disabilities: Finding a Place in the World.* Jessica Kingsley Publishers, London.

Varley, C.K. (1984) Schizophreniform psychoses in mentally retarded adolescent girls following sexual assault. *American Journal of Psychiatry*, **141**, 593–595.

Walmsley, J. (1996) Doing what mum wants me to do: looking at family relationships from the point of view of people with intellectual disabilities. *Journal of Applied Research in Intellectual Disabilities*, **9**, 324–341.

Walsh, A. (1998) Women and mood: biological considerations. In: *Folding Back the Shadows: A Perspective on Women's Mental Health* (ed. S.E. Romans), pp. 165–176. University of Otago Press, New Zealand.

Walsh, P.N., Heller, T., Schupf, N. & van Schrojenstein Lantman-de Valk, H. (2000)

Healthy Aging – Adults with Intellectual Disabilities: Women's Health Issues. World Health Organization, Geneva.

Walters, A.S., Barrett, R.P., Knapp, L.G. & Borden, M.C. (1995) Suicidal behavior in children and adolescents with mental retardation. *Research in Developmental Disabilities*, **16**, 85–96.

Weinman, B., Haydon, S. & Sapan, J. (1990) Behavioral treatment of a food refusal conversion disorder in a mentally retarded adult. *Journal of Mental Deficiency Research*, **34**, 501–508.

Westermeyer, J., Phaobtong, T. & Neider, J. (1988) Substance use and abuse among mentally retarded persons: a comparison of patients and a survey population. *American Journal of Drug and Alcohol Abuse*, **14**, 109–123.

5 Sterilization and Sexual Control

Pamela Block

Introduction

For much of the twentieth century, individuals stigmatized by gender, race, poverty, disability or sexuality were subject to extreme methods of social control in the US and Europe. People with intellectual disabilities (ID) faced compulsory institutionalization and sterilization, as policy makers sought to reduce perceived threats to the social order. The existence of multiple stigmas based on class, race and gender resulted in increased vulnerability to extreme practices. However, theories and approaches to social marginality differed regionally as professional theories were influenced by cultural beliefs in particular social contexts. In Brazil, sterilization and institutionalization were practiced upon individuals but were never mandated by the state. In the absence of official policy, cultural beliefs and professional opinions shaped the practices used by professionals and family members to regulate the sexuality of women and men with ID. This chapter will review the different methods used to control the sexuality and fertility of women with ID throughout the twentieth century and how such practices as eugenic sterilization, institutionalization and other repressive measures of social control grew out of cultural notions of gender, race, class, sexuality and disability.

In 1995–96 I conducted ethnographic and archival research in Brazil on the topic of cultural perceptions and professional theories of ID with a focus on sexuality and fertility control. I collected historical documents, interviewed dozens of professionals, parents and people with disabilities, and conducted participant observation at several vocational and residential programs in two of Brazil's largest cities. Brazil is perceived as 'underdeveloped' (one author even used the term 'retarded') in the realm of economics, politics and in the social service systems (Huggins, 1985: 1). During the course of my research, Brazilian human service professionals expressed to me that Brazil is 20 years behind the US. This implies that Brazil's service system developed through the same evolutionary progression as the system in the US. It also implies that practices in the US are, and have always been, more 'progressive' than practices in Brazil. Both of these assertions are false. Brazil's system developed quite differently than the system in the US and was, in many ways, more 'progressive' and humane. The root of this difference lies in differing cultural definitions of ID, gender and sexuality, and also differences in the eugenics movements of the two countries.

Eugenics and intellectual disability

In the US, the eugenics movement was crucial to the evolution of services for people diagnosed with ID. Eugenics, the science of the genetic improvement of the human race, was influenced by Darwin's theories of heredity in the evolutionary process, and Mendel's research on the transmission of genetic traits over generations. Eugenics was used to establish race and class distinctions as 'natural' and incontrovertible (Fairchild, 1926). The upper class dominated because of their superior genetic heritage; the poor remained in poverty because of their degenerate genes.

Unlike the US, in Brazil there is no cultural legacy supporting the sterilization of people with ID and it was rarely practiced. In the US over 50 000 individuals were systematically sterilized between 1900 and 1950 (Kempton & Kahn, 1991). Because of historical differences, such as the persistence of Lamarckism, religious, and humanist influences, the Brazilian eugenics movement did not unite to lobby for the large-scale segregation of people with ID.

Early diagnoses of ID in Brazil were usually based on observation, and often coincided with regional, class and racial designations. The eugenics movement in Brazil responded to concerns about rapid urbanization caused by the emancipation of the slaves and immigration (Stepan, 1991). The movement included a continuum of eugenics theories, both Lamarckian and Mendelian. In Lamarckian-influenced eugenics, it was thought that genetic traits were influenced by environmental factors, such as improved sanitation, better hygiene, and access to better medical care. Such beliefs led Brazilian eugenicists to adopt slogans such as 'to sanitize is to eugenize' and 'sanitation-eugenics is order and progress'. In 1918, Belisário Penna wrote about the health problems of rural Northeastern Brazilians:

'In a country of sick and illiterate people like Brazil, the greatest primordial worry of conscientious policy makers should be physical, moral and intellectual sanitation of its inhabitants.

There is no prosperity, there can be no progress amongst ignorant individuals, and much less so when ignorance joins with sickness, vice, physical and intellectual deficiency, and the destruction of essential organs.'

(Penna, 1918: 7)

Lamarkists believed this social crisis could be averted through improvements in public health and mental hygiene.

In Brazil a great chasm separated the urban elites from the mass of people living in rural poverty (Stepan, 1991). This gulf is evident in Penna's descriptions of the local population as 'idiots, cretins, crippled or paralytic' (Penna, 1918: 10). Yet, despite preconceptions based on race, class and regional differences, Penna and most other professionals, especially those writing before 1920, were careful to stay away from models of genetic inheritance based on race and class. This differs from the US, where rigid Mendelian models of the transmission of pathological genetic traits across generations, espoused by Goddard (1913) and others, were widely accepted by the 1920s. At a time when institutional models of strict segregation were being put into place in the US, Brazilian professionals sought to use science and technology to improve the lives of people at the margins of society without resorting to institutionalization.

However, in 1920s some factions of the Brazilian eugenics movement considered how sterilization might be used for social control and the prevention of racial degeneration. Individuals with ID were included in lists of social threats alongside criminals, degenerates, vagabonds, psychopaths, etc.

'To create pain is a crime against humanity; to create monstrosity is a crime against the race. The marriage of those ill in spirit and body, freaks … and defectives – the producers of abortions and martyrs – ought to be forbidden, or, at least, should not be sanctioned by law.'

(Dantas, 1930: 5)

Between 1920 and 1940 Brazilian eugenicists discussed three methods to reduce these populations: prenuptial examinations to prevent the 'unfit' from marrying, institutionalization, and eugenic sterilization. Over the course of two decades, Dr Renato Kehl, founder and editor of the *Boletim de Eugenía*, published dozens of books and articles in support of eugenic sterilization citing American, German and English sources in support of his cause:

'In order to achieve thorough results sterilization would need to be applied compulsorily, be of a permanent nature, and on a vast scale, and must not spare even the individuals that appear superficially normal but are, nevertheless, intrinsically defective.'

(Kehl, 1921: 156)

Kehl's work linked nineteenth-century theories of racial degeneration to the twentieth century Brazilian eugenics, claiming that interclass or interracial marriages led to progeny that were physically, psychically and morally inferior. Most eugenicists were less specific on the issue of race, since some of them, including one of the founders of the field, Dr. Juliano Moreira, were themselves mestizo (Stepan, 1991). Kehl (1933: 185) also spoke favorably of institutionalization:

'[I]t would be desirable to have an obligatory exam and register all abnormal children attending school in order to remove them from the daily life of normal individuals, give them adequate instruction, and commit them to special asylum colonies for the time necessary to reveal those that are dangerous or incompatible to a life of complete liberty.'

Kehl advised that only those who had been sterilized should be released from asylums. For example, couples that were capable of taking care of themselves but incapable of taking care of children could be allowed, once sterilized, to exist in childless harmony.

Moreira e Costa (1927: 56), discussed the potential role of negative eugenics in the future of the Brazilian race: 'The future generation of Brazil depends on it; the birth of a new, stronger, healthier, better looking nationality depends on it'. He saw eugenic sterilization as a means to modernize the country, describing Brazil as developmentally delayed on a national level, 'still being served by the bull cart of custom rather than the automobile of Eugenics' (1927: 56). In the 1930s, the Brazilian government passed laws that mandated prenuptial examinations (Stepan, 1991). Such laws were specifically designed to prevent people with disabilities such as deafness or mental deficiency from marrying (Lopes, 1933). However, the Brazilian government declined to legislate more extreme forms of eugenic practice.

Although a supporter of sterilization in some cases, Dr Jefferson Lemos (1933) wrote that large-scale sterilization programs would lead to the destruction of not just degenerates, but also people of genius. Sterilization was acceptable when enacted in individual cases, but Lemos felt legislation would limit the ability of practitioners to make decisions based on individual cases and the dictates of their conscience. He defended the rights of individuals (if they were doctors) to make their own decisions regarding the morality of the practice and its merits in particular cases. Farani (1931: 171) brushed aside such defense of the rights of individuals, stating, 'the *possible* hypothesis of good descendents does not outweigh the *probability* of bad elements' (original emphasis). Farani considered institutionalization inhumane and costly compared to sterilization. He believed that the religious prohibition on interfering with the act of sexual procreation would lead to the degeneration of the Brazilian population.

As Brazilian support for Germany waned in the late 1930s, critics of sterilization became more vocal. In the words of Muniz Neto (1937: 15–

16): 'The ethos of democracy cannot co-exist with this policy grounded in authoritarian-type regimes'. He argued that the majority of the children born to people with ID were themselves normal. He claimed that many 'pathological inheritances' of different ethnic groups could be improved through better nutrition and that the majority of cases of ID were not a result of inheritance but were caused by environmental factors or obstetric traumas (1937: 73). Despite these arguments many Brazilian professionals chose to practice sterilization. Doctors would share information about clandestine procedures using informal networks. According to one informant, older doctors would take younger doctors out for coffee or lunch and tell them where to send patients for sterilization, lobotomy or other illegal or scientifically questionable procedures. Psychosurgery (such as lobotomy) was no longer practiced in public hospitals after 1962, but still could be procured in private hospitals. Sterilization was still conducted, although perhaps obscured – a record might note that a hysterectomy was performed due to infection, for example.

According to several informants, psychiatric patients and those with ID were not consulted about the decision to sterilize. Either the doctors made the decision or their parents requested the procedure. One administrator at a prominent psychiatric hospital believed that the sterilization of patients was a means for the institution to ignore the issue of sexuality and especially sexual abuse. If a patient became pregnant, it was the responsibility of the hospital. If the patient was sterilized, then sex and rape were rendered invisible. I was told that the decision to sterilize was only made after careful evaluation of the patient's intellectual level of functioning. Decisions were made case by case. One informant stated that he had never heard of cases of '*leves*' (the high functioning or 'borderline' individuals) being sterilized, but only people with profound disabilities. Several doctors and psychiatrists informed me that sterilization was a medical 'fashion'. Just as tonsillectomy, once a common practice, fell out of style, so too was sterilization passing out of mode.

Gender and sexuality

After the decline of eugenics ideologies in Brazil, issues of sexuality and ID, institutionalization and sterilization, disappeared from popular and professional discourse until the 1970s. Although Brazilian psychiatrists in the 1920s and 1930s expressed concern about the sexuality of deviants, degenerates and the abnormal, specific constructions of ID as a sexual and social threat never entered the popular culture. In Brazil, most individuals with ID lived with family members and thus were not subject to the increased incidence of sexual abuse linked with institutionalization (Crossmaker, 1991). Sexuality remained a concern of parents and professionals but was not discussed openly. Many parents denied the sexuality of their adult children. Adults with ID were portrayed as child-like and asexual in parent narratives such as *Menino Sempre* (*Perpetual Child*) (Celentano, 1977). In Brazil, sexual repression of people with ID by parents and professionals was widespread until the late 1980s, and is still common. In the 1990s the discourse of professionals changed, with classes, articles and books now stating that people with ID had the same dreams and sexual desires as anyone in their society (Glat, 1992). Yet the practices of many vocational facilities and parents remained controlling and repressive. Individuals with ID were often held to rigid standards of sexual morality. Brazilian parents were overwhelmed and panicked by sexual manifestations ranging from masturbation and menstruation, to homosexuality and sexual aggression.

Although it is accepted that Brazilian parents will often oppose the sexual activities of unmarried children (especially daughters), people with ID lack the ability, opportunity or financial capacity to circumvent the sexual repression. They often lack permission to date, the money to go to a hotel, or even the social opportunity to meet people with whom a relationship might develop. The concerns of parents and professionals vary depending on the gender of the person with the ID. Fewer adult women with ID participate in vocational programs because, if they have the skills, they are kept at home to clean, cook and care for nieces, nephews or aging parents. These women are allowed to perform such traditional roles (typical for any unmarried daughter regardless of intellectual ability) but are not allowed, or not considered capable of, having a sexual life. Some families control the social interactions of their daughters to ensure that they will not be 'seduced'. Parents fear that immoral individuals will use their daughters sexually. There are some representations linking ID with seduction or prostitution, but only because the women have been 'corrupted'. Sterilization is sometimes a response to sexual activity, but more for the convenience of the family than from any perceived social threat. However, when interviewed, some professionals continued to express concerns about the transmission of pathological genes.

During my research in Brazil I found that boys and men with ID were judged by different standards than women. Fathers often considered the sexual experiences of their sons acceptable if their experiences were heterosexual. It was not uncommon for fathers to take their sons to prostitutes. The practice served a function of reinforcing masculinity despite the presence of a disability (at least in this way, my son is like any other man). I met several men with ID whose families encouraged visits to prostitutes, including one adolescent who was traumatized after being forced to visit a brothel on his eighteenth birthday.

D'Abreu (1974: 45) noticed that the parents interviewed mentioned menstruation, masturbation, heterosexual contact, homosexual contact, using parents or servants as 'objects of excitation', exhibitionism, using clothes or dolls for 'sexual ends', and visits to prostitutes as sexual concerns. D'Abreu (1974: 50) suggested that many parents projected their own sexual insecurities on to their child when they expressed fears 'that they were not capable of controlling themselves sexually', 'that they were not capable of being satisfied', 'that they will not know how to defend themselves', etc. The professionals interviewed by D'Abreu were more accepting of the idea of adults with ID having sexual lives, but only if pregnancy could be avoided through sterilization or other forms of contraception (D'Abreu 1974: 49). His most significant departure from earlier beliefs held by Brazilian professionals was a shift from biological to cultural explanations for the behavior of individuals with ID. The 'problematic' was not an inherent part of the nature of disabled individuals, but rather a function of repressive social and cultural contexts.

Brazil never practiced wide-scale institutionalization of children and adults with ID, but the service system attempted to provide for those who had been orphaned or abandoned. Usually they were sent to regular state orphanages or to the children's (or chronic) wards of psychiatric hospitals. Sexual violence was common in these contexts. During interviews, some professionals told me heartbreaking stories of sexual abuse, but also expressed the belief that ID serves to protect individuals from long-term trauma associated with sexual assault ('the memory will fade...'). In the 1980s and 1990s some orphanages attempted to prevent abuse by segregating individuals diagnosed with ID from the other children. This did not stop abuse – the older, stronger and higher functioning individuals continued to victimize those who were younger and weaker. In the 1990s collusion and silence were the usual institutional response to abuse in Brazil. I found that only one psychiatric facility had adopted a formal procedure for investigating suspected abuse and rape and punishing the perpetrators, but only in cases where the perpetrators were employees.

Some professionals implied that abuse and incest only exist in families 'of an inferior socio-economic-cultural level' (Coelho 1987: 39). However, a venerable Brazilian psychiatrist told me of a socially prominent man who raped his daughter who had an ID, and then institutionalized her in a psychiatric facility in order to hide the evidence. In the 1980s and 1990s the topic of sexual abuse was virtually absent from the Brazilian literature, except for a few statements denying it was the problem. Yet, 27 out of the 30 professionals that I interviewed worked with individuals who were sexually abused and they felt that this population was particularly vulnerable to sexual exploitation. I was told of dozens of cases of abuse and incest of Brazilian adults and children with ID. In all cases the individuals knew the perpetrators; they were family members, neighbors, fellow-students or other acquaintances.

Coelho (1987) considered the problems faced by individuals with ID as products of social, economic and cultural context. He discussed abandonment, prostitution and homosexuality as resulting from corrupting influences, and concluded that institutionalization in special schools for abandoned youth and psychiatric hospitals was no solution. He believed some individuals might be capable of marriage, but stressed the necessity of considering the emotional maturity and financial security of the individuals, stating that, in Brazil, survival is difficult for those of average intelligence and doubly difficult for those with ID. He concluded that Brazil lacks the social infrastructure to provide adequate economic support and education about birth control.

In my research, I found that people with ID who came from middle-class backgrounds often encountered more substantial barriers to marriage and children than those living in or near poverty. Prosperous parents had a greater ability to control (and limit) the social lives of their children, since they could arrange for constant supervision. Even if parents encouraged their children to have typical life experiences, there were virtually no opportunities for gainful employment to support a middle-class lifestyle. The responsibility for support fell entirely on the family. Parents with enough money sometimes chose to support a married child with disabilities and any grandchildren who might follow. Others made sterilization a precondition before marriage was allowed. Such parents were considered liberal, since they were at least allowing their child to have a sexual life. I was told of a grandmother who sought custody of her grandchild on the grounds that the mother was incapable of caring for it. The judge supported the mother's right to keep her child.

Contemporary thinking

By 1981, disability-rights activists began exchanging information about sexuality and disability. Sexuality was recognized as a human right which included the right to information, education and training, the right to marry and have children, and the right to receive counseling for family planning, marital or sexual dysfunction, and genetic counseling (Sassaki 1981: 9). At first these discussions involved individuals with physical disabilities, but slowly people with ID became involved. Lipp (1986) wrote that with the appropriate education and training, individuals with ID were capable of fulfilling sexual relationships. She recognized that individuals with ID were vulnerable to sexual abuse, but stressed that parents should not allow fear of this possibility to control and constrain people's lives. However, her solution to the possibility of unwanted pregnancy resulting from sexual activity was sterilization.

Grounding their argument in theories of family, culture and society, Assumpção Jr and Sprovieri (1993) concluded that individuals with ID lack the emotional and psychological capacity to form lasting sexual relationships, marriage and family. They present case studies of ten married (or formerly married) couples with ID. None of the unions lasted more than five years and most caused great difficulties for family members and professionals. Their analysis showed a complex understanding of the social barriers preventing individuals with ID from living 'normal' lives. Though they decried the injustice, their solution was not social change but a recommendation that individuals with ID and their families accept the existing constraints and learn to function within them. Thus they strongly advocated sterilization and abortion for the benefit of responsible family members and professionals.

In contrast to these assertions, 20 out of 25 professionals that I interviewed believed that marriage by individuals with ID could succeed when given the appropriate support; 18 out of 20 felt that raising children was also possible, with support. Many of these professionals gave examples of couples with ID who succeeded in both marriage and parenthood. Despite the barriers depicted by the above authors some individuals with ID manage quite well for themselves. They get jobs, marry, have children and live typical lives for people of their socioeconomic backgrounds. The Brazilian social system may not be capable of supporting them, but it is also incapable of preventing them. Probably the vast majority of those who might be considered to have intellectual disabilities (through diagnostic measurements) will never be in a position to receive an official diagnosis. Some Brazilian professionals fight to keep individuals out of a system that will segregate them from their family and community. In one case, a young woman was to be sent a long distance in order to receive specialized educational services. The director of the program argued that the woman was happy and functioning quite well in her community. If disability is a function of context and labeling, then the director argued that this woman was not disabled. She did not want this woman to commute six hours every day in order to learn how to be disabled.

Glat (1989) collected the life histories of 35 women with ID of different ages and social backgrounds, asking questions about all aspects of their daily lives, including family, work, friendships and romance, and their perceptions of their own disabilities. Like Lipp (1986), Glat stresses that individuals with ID do not differ from anyone else in their desire for sexual and non-sexual relationships. The only difference is the repression experienced by these individuals. Glat (1989) found that women with ID are receiving messages from family and professionals that marriage, children and an active sexual life are forbidden. Glat (1989: 134) provides examples of the desire and subsequent familial repression, such as Ivone, 35 years:

> 'Why can't you marry, Ivone?'
> 'It's like this, I can't marry because, because of my mother. Because of our, because of our, like, it's, it's, retardation [silence]. It's because of this that we can't marry.'

Glat finds that individuals with ID are being held to standards of behavior that people without disabilities would find difficult to maintain. Based on interviews with 25 men and 26 women, Glat (1992) stated that, although all individuals with ID had fewer social opportunities than others, this was particularly true for women.

Sexuality has become a fashionable topic and is being discussed with more frequency and openness than in the past, but it is questionable whether practices are changing. During the course of my observations and interviews, professionals who spoke progressively often acted repressively. In the parent-controlled vocational organizations that I visited, founding parents over the age of 70 controlled policies on sexuality. These policies lagged far behind the current professional discourse, with a generation gap between the founder-controlled administration, the younger parents whose children were currently receiving services and the professionals employed within the organizations. Omote (1993) concluded that special education instructors are inconsistent in their practice and ill prepared to teach and counsel their students on the issue of sexuality. Professionals often recognized that individuals with ID had a right to sexual expression but feared the consequences of allowing it (Omote, 1993). Ribeiro and Nepomuceno (1992: 168) report that parents sometimes resort to extreme actions to prevent their adult children from having sexual lives. Upon learning that their daughter had sexual relations, one set of parents beat her and kept her imprisoned in their home for many years, with long term consequences to her emotional stability:

> '... when someone speaks about sex near her, she covers her ears and starts to cry. She will not allow anyone to change clothes in front of her, and she screams and cries desperately if scenes appear on soap operas or television films with couples kissing, speaking words of love, in the nude, or having sexual relations.'

One professional told me of a mother who, upon learning her daughter had been sexually active, placed a hot hard-boiled egg in her vagina as punishment.

There is something about the nature of ID, both in Brazil and in the US, that leads parents and professionals to assume they are justified in having complete control over the fates of their children or charges (Block, 2000). Unfortunately, in both countries, cases where important life decisions were made by people with ID, rather than by parents or professionals, were the exception rather than the rule. In the last two decades of the twentieth century self-advocacy movements led by people with ID formed internationally to address this injustice. Individuals with ID are now demanding the right to control their own lives and make their own decisions. A few such groups exist in Brazil. In one vocational program, the adults successfully lobbied to change institutional policy and be allowed to have (heterosexual) romances that could (in socially appropriate ways) have expression in public. Other groups that I observed had become another medium through which professionals could castigate and criticize the actions (particularly sexual and 'antisocial' behavior) of the group members. Thus the groups meant for self-actualization were transformed into another means of social control. There were few sanctioned ways that sexuality or romance could be expressed. Homosexual activity was especially discouraged, but heterosexual romances were also repressed. A flirtatious woman was seen as a troublemaker.

Because higher functioning adult women were more likely to be kept at home to care for family, one vocational facility had more than four times the number of men than women in attendance. Although there had recently been moves to reintegrate gender-segregated vocational activities, most women still worked at gender-traditional tasks such as sewing, weaving, knitting and embroidering, while most men worked at painting, woodworking, printing and bookbinding. The professionals sought to desegregate the workshops not just to broaden the experiences of the women, but in an attempt to avoid all-male contexts conducive to men engaging in sexual activities with each other. Professionals feared that individuals known to engage in these behaviors would 'contaminate' others, and hoped that the presence of women in every workshop would inhibit this behavior.

Several professionals that I interviewed discussed the process by which young women and men entering a vocational facility were 'trained' in rules of acceptable conduct, being told: 'This is a professional work situation. No romance is allowed. If you want to romance, do it somewhere else'. One psychologist stated that new students could be 'a little wild' at first, but usually 'calmed down' after they learned the rules. Many of the adults attending the vocational facilities I visited had boyfriends and girlfriends in the community, but the majority were not allowed the social freedom, opportunity or privacy. For many, the vocational centers were the only social space available outside of home and family. Some chose to use this opportunity to do what they could. Some professionals told me that this was to be expected because individuals with ID had '*a flora da pele*' (were easily excitable with hypersensitive sexual responses).

Although the more recent literature on sexuality and disability in Brazil was remarkably consistent in its progressivism, there was no indication of a unified professional practice. In interviews with parents and professionals, I found that responses to the issue of sexuality were extremely individualized, depending on training, religion and personal opinions. There did seem to be a generational shift in regard to parental and professional perceptions (younger parents and professionals being more accepting), but even this was often less a factor of age than of personal opinion. Many of the older parents and professionals that I interviewed were very open-minded, and some of the younger parents quite repressive.

Despite the relative rarity of sterilization and institutionalization, I saw the effects of powerlessness on the individuals with ID that I befriended in Brazil. I saw the unhappiness caused by infantilization, social and sexual repression, exclusion and isolation. Though no longer practiced for eugenic purposes, involuntary sterilization remains a distressing common practice in Brazil with many prominent professionals advocating its continued use. However, such practices were never legislated or mandated by the state, nor did they become incorporated into the popular culture (as was the case in the US). As institutionalization was never common, individuals with ID were not perceived as dangerous outsiders. Brazilian men and women with ID were sometimes perceived as sexual vessels to be used at will, and sometimes experienced sexual violence. However, the fact that most individuals lived with their families, rather than in institutions, lessened the probability of sexual victimization (Crossmaker, 1991).

In Brazil, the stigma of disability is enmeshed within established and well-recognized power hierarchies of gender, class and race. Sexual repression exists, but unlike in the US, it does not include an ethos of sexual threat. Individuals with ID are not commonly perceived as sexual monsters that need to be controlled for the good of society. However, the fact that they are kept 'sheltered' from the significant life experiences of sexual relationships, marriage and procreation does indicate a continuing struggle between social marginality and citizenship.

References

Assumpção, F.B. & Sprovieri, M.H. (1993) *Deficiência Mental, Familia, e Sexualidade.* Memmon, São Paulo.

Block, P. (2000) Sexuality, fertility, and danger: twentieth-century images of women with cognitive disabilities. *Sexuality and Disability*, **18** (4), 239–254.

Celentano, Y.O. (1977) *Menino Sempre.* Published by author, Sao Paulo.

Coelho, E.F. (1987) *Deficiência Sexual (do Proibido ao Permitido).* Luzzatto Editora, Porto Alegre RS.

Crossmaker, M. (1991) Behind locked doors: institutional sexual abuse. *Sexuality and Disability*, **9** (3), 201–219.

D'Abreu, A. (1974) A problemática sexual do excepcional. *Mensagem da APAE*, **1** (1), 42–53.

Dantas, J. (1930) A proposito de eugenía: degenerados. *Boletiim de Eugenía*, **2** (18), 5–6.

Fairchild, H.P. (1926) *The Melting Pot Mistake.* Little Brown and Company, Boston.

Farani, A. (1931) Como evitar as proles degeneradas. *Archivos Brasileiras de Hygiene Mental*, **4** (3), 169–179.

Glat, R. (1989) *Somos Iguais a Vocês.* Livraria Agir Editora, Rio de Janeiro.

Glat, R. (1992) Sexualidade da pessoa com deficiência mental. *Revista Brasileira da Educação Especial*, **1** (1), 65–73.

Goddard, H.H. (1913) *The Kallikak Family: A Study in the Heredity of Feeble-Mindedness.* The MacMillan Company, New York.

Huggins, M.K. (1985) *From Slavery to Vagrancy in Brazil: Crime and Social Control in the Third World.* Rutgers University Press, New Brunswick.

Kehl, R. (1921) A esterilzação sob o ponto de vista eugenico. *Brasil Medico*, **35** (13), 155–157.

Kehl, R. (1933) *Sexo e Civilização.* Livraria Francisco Alves, Rio de Janeiro.

Kempton, W. & Kahn, E. (1991) Sexuality and people with intellectual disabilities: a historical perspective. *Sexuality and Disability*, **9** (2), 93–111.

Lemos, J. (1933) Considerações sobre a esterilização dos anormais e a formação dos homes de génio. *Archivos do Manicômio Judiciário*, **4** (1 & 2), 21–31.

Lipp, M.N. (1986) *Sexo para Deficientes Mentais: Sexo e Exceptional Dependente e Não Dependente.* Cortez, São Paulo.

Lopes, J.M. (1933) Em torno do exame pre-nupcial. *Archivos Brasileiros de Hygiene Mental*, **6** (2), 103–121.

Moreira e Costa, P.G. (1927) *Eugenia e Seléção.* Téze de Doutoramento, Faculdade de Medicina de São Paulo.

Muniz Neto, E. (1937) *Esterilisação e Direito Penal.* Imprensa Industrial, Recife.

Omote, S. (1993) Relações afetivo-sexuais e o portador de deficiência. In: Deficiencia mental: *Temas em Educação Especial 2* (eds T.R. da Silveira Dias, F.E. Denari & O.M.V. Kubo). UFSCAR, São Carlos.

Penna, B. (1918) *Saneamento no Brasil.* TyRevista dos Tribunaes, Carmo 55, Rio de Janeiro.

Ribeiro, P.R. & Nepomuceno, D.M. (1992) Sexualidade e deficiência mental: um estudo sobre o comportamento sexual do adolescente excepcional institucion-alizado. *Jornal Brasileiro de Psiquiatria*, **41** (4), 167–170.

Sassaki, R.K. (1981) Integração social da pessoa deficiente: o fator sexualidade. *CÉDRIS* (found in the archives of REINTEGRA (Rede de Informação Integral Sobre Deficientes)).

Stepan, N.L. (1991) *The Hour of Eugenics: Race, Gender, and Nation in Latin America.* Cornell University Press, Ithaca.

6 Sexuality

Michelle McCarthy

Introduction

Although there has been growth in research and practice on sexuality issues for women with intellectual disabilities (after years of neglect), there are still huge gaps in our knowledge. This chapter begins by outlining those areas we know relatively little about: it first looks at this from a life span perspective and examines the evidence available about sexuality specifically in relation to young and old women with intellectual disabilities. It then looks at sexuality from an equal opportunities perspective and presents what is known about sexuality for women from minority ethnic backgrounds, women with profound and multiple disabilities and lesbian women. The chapter then moves on to examine those sexuality-related issues that *have* been researched with women with intellectual disabilities, both consented and abusive experiences. The chapter concludes with suggestions, based on holistic and feminist principles, for improving the disadvantaged situation that many women with intellectual disabilities find themselves in.

Taking a life span perspective

Sexuality and young women with intellectual disabilities

There is no research I am aware of which explores what girls and young women with intellectual disabilities want for their current or future sexual lives. What we do know is that parents and other carers often have deep concerns about the emerging sexuality of girls and young women. These concerns focus on vulnerability to sexual abuse and fears of pregnancy (Heyman & Huckle, 1995). With regards to teenage pregnancy, it is well established that girls most at risk of becoming pregnant often have low educational achievements, low expectations for their futures and low socioeconomic status (Corcoran, 1999). Clearly, many girls with intellectual disabilities would come into these categories, although there are no national or international statistics on pregnancies in girls and young women with intellectual disabilities.

Occasionally, the pregnancy of a girl with intellectual disabilities causes a public scandal and makes newspaper headlines (such as 'Court bans abortion for girl with mental age of six', *The Guardian*, 17 December 1999).

Proposed or actual hysterectomies of young girls, usually in the context of a suggested strategy for menstrual management, are also discussed in the literature. The views of parents of girls and young women are prominent in these debates (Bambrick & Roberts, 1991; Carlson & Wilson, 1994); this is understandable given their caring roles and responsibilities. However, the voices of the young women themselves are missing from the literature, although older women with intellectual disabilities often speak with bitterness and regret about having been sterilized at an early age.

Sexuality and old(er) women with intellectual disabilities

Until relatively recently, aging as a topic in its own right was generally neglected in relation to people with intellectual disabilities, although this has clearly changed. However, within the aging and intellectual disabilities field, sexuality is largely neglected. Sexuality has been, and is likely to remain, relatively neglected for old(er) women with intellectual disabilities for the following reasons: it is still a relatively low priority within intellectual disability services generally; strong beliefs still prevail in society which regard older people generally as asexual; once women with intellectual disabilities reach an age where their fertility is no longer a 'threat', the issue can be safely forgotten. However, research evidence shows that many older women with intellectual disabilities do not understand the impact of the menopause on either their sexuality generally or on their fertility specifically (McCarthy, in press). For instance, some older women have picked up information from the media and believe they can still get pregnant after the menopause: 'Women like me *can* still have children, I've seen it on the television' (with reference to a news item about a 60 year old woman having a baby through in vitro fertilization). Other older women who have understood that menopause means the end of their fertility have expressed understandable but unrealistic ideas about the alternatives (e.g. ' I thought I could adopt one').

Regardless of age considerations, we lack knowledge generally about how women with intellectual disabilities feel about their fertility, about having or not having babies and raising or not having the opportunity to raise children. We also lack information about the sexual experiences and feelings of women with intellectual disabilities who have not experienced some form of abuse.

Taking an equal opportunities/inclusive perspective

Sexuality and women from minority ethnic backgrounds

Again relatively little is known about sexuality and women from minority ethnic backgrounds, and if assumptions are made at all, it is that women from different ethnic backgrounds have the same experiences, hopes and desires as women from majority white communities. Some recent research (Alam & Aziz, 2000) on sexuality issues with women with intellectual disabilities from black and Asian communities in Britain seems to substantiate this. These women reported that they experienced high levels of sexual abuse; that they lacked choice regarding their reproductive rights, but that they nevertheless had strong desires to have children; that they lacked knowledge about women's sexual pleasure; and that relationships were as important as, if not more important than, sex. All these factors compare very well to what white women with intellectual disabilities have said about their sexual lives; yet obviously there is the added layer of racism for the minority ethnic women to contend with, as well as all their struggles around sexuality.

Sexuality and women with profound and multiple disabilities

Of all people with intellectual disabilities, those with the most severe disabilities are the most neglected when it comes to consideration of their sexual needs and feelings (Downs & Craft, 1997). In the past it was considered that the severity of their disabilities would override all and any aspects of their sexuality. Yet this is a misguided view: 'sexuality is not an optional extra which we in our wisdom can choose to bestow or withhold according to whether or not some kind of intelligence test is passed' (Craft, 1987). For most people it is the case that a profound intellectual impairment and the associated life-long dependency on others, means that they are unlikely to be in a position to engage in consenting sexual relationships with other people. As society tends to view this kind of sexual expression as the most 'legitimate' form, it goes some way to explain why the sexual needs of profoundly disabled people have been ignored. But if sexuality is seen in a wider context, it also encompasses feelings of love and sexual arousal, understanding what touch does and does not give pleasure, masturbation, sexual health, self-awareness and self-image, identity, communication, personal development, gender issues and age appropriateness. All these things are as relevant for people with profound and multiple disabilities as they are for anyone else.

Sexuality and lesbian women with intellectual disabilities

Lesbian sexuality is one of the least researched and least understood forms of sexual expression for women with intellectual disabilities (McCarthy, 1999). This contrasts strongly with sex between men with intellectual disabilities about which far more is known (Thompson, 1994). The fact that little is known about lesbian sexuality does not mean there are no lesbians with intellectual disabilities. However, lack of positive information, lack of role models and lack of comprehensive sex education about the range of possibilities, means that it does become 'exceptionally difficult for women with intellectual difficulties to recognize themselves as lesbians' (Walmsley, 1993: 94). Nevertheless, some sex education support materials for people with intellectual disabilities include positive images of lesbian sexuality (FPA Auckland, 1997). Some supportively discuss homophobia (Twentieth Century Vixen Productions, 1988), and gradually a few courageous women with intellectual disabilities are speaking out publicly about their sexual desires for other women (Teuben & Davey, 2000).

What we do know about sexuality and women with intellectual disabilities

Essentially the research that has been done relates to the heterosexual experiences of mainly white women with mild and moderate intellectual disabilities in early and middle adulthood. This reflects feminist work more broadly, which despite taking a holistic approach to individual women's lives and circumstances, has tended to focus on mostly white, middle-class, younger women's experiences. Also, women with disabilities have traditionally been left out of feminist analysis:

> 'Women with disabilities have traditionally been ignored not only by those concerned about disability but also by those examining women's experiences. Even feminist scholars to whom we owe great intellectual and political debts have perpetuated this neglect. The popular view of women with disabilities has been one mixed with repugnance. Perceiving disabled women as childlike, helpless and victimized, non-disabled feminists have severed them from the sisterhood in an effort to advance more powerful, competent and appealing female icons.'

> (Fine & Asch, 1988: 3-4)

Notwithstanding the above observations, there are now many aspects of the sexual experiences of women with intellectual disabilities that we can analyze and reflect upon.

Sexual abuse

There is now ample research evidence from various countries, demonstrating the high prevalence of sexual abuse among women with intellectual disabilities; 82% of the women in the author's recent qualitative study described at least one, and in some cases several, act(s) of sexual abuse (McCarthy, 1999), as did 61% of the women in an earlier, larger prevalence study (McCarthy & Thompson, 1997), 83% in an American prevalence study (Hard & Plumb, 1987), and 79% in another qualitative study from the US (Stromsness, 1993).

The above is not an exhaustive list of all the sexual abuse research studies in the intellectual disability field. It includes only prevalence, and not incidence, studies and only those studies that delineate separate figures for women and men. Women almost always experience sexual abuse more frequently (McCarthy & Thompson, 1997)). Despite the above not being an exhaustive list, it indicates that the prevalence rates of sexual abuse for women with intellectual disabilities are very high. It is important to remember that although these figures are considerably higher than the reported rates for other women, figures for abuse of women without disabilities are also shockingly high. For example, Hall's London study (Hall 1985) reported a prevalence rate of 17% for rape and 20% for attempted rape. Russell's (1984) research in the US reported 41% of women experiencing rape or attempted rape. Randall and Haskell's study (1995) in Canada found that 56% of women had experienced rape or attempted rape at some point in their childhood or adulthood. This rate rose to two out of three women when the definition of sexual abuse was broadened to encompass all forms of unwanted sexual touch or intrusion. Sexual abuse research studies in the intellectual disability field often use broad definitions of abuse.

Sexual abuse can have many short and long term effects on those who experience it, but one of the most relevant for people with intellectual disabilities is the effect on women's sexuality in a broad sense, i.e. the difficulties they may have in experiencing other sexual encounters positively. Research concerning women without disabilities (Kelly, 1988; Orlando & Koss, 1983; Wyatt et al., 1993) and women with disabilities (Kiehlbauch Cruz et al., 1988) suggests that abusive sexual experiences can have a negative impact on women's subsequent consented sexual experiences. It is important to try to understand what links there may be between the two different types of experiences. Although it is difficult to integrate the experiences of women with intellectual disabilities in relation to both consented and abusive sex, this has been my intention in previous work (McCarthy, 1999).

Masturbation

Relatively little is known about women with intellectual disabilities and masturbation. Generally in intellectual disability services the issue is given greater priority for men, as is reflected in referrals to specialist sex education services (McCarthy, 1996). Clearly, many women with intellectual disabilities find it difficult to talk about masturbation, more so than their male peers, and this is to be expected given the strong social taboos which still exist for all women in talking about the sexual pleasure they can give themselves (McNeil, 1992). Where the issue has been sensitively explored with women with intellectual disabilities, there is a low reported level of masturbation (one-third of women with intellectual disabilities report that they did or had done this) (McCarthy, 1999). This is much lower than other reported surveys involving women without disabilities, but caution needs to be taken in making comparisons, due to the much larger sample sizes in other studies and the differences in research methodology. Therefore, it is not possible to ascertain that women with intellectual disabilities really do masturbate less than other women; an alternative explanation may be that they feel less able to say so. Until all women, and especially those with intellectual disabilities, feel more comfortable talking about the subject (which could possibly be achieved by sensitive sex education which encourages it and from more openness about it generally), further insights into this are unlikely to be gained.

Sex with men

From my practice-based discussions and research with women with intellectual disabilities, a picture emerges of a relatively narrow range of sexual activities with men, the most common activities being those which afford men relatively quick and easy routes to orgasm (see Fig. 6.1, from McCarthy, 1999):

The women with intellectual disabilities I have spoken to have reported that their sexual experiences with men are generally devoid of those non-penetrative activities which other women often name as sources of pleasure, for example, kissing, caressing, skin contact and stimulation (with partner's hands and mouth) of breasts, genitals and other erogenous zones. This does not imply that women generally do not like or want penetrative sex and would prefer these other activities. Most women report to researchers that they desire both types of sexual activities. Hence, few women would be satisfied with what is offered to most women with intellectual disabilities (i.e. vaginal and/or anal

Most common

Penetrative sex
(always vaginal, often anal)

Woman touching man's genitals

Oral sex from woman to man

Man touching woman's genitals

Oral sex from man to woman

Least common

Fig. 6.1

penetration with little or nothing else to arouse the woman prior, during or after it).

Aside from my own work, there is little research on precisely what kinds of heterosexual activity women with intellectual disabilities engage in and what they think and feel about it. However, Andron (1983) and Andron & Ventura (1987) report from their work with married couples with intellectual disabilities, that most of the women did not know about their clitoris, did not experience orgasm or indeed have any concept of what it involved, and that 'sex play was basically non-existent. Sex was understood as penis-vagina intercourse' (1987: 33). Also, Millard (1994) provides accounts of women with intellectual disabilities talking about heterosexual sex in negative and male-centered terms.

Sexual relationships with men

From my experience in talking to women with intellectual disabilities, many who did not have boyfriends wished for one and those who did have male partners valued their relationships very highly and wanted them to continue (see also Stromsness, 1993). Again this should not be a surprise, given the social pressures on adults to be in relationships. However, there are particular pressures for many women with intellectual disabilities. Burns (2000) described how achieving a valued identity as a woman is in itself a way of shaking off the devalued identity of a person with intellectual disabilities. As other valued roles for women, such as those of wife, mother/grandmother and career woman are usually denied to women with intellectual disabilities, embracing the role of sexual partner to a man, especially a more intellectually able man, is one of the few positive choices open to some women.

Men in heterosexual partnerships with women with intellectual disabilities are generally more intellectually able than their partners (McCarthy, 1999). It would be wrong to characterize all such relationships as exploitative, for there are positive aspects to such relationships for some women. But there are legitimate concerns that the person with the intellectual advantages may use those to shape the relationship to meet his own needs at the expense of his partner's. When the more intellectually able partner is the man, these advantages compound some of the more obvious ones already there on the basis of his gender. As Burns' work (2000) has demonstrated, this can make women with intellectual disabilities especially vulnerable. If being exploited, oppressed or even abused is the price to be paid for having a relationship with a man, then it can be a worthwhile trade-off in the eyes of many women with intellectual disabilities (see also Stromsness, 1993).

Sexual pleasure

The vast majority of women with intellectual disabilities interviewed by the author have spoken of lives which are largely devoid of sexual pleasure. However, as outlined above, this is not to say that their sexual relationships more broadly do not give them various kinds of pleasure and satisfaction, but the bodily experience of sexual pleasure and specifically of orgasm is not among them. Only one woman out of approximately 75 appeared to know what a clitoris was and what it was for. None of the women appeared to know what I was talking about when I tried to describe strong feelings of sexual pleasure, particularly orgasm. These findings support the findings of other similar research studies from the US (Andron, 1983; Andron & Ventura, 1987) and from practice-based work with women with intellectual disabilities (Millard, 1994).

Few of the women in my studies gave any indication that sexual attraction or sexual arousal were reasons for them engaging in sexual contact with men (it is acknowledged that these are difficult things for anyone to discuss). Indeed it was often very difficult for the women to say *any* reasons why they had sex with men. When they did offer reasons, however, most referred to the fact that they liked or loved the man. Most women gave a very strong impression that their relationships with men were extremely important to them. Very often they felt that in order to develop and maintain a relationship they had to engage in sex, even if the kind of sex they were having did not afford them much personal pleasure. In other words, sex was seen by many women as a means to an end, the end being the relationship, not sexual pleasure. It is of course the case that many other women, who do not have intellectual disabilities, have throughout history and across many cultures found themselves in a similar position. Despite the 'girl power' rhetoric of recent times, many young women still find themselves understanding and experiencing sex in terms of men's needs, rather than their own pleasures (Holland *et al.*, 1998).

Improving the way women with intellectual disabilities experience their sexuality

Given the rather negative picture that emerges when women with intellectual disabilities speak about their sexual lives, there is a need for sex education to improve the situation. The following are brief suggestions that would be at least partially conducive to women with intellectual disabilities experiencing their sexuality more positively.

- Those concerned with supporting women with intellectual disabilities in their sexual lives need to develop an understanding of gender power relations and the impact of this on the motivation of women and men to engage in sexual activity in the first place and on their subsequent experiences.
- Sex education needs to emphasize (for both women and men) a positive sexual discourse for women, explaining why and how women can and do enjoy sex, either alone or with a partner.
- Formal sex education and informal sexuality support need to give more emphasis to masturbation as an activity in its own right and as a way in which women can learn about their bodies, their desires and their capacity for pleasure alone or with a partner.
- Sex education needs to focus not only on sex and relationships, but also on developing women's self-esteem and sense of themselves as valued people in the broadest possible terms.
- Without the above, education regarding safer sexual practices is unlikely to be effective.

Case study: Maria

Maria is a 50-year-old woman with moderate intellectual disabilities. She spent her childhood and teenage years at home with her family and was first sent to an institution for people with intellectual disabilities at the age of 19, after she had a baby (which was taken into care and adopted). Maria was not able to say who the father was and, when questioned, had apparently very little understanding of how conception took place. During the many years she spent in the institution, Maria had several boyfriends and other more casual sexual encounters. As far as the staff was aware, these took place only with other residents. However, during sex education, Maria talked about men coming into the institution's grounds from the local community and having sex with women residents, herself included. These men would often promise, and sometimes give, rewards to the women for their sexual favors (Maria reported this could be small sums of money, sweets, a car ride, etc.). Maria never experienced any more pregnancies as she used various forms of contraception over the years, including an IUD, the Pill and the Depo-Provera injection.

   Maria finally left the institution when she was in her early 40s. She moved to a small group home, which she shared with three other women. She attended a day center, college classes and community groups, where she occasionally became sexually involved with men. Maria became a rather sad and withdrawn person and showed signs of depression. At one point she bought herself a doll and would spend long periods in her bedroom, cuddling and talking to it. This was strongly discouraged by staff, who saw it as an age-inappropriate activity.

   Maria joined a women's health group, the primary purpose of which was to prepare women with intellectual disabilities for the changes they may experience as they went through the menopause. However, group discussions were broad and covered social and emotional, as well as physical, health issues. Maria used the time well to talk about her previous relationships with men, both the exploitative and positive ones. She was able to say that although she never experienced much sexual pleasure, she nevertheless missed the physical and sexual contact she had been used to. She was helped to see how she put herself at risk in her efforts to seek these out, and to consider safer strategies. Maria became very distressed at the realization that menopause would mean she could not have a baby in the future, and spoke about the one she had lost many years earlier. Her current staff team was shocked to hear of this, as they had no knowledge of this part of Maria's life. Maria was referred to a psychologist for support and counseling to help her with her feelings about this. Maria formed some strong friendships with other women in her group and began to be less depressed, as new avenues for socializing and support opened up in her life. Maria's hope for her future is that she will get married and live independently with her husband.

Conclusion

Why is it that, despite the large body of literature on sexuality and intellectual disability which now exists, there is so little research on how women (and men) with intellectual disabilities actually experience their sexual lives? Clearly there are many considerations regarding the appropriateness and the ethics of researching sensitive and private experiences with anybody (Renzetti & Lee, 1993) and particularly with people with intellectual disabilities who may be less able than most to protect themselves from researchers' intrusive questions (Swain *et al.*, 1998). However, there is also a clear imperative to base sexuality support on the actual, not presumed, needs of the women who use intellectual disability services.

My research with women with intellectual disabilities has been from an explicitly feminist perspective. I have sought to give a voice to women who are, and have long been, 'socially and politically silent' (McRobbie, 1982: 52) by adopting research and practice methods within which, together, we could articulate their experiences. But merely giving a voice to an excluded and oppressed group, although essential, is not enough. It is necessary to provide some theoretical context to this, especially as so many women with intellectual disabilities who have spoken about their sexual experiences have done so in negative terms. Failure to provide this can lead to essentialist views being taken that many women with intellectual disabilities do not enjoy sex either because they are women and/or because they have a disability. Instead I have provided a framework for understanding individual women's experience of sexual oppression by reference to aspects of patriarchy (the privileging of male sexuality) and to oppression based on disability.

For those who do not take a feminist position in interpreting women's experiences, it is still nevertheless important to explore sexuality issues in a holistic way. The following factors are inextricably linked to most women's sexuality:

- The way women think and feel about their bodies (i.e., how they perceive their attractiveness or lack of it)
- Their self-esteem more generally
- Their ability to make decisions which other adults take for granted (such as who to live with, who to associate with)
- Their opportunity and ability to control (or not) their fertility specifically and their sexual and reproductive health more broadly
- Their experiences of sexual abuse and coercion

All these factors, and more, need to be explored with women with intellectual disabilities, to enable them to maximize their chances of being able to enhance their lives through the potential pleasures which are available from sexual relationships and private sexual expression. Trying to give such an advantage to women with intellectual disabilities in this one sphere of life would be no small achievement for women who are disadvantaged in so many other spheres (i.e. intellectually, economically, socially and politically).

References

Alam, A. & Aziz, R. (2000) *Reach Out: Looking At the Personal Relationships, Sexuality and Needs of African and Asian Descent Learning Disabled Women*. Family Planning Association, London.

Andron, L. (1983) Sexuality counselling with developmentally disabled couples. In: *Sex Education and Counselling for Mentally Handicapped People* (eds M. Craft & A. Craft), pp. 254–286. Costello, Tunbridge Wells.

Andron, L. & Ventura, J. (1987) Sexual dysfunction in couples with learning handicaps. *Sexuality and Disability*, **8** (1), 25–35.

Bambrick, M. & Roberts, G. (1991) The sterilization of people with a mental handicap: the views of parents. *Journal of Mental Deficiency Research*, **35**, 353–363.

Burns, J. (2000) Gender identity and women with learning disabilities: the third sex. *Clinical Psychology Forum*, **137**, March.

Carlson, G. & Wilson, J. (1994) Menstrual management: the mother's perspective. *Mental Handicap Research*, **7**, 51–64.

Corcoran, J. (1999) Ecological factors associated with adolescent pregnancy: a review of the literature. *Adolescence*, **34**, 135, 603–619.

Craft, A. (1987) *Mental Handicap and Sexuality: Issues for Individuals with a Mental Handicap, their Parents and Professionals*. Costello, Turnbridge Wells. Cited in Downs, C. & Craft, A. (1997) *Sex in Context*. Pavilion Publishers, Brighton.

Downs, C. & Craft, A. (1997) *Sex in Context*. Pavilion Publishers, Brighton.

Fine, M. & Asch, A. (1988) *Women with Disabilities: Essays in Psychology, Culture and Politics*. Temple University Press, Philadelphia.

FPA Auckland (1997) *Four Stories: A Video about Relationships for People with Intellectual Disabilities*. Family Planning Association, Auckland.

Hall, R. (1985) *Ask Any Woman*. Falling Wall Press, Bristol.

Hard, S. & Plumb, W. (1987) Sexual abuse of persons with developmental disabilities. A case study. Unpublished manuscript. Association for Retarded Citizens, CA.

Heyman, B. & Huckle, S. (1995) Sexuality as a perceived hazard in the lives of adults with learning disabilities. *Disability and Society*, **11** (2), 139–155.

Holland, J., Ramazanoglu, C., Sharpe, S. & Thomson, R. (1998) *The Male in the Head: Young People, Heterosexuality and Power*. Tufnell Press, London.

Kelly, L. (1988) *Surviving Sexual Violence*. Polity Press, Cambridge.

Kiehlbauch Cruz, V., Price-Williams, D. & Andron, L. (1988) Developmentally disabled women who were molested as children. *Social Casework: The Journal of Social Work*, September, 411–419.

McCarthy, M. (1996) The sexual support needs of people with learning disabilities: a profile of those referred for sex education. *Sexuality and Disability*, **14** (4), 265–279.

McCarthy, M. (1999) *Sexuality and Women with Learning Disabilities*. Jessica Kingsley Publishers, London.

McCarthy, M. (in press) Going through the menopause: perceptions and experiences of women with learning disabilities. *Journal of Gerontological Social Work*.

McCarthy, M. & Thompson, D. (1997) A prevalence study of sexual abuse of adults with intellectual disabilities referred for sex education. *Journal of Applied Research in Intellectual Disability*, **10** (2), 105–124.

McNeil, P. (1992) Doing it on my own. In: *Women Talk Sex* (ed. P. McNeil, B. Freeman & J. Newman), pp. 88–102. Scarlett Press, London.

McRobbie, A. (1982) The politics of feminist research: between talk, text and action. *Feminist Review*, **12**, 46–57.

Millard, L. (1994) Between ourselves: experiences of a women's group on sexuality and sexual abuse. In: *Practice Issues in Sexuality and Learning Disabilities* (ed. A. Craft), pp. 135–155. Routledge, London.

Orlando, J. & Koss, M. (1983) The effect of sexual victimisation on sexual satisfaction: a study of the negative-association hypothesis. *Journal of Abnormal Psychology*, **92** (1), 104–106.

Randall, M. & Haskell, L. (1995) Sexual violence in women's lives: findings from the Women's Safety Project, a community based study. *Violence Against Women*, **1** (1), 6–31.

Renzetti, C. & Lee, R. (1993) The problems of researching sensitive topics: an overview and introduction. In: *Researching Sensitive Topics*. (eds C. Renzetti & R. Lee), pp. 3–13. Sage Publications, London.

Russell, D. (1984) *Sexual exploitation: Rape, Child Sexual Abuse and Workplace Harassment*. Sage, London.

Stromsness, M. (1993) Sexually abused women with mental retardation: hidden victims, absent resources. *Women and Therapy*, **14** (3–4), 139–152.

Swain, J., Heyman, B. & Gillman, M. (1998) Public research, private concerns: ethical issues in the use of open-ended interviews with people who have learning difficulties. *Disability and Society*, **13** (1), 21–36.

Teuben, S. & Davey, M. (2000) Gina's Story. In: *Women with Intellectual Disabilities: Finding A Place In the World* (eds R. Traustadottir & K. Johnson), pp. 162–171. Jessica Kingsley Publishers, London.

Thompson, D. (1994) Sexual experience and sexual identity for men with learning disabilities who have sex with men. *Changes*, **12** (4), 254–263.

Twentieth Century Vixen Productions (1988) *Between Ourselves* video. Twentieth Century Vixen Productions, Brighton.

Walmsley, J. (1993) Women first: lessons in participation. *Critical Social Policy*, **13** (2), 86–99.

Wyatt, G., Newcombe, M. & Riederle, M. (1993) *Sexual Abuse and Consensual Sex: Women's Developmental Patterns and Outcomes*. Sage, Newberry Park, CA.

7

Parenting

Susan L. Parish

Introduction

Women with intellectual disabilities in the US have endured a repressive history of coercive sterilization and segregation in order to prevent them from procreating. At the outset of the twentieth century, parenting by these women was identified by professionals in the field as one of the prime threats to the continued success and stability of the nation. Beliefs that women with intellectual disabilities cannot successfully parent have continued, and this topic remains deeply controversial. Today, as for no other group, their disability label alone is sufficient in some states to facilitate the termination of their parental rights. Despite the rhetoric, mothers with intellectual disabilities are quite diverse and they represent one of the most underserved populations in the US.

The objective of this chapter is to evaluate the circumstances surrounding mothering by women with intellectual disabilities in the US, including an assessment of the economic and sociopolitical context in which mothers with intellectual disabilities parent. A review of the research on mothers with intellectual disabilities is presented, followed by a discussion of the legal status of parenting and intellectual disabilities in the US. The chapter concludes with a consideration of the policy implications of the preceding analysis.

Parenting in context

On an array of measures, the well-being of children is widely recognized to be affected by individual characteristics of the child, the mother and the father, and the interplay between the sociocultural context and environment in which the family lives (Lanata, 2001). As is not always apparent from the research on mothers with intellectual disabilities, parenting occurs in a context influenced by the family's socioeconomic status, emotional and social resources, and relationships to the larger community. Many investigations of parenting by women with intellectual disabilities focused on the attributes or individual situation of the mothers or their children, ignoring the larger environment in which they lived. This is particularly problematic in that mothers with intellectual disabilities often face circumstances in their lives that include psychiatric disabilities, discrimination, poverty and violence. Perhaps the greatest need for further research concerning mothers with intellectual disabilities is into the implications of these larger issues for their parenting.

Numerous studies have reported that the life circumstances of mothers with intellectual disabilities are often characterized by overwhelming problems. Parents' lives represent a constant onslaught of crises, including such things as eviction and homelessness, insufficient money for food, mental health problems, victimization from community members, disconnection of power and water, spousal/partner abuse, rape, and undiagnosed medical problems (Booth & Booth, 1993b; Whitman *et al.*, 1989). While these issues may be seen as common results of poverty, and they may be experienced by a large subset of the general population, mothers with intellectual disabilities, due to their cognitive limitations, may lack the coping and problem-solving abilities that enable other poor people to survive. This section will discuss the scope and implications of the larger context in which mothers with intellectual disabilities live.

There is a dearth of resources allocated to supporting parents with intellectual disabilities, which occurs in a context in which services for adults with intellectual disabilities generally are quite limited. In 1998, only 17% of the US population with intellectual disabilities received some form of long-term care (defined as family support or residential care). The majority of people with intellectual disabilities are not receiving formal services and most of the services that are provided are not directed at mothers with intellectual disabilities.

The most prevalent support provided to people with intellectual disabilities in the US is disability-based income maintenance, through the Supplemental Security Income (SSI) and Disability Insurance (DI) programs. SSI is a means-tested monthly income program for the elderly and persons with disabilities. SSI eligibility for persons with disabilities is predicated upon the individual having a disabling condition that results in work incapacity. DI is an income replacement program for persons with disabilities who previously worked and are no longer able to perform substantial gainful activities (Mashaw, 2000; Social Security Administration, 2000a), which were defined in 2001 as monthly earnings in excess of $740 (Social Security Administration, 2000b).

In fiscal year 2000, an estimated $6.5 billion was paid in SSI benefits to 776 000 adults with intellectual disabilities. An additional $3.2 billion in DI benefits was paid to 536 000 adults with intellectual disabilities (Parish & Braddock, 2001). Averaging $512 for SSI, and $498 for DI, the monthly amount received by adults with intellectual disabilities left most individuals well below the federal poverty level of $746 for a single person (US

Census Bureau, 2001). While it is not possible to identify the unduplicated count of people receiving income maintenance payments and long-term care services, it is clear that a significant proportion of those individuals with intellectual disabilities (by the author's conservative estimate, at least 50%) in the US are not receiving either. It is unknown how many mothers with intellectual disabilities are among this group.

Research has shown that people with intellectual disabilities are substantially more likely to be living below the poverty level than people without intellectual disabilities. An analysis of the National Health Interview Survey Disability Supplement (NHIS-D) indicated that 33% of all persons with intellectual disabilities are living below the poverty level, compared to 13% of persons without intellectual disabilities (Larson *et al.*, 2000). The complex nature of the relationship between poverty and disability is not wholly understood. The risk of disability appears to be growing, and that risk is elevated in poor homes and single-parent families (Fujiura & Yamaki, 2000). There are numerous risks associated with poverty, including violence, limited access to health care, and reduced quality of life. These figures suggest that a substantial portion of the population with intellectual disabilities is grappling with an array of issues related to poverty, in addition to the difficulties they face due to their impairments.

In the US, employment rates for adults with intellectual disabilities are substantially lower than for the general population. Yamaki's (1999) analysis indicated that the employment rate for women with intellectual disabilities (operationalized as 'mental retardation') was 23.5%, while the employment rate for men with intellectual disabilities was 27.4%. The employment rate of people with disabilities has consistently ranged between 23% and 45% (Daniels & West, 1998), indicating that people with intellectual disabilities have among the lowest employment rates of any individuals in our society. These individuals are likely to be working in jobs at the fringe of the economy, and will be among those hardest hit in an economic downturn.

Another important aspect of the lives of mothers with intellectual disabilities is the extent to which they have been abused, either as children, adults or both. While it is very difficult to determine the rates of abuse for the general population (Pagelow, 1984), it is even more difficult to ascertain abuse rates for people with disabilities, and particularly those with intellectual disabilities (Sobsey, 1994). There is widespread belief that rates of abuse for persons with disabilities are significantly higher than those for the general population, particularly those individuals with intellectual disabilities, although the number of studies are limited and have had variable results (Sobsey, 1994). Children with disabilities are believed to be maltreated at rates that are an estimated 1.7 times greater than children without disabilities (National Center on Child Abuse and

Neglect, 1993). However, a number of researchers believe this estimate to be quite low (Sobsey, 1994). In Spain, Verdugo *et al.* (1995) found that 11.5% of children with intellectual disabilities were abused as compared to 1.5% of a contrast group of children without disabilities.

A related issue is the sexual abuse and exploitation of people with intellectual disabilities. Anecdotal evidence from many of the intervention studies reported that some of the children born to mothers with intellectual disabilities are the result of rape or incest, and many women spontaneously reported having been sexually victimized at some point in their lives. People with intellectual disabilities are believed to be much more vulnerable than the general population to sexual abuse, due to their cognitive limitations, reliance on carers, desires to be compliant in order to 'pass' as normal, and limited access to sex education. There is evidence that people with intellectual disabilities are often abused by relatives, family friends and paid carers, and that the abuse is often long-standing (Tharinger *et al.*, 1990). There are tremendous difficulties in the identification and reporting of sexual abuse, including memory and communication difficulties faced by people with intellectual disabilities, perceived lack of credibility of victims, limited interest on the part of law enforcement in prosecuting these types of cases, and a host of other issues (Mitchell & Buchele-Ash, 2000; Tharinger, *et al.*, 1990). As might be suspected, rates of sexual abuse for girls with disabilities are significantly higher than for children without disabilities and for boys with disabilities (Sobsey *et al.*, 1997). However, it is unknown if this trend is consistent for girls with intellectual disabilities.

Abuse in the lives of people with intellectual disabilities is of enormous concern, particularly as related to parenting ability. The fact that they have been abused as a child increases the likelihood that individuals will in turn abuse their own children (Hall *et al.*, 1993). There is also evidence that parents are more likely to be abusive if the child was unwanted (Pagelow, 1984). As has been reported anecdotally in the intervention research, this is often the case with mothers with intellectual disabilities whose children are conceived by rape or incest.

Another critical issue in understanding the life context of mothers with intellectual disabilities is related to mental illness. At least one-third of people with intellectual disabilities have mental illnesses or psychiatric disorders, rates that far exceed those for the general population (Reiss, 1994). Depression and other mental illnesses are widely recognized to impact negatively the nurturing and parenting abilities provided by affected mothers. In an investigation of depression, significantly more mothers with intellectual disabilities exhibited depressive symptoms than did a control group of women without disabilities from the same socioeconomic background and local community (Tymchuk, 1994). Of the mothers with intellectual disabilities, 39% had depressive symptoms as compared to 13% of the 97 contrast mothers.

Another important aspect of the mental health issues related to mothers with intellectual disabilities is their self-esteem. There is long-standing evidence that individuals with intellectual disabilities generally have poorer self-concepts than individuals without disabilities (Edgerton, 2001). Studies of mothers with intellectual disabilities have indicated that their self-esteem is often substantially damaged. Tymchuk (1991) found that 67% of mothers with intellectual disabilities, as compared with 28% in a contrast group of mothers from the same neighborhoods, had poor self-esteem. An intervention project with mothers with intellectual disabilities found that low self-esteem was 'a major factor in all the interactions the parents had with their children, each other, and the staff in the program. A number of the parents raised issues related to their cognitive limitations and the constant negative comments they experienced as a result' (Whitman *et al.*, 1989: 432). The mental health of mothers with intellectual disabilities is very much related to the resources they bring to their parenting, and is an issue to which service providers and policy-makers must attend.

Research on parenting by women with intellectual disabilities

Historically, opposition to parenting by women with intellectual disabilities was lodged out of concern for the genetic material that would be transmitted to their children. Currently, opposition and concern about mothers with intellectual disabilities is related to their supposed incompetence and deficiencies in providing appropriate parenting to their children. Different authors have argued that children whose mothers have intellectual disabilities face greater risks of an array of negative outcomes, including lowered intelligence, abuse and neglect, poor educational attainment, and greater levels of psychiatric problems. As this section will demonstrate, interpreting the literature and explaining the extent or causes of poor parenting by these mothers, is problematic.

Parenting is complex and there is no agreement, either legally (Hayman, 1990) or clinically (Pagelow, 1984), as to what constitutes parental competence or adequacy. The lack of agreement on a minimum set of skills, behaviors and knowledge for parenting competence has profound implications for research on mothers with intellectual disabilities. Today, the construct of competence lies at the heart of all discussions of mothers with intellectual disabilities. Investigators have used a plethora of different and sometimes incompatible measures of adequate or inadequate parenting. This variability has resulted in a body of research from which it is very difficult to distill meaningful, and valid, understandings of these women's competence.

The quantity of research on parenting by women with intellectual disabilities is quite limited in relation to other intellectual disabilities research. There are tremendous difficulties in drawing summative conclusions from this body of research, both due to its limited scope and because of frequently serious methodological flaws. A number of authors have conducted relatively extensive discussion of these works (e.g. Espe-Sherwindt & Crable, 1993; Tymchuk & Feldman, 1991), and an exhaustive assessment of each study is beyond the scope of this chapter. The discussion in this section will address larger trends, and point to areas in which further research is needed.

The research on parenting and intellectual disabilities can be generally characterized within five categories: parental skill or knowledge assessments, intervention evaluations, child outcome inquiries and service needs, investigations of mothers' individual or interpersonal traits, and studies of parents' own perspectives. The vast majority of these studies have been done with mothers, and not fathers with intellectual disabilities.

Assessments of parental skill or knowledge (e.g. Tymchuk *et al.*, 1990), typically evaluate different aspects of mothers' knowledge of necessary parenting skills, such as child safety, emergency responses, nutrition, or decision-making. Intervention evaluations (e.g. Greene *et al.*, 1995; Whitman *et al.*, 1989) include assessments of mothers' abilities to improve their parenting, by participation in support groups, training programs or therapy. Child outcome inquiries (e.g. Booth & Booth, 2000; Feldman & Walton-Allen, 1997) evaluate the impact of parenting by a mother with intellectual disabilities on the well-being of their children, most often operationalized as measured IQ, educational attainment, reported abuse/neglect incidents, or outright removal of the child from the home. Assessments of mothers' interpersonal characteristics (Tymchuk & Andron, 1990) generally have sought to describe attributes of mothers with intellectual disabilities, particularly as compared to a contrast group of mothers without disabilities, on measures such as depressive symptoms or decision-making ability.

There is evidence that mothers with intellectual disabilities can benefit from intervention services that are respectful, supportive and tailored to learners with cognitive limitations and lower literacy levels. Children born to mothers with intellectual disabilities seem to be at the same risk for impaired development, poor health and educational outcomes as other poor children (Tymchuk, 1990; Tymchuk & Feldman, 1991). In fact, in studies comparing mothers with intellectual disabilities with mothers from similar socioeconomic backgrounds, no significant differences in decision-making ability or maternal knowledge have been found (e.g. Tymchuk *et al.*, 1990).

The greatest parenting concerns for women with intellectual disabilities have usually been related to perceptions of increased child abuse or neglect of their children. While neglect in these families occurs, it is frequently related to inadequate training and supports (Tymchuk & Feldman, 1991). It is not possible to know from the research if rates of neglect for these mothers are higher than for mothers with similar socioeconomic backgrounds. Neglect has long been identified as related to poverty (Pagelow, 1984).

Mothers with intellectual disabilities are significantly less likely to abuse their children than the general population (Tymchuk, 1990; Tymchuk & Feldman, 1991). Twelve factors that increase the likelihood of child abuse by mothers include young motherhood, single motherhood, unwanted pregnancy, difficult birth, other young children at home, low birth weight infant, mother's health problems, child's health problems, lack of respite from child care, irritable or unresponsive infant, social isolation, low education of parent, and poverty (Pagelow, 1984: 262). What is known about the lives of many people with milder levels of cognitive limitations is that social isolation, poverty and low education are frequently issues that loom large in their lives (Edgerton, 2001; Tymchuk *et al.*, 2001). Perhaps this makes it even more remarkable that abuse rates are lower for mothers with intellectual disabilities than for the general population.

A final, and quite different category of research involves in-depth examinations of parents' own perspectives of their lives (e.g. Booth & Booth, 1993a; Llewellyn, 1995). In these investigations, qualitative research methods are employed to gain an extensive understanding of the parents' own feelings about their experiences, the services they receive, and the supports that are most helpful to them. While very few of these studies have been conducted, they offer the greatest possibilities for truly understanding the complexity of parenting by women with intellectual disabilities. These studies also shine a harsh light on much of the other research that has been done, illuminating what has so often been missing in it – detailed investigations of the magnitude and importance of social support networks, the relationship between poverty, inadequate home environments and neglect, and the impact of stigma, violence and society's prejudice on these women. Unfortunately, research on mothers with intellectual disabilities frequently fails to account for the ways in which these women's parenting experiences are embedded in a complex, and often unforgiving, larger environment.

This body of research has frequently included methodological problems arising when mothers with intellectual disabilities were compared with women whose educational levels and socioeconomic backgrounds were quite dissimilar. Many of the studies have also used extremely small samples, often with fewer than ten subjects, effectively invalidating their generalizability to other mothers with intellectual disabilities. Another serious methodological problem faced by many of these studies is that participants were often recruited from Child Protective Service registries or other social service agency rosters. The results of these studies cannot possibly be generalized to women who have successfully managed to evade detection by social service agencies.

One problematic illustration of this type of research examined placement outcomes for children whose mothers were referred to their clinic for substantiated findings of abuse or neglect (Seagull & Scheurer, 1986). Reviewing case records, the authors found 20 of the 1500 families that had been referred to their clinic were headed by a parent with intellectual disabilities, for a total of 64 children. After seven years, all but 17% of the children had been removed from their family homes either temporarily or permanently. The authors note that the families received between 6 and 17 community services in addition to AFDC (the former welfare program in the US) and Medicaid (public health insurance for the poor and disabled). They conclude 'few maltreated children of intellectually low functioning parents were ultimately able to remain with their parents if they were to be adequately cared for' (Seagull & Scheurer, 1986: 498). They then report that the termination rates for these families are substantially higher than those for other families receiving protective service. They also argue that if their results are replicated in subsequent studies, 'the general right of retarded adults to marry and bear children may be called into question' (Seagull & Scheurer, 1986: 499).

The methodological problems with this study are significant. Placement rates were not evaluated for any of the parents without disabilities, so it is impossible to conclude that termination is greater for mothers with intellectual disabilities than for other parents. The authors suggest that these women were unable to benefit from the generic services offered to parents without disabilities, which may seem obvious given that the entire field of special education emerged in recognition that people with intellectual disabilities have learning difficulties. Furthermore, non-probability samples like these, recruited from child protective or social service agencies, will always over represent those whose parenting has resulted in intervention, and will certainly not represent women who have managed to avoid detection by social service agencies.

Perhaps the most serious issue in research on mothers with intellectual disabilities, however, is what has not been studied. With the notable exceptions of Booth and Booth (2000) and O'Neill (1995), nearly all studies have focused on parents of children, and not parents of adolescents or adults. These two studies offered very interesting support for the fact that over the long-term, some children of mothers with intellectual disabilities fare very well and have quite positive assessments of the care that they received from their parents. Another striking issue that arises from these two studies is that a number of the children (all in the O'Neill study) had very successful outcomes, as measured by educational attainment, employment and general well-being (Booth & Booth, 2000; O'Neill, 1995). Both sets of researchers did not use families referred by Child Protective Services, and the positive outcomes achieved by their children are quite telling.

Longitudinal investigations of the dynamics of parenting by these women over time do not exist. Studies have also almost exclusively approached their research questions from a deficit perspective. Some researchers have simply sought to catalogue the deficits of these mothers. Attempts to seek evidence of resilience, achievement of mastery in the face of extraordinary stress, and triumphs over discrimination, are not generally present in the literature.

Except for work by Booth and Booth (1993a, 2000), Llewellyn (1995) and O'Neill (1995), the research has focused on relatively superficial accounting of behavior, deficits and child outcomes. For instance, Dowdney & Skuse (1993) found that assessments of parenting based on observed behavior relied on observational periods that did not exceed ten minutes. Study samples drawn from Child Protective Services cases proliferate, and are doubtless not representative of the larger population of mothers with intellectual disabilities. Researchers Booth and Booth have suggested that:

> 'Parenting cannot be reduced to a set of tick boxes or rendered in terms of numbers alone. There is a need to move beyond blanket descriptions of parents with learning difficulties that allow them no say in their own destiny. People's qualities as parents are more surely revealed in their lived lives than by standardized assessment schedules or behavioral tests ... Research or practice devoid of such familiarity runs the risk of seriously misrepresenting the quality of parenting provided by people with learning disabilities as well as the nature of their family life ... alerts us to the danger of making easy generalizations on the basis of a superficial knowledge of parents as people.'

(Booth & Booth, 1993a: 111)

We cannot say with confidence how mothers with intellectual disabilities or their children fare over time. The research must delve more deeply into the lives of these women and their families, and evaluate the strengths they bring to their parenting tasks and how the larger context of their lives influences their parenting, particularly the degree to which they experience social isolation, poverty, violence and discrimination. The research should also focus on how these families can be supported in ways that do not disempower the parents and perpetuate stereotypical assumptions about disability.

In court cases involving mothers with intellectual disabilities, as will be discussed shortly, the justice system has a tendency to rely on the testimony of experts, to the exclusion of evidence regarding the actual parenting experiences of the women themselves (Hayman, 1990; Watkins, 1995). In their testimony, professional witnesses have often relied on the very problematic research addressing these women, clearly exceeding the limits of the research's applicability.

Mothers with intellectual disabilities and the justice system

Currently, public policy toward mothers with intellectual disabilities most often is manifested in court intervention to terminate their parental rights. Most marriage restrictions have either been repealed or are not enforced, and compulsory sterilization of women with intellectual disabilities is no longer widespread. This is not to say that involuntary sterilization for women with intellectual disabilities is not sought or does not exist (e.g. Cleveland, 1997), but a wide-scale program of coercive sterilization is not in place.

There is evidence that children of parents with intellectual disabilities are significantly more likely to be removed from their family home than are children of parents without disabilities. This is often the basis for conclusions that parenting provided by people with intellectual disabilities is inadequate. There is considerable evidence that in some American states mental disability is, by itself, a sufficient reason for the removal of children from the home (Levesque, 1996; Watkins, 1995).

In 1980, the United States Congress adopted the Adoption Assistance and Child Welfare Act, which included a goal of providing families with the services necessary to preclude removal of children from the family home. States that comply with the mandates of the federal law receive federal funds for their child protection systems. The Act also compels states to make 'reasonable efforts' to reunite parents with their children. This Act established a national standard that a key goal of child welfare services is the preservation of the family (Buchele-Ash et al., 1995; Public Law 96-272, 1980). This so-called family preservation strategy is a policy whereby families that face possible dissolution by the courts are provided with services and supports that enable them to meet minimum standards for providing adequate care to their children.

In spite of the family preservation policy, and the US Supreme Court's articulation of parenting as a fundamental right (Gilhool & Gran, 1985), states absolutely have the right to remove children from their family homes, if necessary. One of the Supreme Court's most influential custody termination decisions upheld states' rights to terminate parental custody if 'clear and convincing' evidence is presented regarding harm to the child, inability of parents to care for the child, and probability that the inadequacies of care will persist (Levesque, 1996). The standards for protecting parental rights are based on the belief that parental rights are fundamental and should only be terminated after due-process protections have been followed, and the welfare of the children demands termination.

For women with intellectual disabilities, however, the intersection of family preservation policy and the state's child protection responsibility frequently leads to the dissolution of their families. A litany of cases across the nation indicates that mothers with intellectual disabilities routinely have their parental rights terminated, often without any evidence that they have abused or neglected their children (Hayman, 1990; Watkins, 1995). This is the case in spite of Supreme Court mandates that such actions are unconstitutional. Inadequate parenting is presumed to be an automatic result of intellectual disability itself (Hayman, 1990; Watkins, 1995). In several states, the existence of mental disability in a parent is sufficient to terminate his or her custody, regardless of the care provided to the child. It is far more common, though, that states use standards that are significantly more strict for parents with intellectual disabilities than for other parents. Presumptions of incompetence by the courts and child welfare workers result in termination cases in which other circumstances, including domestic abuse, poverty, inadequate social supports and successful completion of rehabilitation or training programs are not considered.

Characterizing termination proceedings for parents with intellectual disabilities, Hayman (1990: 1237) has articulated four main features of these child welfare cases:

> '[The courts] display a remarkable degree of deference to expert testimony about the nature and impacts of the alleged disability. Second, the fact of mental retardation, once established, often has the effect of shifting the various burdens of proof from the state to the parent. Third, in assessing the fitness of the parents, courts tend to utilize a variety of norm-references, including some already implicit in the mental retardation construct. Finally, courts demonstrate an extraordinary resourcefulness for legitimating termination decisions with formal findings regardless of the meaningfulness of the process.'

These four issues create a clear foundation of a system that is indefensibly discriminatory toward these women, and against which most mothers with intellectual disabilities are literally powerless. What is particularly pernicious is that the use of expert testimony serves to shift the trial to an evaluation of the notion of parenting by women with intellectual disabilities, and evidence of the individual woman's parenting becomes irrelevant (Hayman, 1990; Levesque, 1996). This expert testimony is frequently grounded in the problematic body of literature previously discussed.

Watkins (1995) has argued that Title II of the Americans with Disabilities Act 1990 explicitly prohibits states from utilizing such discriminatory double standards against parents with disabilities, including intellectual disabilities, in child welfare cases. He suggests that the ADA's requirement that states make reasonable modifications to meet the needs of people with disabilities should assist parents with intellectual disabilities. However, the ADA is a voluntary compliance law, which means that the burden of securing enforcement of its mandates falls upon the injured party. Women with intellectual disabilities frequently do not have the resources to successfully advocate for their own interests.

Discussions of court-authorized proceedings fail to examine the extent to which custody is terminated outside the courts. In 1997, a 27-year-old woman gave birth to her first child in a New Jersey hospital. The woman had been diagnosed with a moderate level of intellectual disabilities, and was living in a supervised residential setting. Her boyfriend refused to have anything to do with the child, but she wanted to keep the baby. She was living in an apartment setting that provided considerable social supports and might have facilitated learning to care for the child. At the hospital, the baby was immediately removed to foster care and the new mother never saw the infant again.

What is striking about this woman's experience is that she had never been found to be an abusive or neglectful parent; she never got the chance to parent her child at all. It is impossible to conclude from this anecdotal story that this practice is widespread, but it is illustrative of the barriers that confront young women with intellectual disabilities who become parents. This woman clearly did not have the resources, financial, emotional or otherwise, to fight a court battle to keep her child. Indeed, she did not even know she could refuse to sign the consent form, in spite of the fact that she did not want to give up her child. The bottom line for this woman was that her diagnosed disability was sufficient by itself to facilitate the abrogation of her rights. No research has been conducted to date that examines the extent to which this type of practice occurs in the US.

Steps must be taken to ensure that the due process rights of mothers with intellectual disabilities are protected, and that the level of care they provide is fairly assessed. Intellectual disability is not a sufficient reason for the termination of parental rights.

Policy recommendations

A number of central policy recommendations emerge from the preceding analysis of the issues surrounding parenting by women with intellectual disabilities. At the societal level, these recommendations include implementation of global school curricula addressing:

- Sex education, parenting skills, and violence and abuse prevention
- Enactment of measures that address the causes and consequences of poverty
- Expansion of research related to parenting and intellectual disabilities
- Immediate enforcement of the due process protections that are constitutionally given to these women, as citizens
- Educational campaigns targeting an end to the stigmatization and prejudice against people with disabilities.

At the micro or family level, there needs to be an expansion of appropriate, respectful and effective services available to these women and their families.

This discussion is addressed at filling an enormous vacuum, and if present US political trends continue, it is unlikely to be realized anytime in the near future. First, services must be developed that are widely available and appropriate for mothers with intellectual disabilities. Parenting programs, in addition to being tailored to people with generally low literacy levels and slower learning rates, should be devised that address the complexities of these women's lives. Many of these women may have unaddressed needs for therapeutic interventions related to often long-term sexual victimization or physical abuse. These women may also need particular supports to navigate an increasingly complicated world of welfare and disability benefits. It is apparent from the anecdotal evidence published by many of the intervention researchers that formidable challenges are a constant part of these women's lives.

The other critical need for services is in the arena of child protective services, which routinely offer interventions to families without disabilities to facilitate nurturing and appropriate caring for their children. Family preservation programs must be developed to address the needs of mothers with intellectual disabilities, whose learning styles necessarily differ from those of mothers without learning disabilities. Watkins (1995) has suggested that in compliance with the reasonable accommodations mandate of the Americans with Disabilities Act 1990, states should fund child welfare programs that are offered by service providers with experience in supporting people with intellectual disabilities.

Global programs aimed at reducing victimization should be implemented in schools, addressing sex education, violence and abuse prevention, and parent training programs. Rates of child abuse and neglect are indicative that the knowledge and skills of too many parents (both with and without disabilities) were shaped by their victimization experiences. Sex education is particularly critical for students with disabilities, who frequently lack access to information and are at greater risk of sexual victimization. Importantly, community-based projects have had considerable success in reducing child abuse and neglect using a home visitor model. Two different pilot projects are being replicated in 565 sites across the US (Leventhal, 2001).

Across intervention studies, researchers have found that mothers with intellectual disabilities were ill-prepared to nurture and provide care for their children (Tymchuk & Feldman, 1991). It is very unclear, due to the lack of appropriate contrast groups, whether this lack of preparation is characteristic only of the women with intellectual disabilities, or of the larger population as well. Arguably, the high rates of substantiated cases of child abuse and neglect and the ever-increasing expansion of child protective service cases are adequate justification for introducing parent skills training into the regular education programs in all schools.

Another major set of recommendations is the importance of addressing poverty and its consequences in a meaningful way. The connections between poverty and poor child outcomes have been extensively studied (Duncan & Brooks-Gunn, 1997). Any serious proposal to mitigate the problems encountered by mothers with intellectual disabilities must consider the often extreme poverty in which they live. The time-limited benefits of the US's current TANF (Temporary Assistance to Needy Families) welfare program are causing great concern for those individuals who are most vulnerable, particularly low-skilled women (DeBell et al., 1997). A sound and comprehensive program to address poverty would be based on research that has delved deeply into the lives and needs of poor people, and has identified the real issues that underlie the political rhetoric. At an absolute minimum, such a program would address disentangling health care from employment, because much of the low-skilled work done by women does not provide health insurance. In addition, solutions must be found to the pressing need for high quality, affordable child care, for education and training to provide women with marketable skills that lead to livable wages, and for transportation to jobs. The best solutions would be cognizant of the role in poverty played by men who cannot or will not provide support to their families, and would establish minimum benefit levels that allow people to avoid living in squalor.

Also related to addressing the causes and consequences of poverty is the need for more adequate funding of early intervention programs for high-risk children. Tremendous successes have been realized in demonstration projects, including reduction of school dropout rates, reduced rates of grade repetition, reduced rates of special education utilization, better overall school achievement, reductions in juvenile delinquency, and reductions in juvenile arrest (Ramey *et al.*, 2000; Reynolds *et al.*, 2001; Zigler *et al.*, 1992). While these quality programs are widely recognized to be economically sound (Council of Economic Advisors, 1997), their implementation is still quite limited. Greater investment on this front would doubtless result in large pay-outs from reduced prison and welfare expenditures.

Another important recommendation comes from Tymchuk (1990), who urged an expanded program of research into the needs of mothers with intellectual disabilities and their children. There is a need for methodologically rigorous research devoted to developing a comprehensive understanding of the lives of these women, how they and their families fare over time, and the types of services that are most effective in assisting them to succeed in their parenting. There is some promising research that has evaluated the ways different interventions are and are not successful (e.g. Tucker & Johnson, 1989), but this research must be expanded.

A final policy recommendation calls for an aggressive national education plan to combat discriminatory and prejudicial attitudes toward persons with disabilities. The suffering that has been endured by persons with disabilities at the hands of an indifferent and abusive society is a shameful part of the history of the US (Braddock & Parish, 2001). Immediate steps should be taken to combat this tradition. Related to this, the civil rights of mothers with intellectual disabilities must be enforced. It is imperative that an end be brought to discriminatory judicial practices that enable women with intellectual disabilities to have their parental rights terminated on the basis of their diagnosis, and not their parenting.

References

Booth, T. & Booth, W. (1993a) *Parenting Under Pressure. Mothers And Fathers With Learning Difficulties.* Open University Press, Buckingham, UK.

Booth, T. & Booth, W. (1993b) Parenting with learning difficulties. Lessons for practitioners. *British Journal of Social Work*, **23**, 459–480.

Booth, T. & Booth, W. (2000) Growing up with parents who have learning difficulties. *Mental Retardation*, **38**, 1–14.

Braddock, D. & Parish, S. (2001) Disability history from antiquity to the Americans with Disabilities Act. In: *Handbook of Disability Studies,* (eds G.L. Albrecht, K.D. Seelman & M. Bury), pp. 11–68. Sage, Thousand Oaks, CA.

Buchele-Ash, A., Turnbull, H.R. & Mitchell, L. (1995) Forensic and law enforcement issues in the abuse and neglect of children with disabilities. *Mental and Physical Disability Law Reporter*, **19**, 115–121.

Cleveland, S.J. (1997) Sterilization of the mentally disabled. Applying error cost analysis to the 'best interest' inquiry. *Georgetown Law Journal*, **86**, 137–153.

Council of Economic Advisors (1997) *The First Three Years. Investments that Pay.* Executive Office of the President, Washington, DC.

Daniels, S. & West, J. (1998) Return to work for SSI and DI beneficiaries: Employment policy challenges. In: *Growth in Disability Benefits: Explanations and Policy Implications* (eds K. Rupp & D. Stapleton), pp. 359–371. Upjohn Institute for Employment Research, Kalamazoo, MI.

DeBell, M., Yi, H., & Hartmann, H. (1997) Single mothers, jobs, and welfare: what the data tell us. *Research-in-Brief*. Institute for Women's Policy Research, Washington, DC.

Dowdney, L. & Skuse, D. (1993) Parenting provided by adults with mental retardation. *Journal of Child Psychology & Psychiatry*, **34**, 23–47.

Duncan, G. & Brooks-Gunn, J. (1997) *Consequences of Growing Up Poor.* Russell Sage Foundation, New York.

Edgerton, R.B. (2001) The hidden majority of individuals with mental retardation and developmental disabilities. In: *The Forgotten Generation: The Status and Challenges Of Adults with Mild Cognitive Limitations* (eds A.J. Tymchuk, K.C. Lakin & R. Luckasson), pp. 3–19. Brookes, Baltimore, MD.

Espe-Sherwindt, M. & Crable, S. (1993) Parents with mental retardation. Moving beyond the myths. *Topics in Early Childhood Special Education*, **13**, 154–174.

Feldman, M.A. & Walton-Allen, N. (1997) Effects of maternal mental retardation and poverty on intellectual, academic, and behavioral status of school-age children. *American Journal on Mental Retardation*, **101**, 352–364.

Fujiura, G.T. & Yamki, K. (2000) Trends in demography of childhood poverty and disability. *Exceptional Children*, **66**, 187–199.

Gilhool, T.K. & Gran, J. (1985) Legal rights of disabled parents. In: *Children of Handicapped Parents: Research and Clinical perspectives* (ed. S.K. Thurman), pp. 11–34. Academic Press, Orlando, FL.

Greene, B.F., Norman, K.R., Searle, M.S., Daniels, M. & Lubeck, R.C. (1995) Child abuse and neglect by parents with disabilities. A tale of two families. *Journal of Applied Behavioral Analysis*, **28**, 417–434.

Hall, L.A., Sachs, B., Rayens, M.K. & Lutenbacher, M. (1993) Childhood physical and sexual abuse. Their relationship with depressive symptoms in adulthood. *Image: The Journal of Nursing Scholarship*, **25**, 317–323.

Hayman. R.L. (1990) Presumptions of justice. Law, politics and the mentally retarded parent. *Harvard Law Review*, **103**, 1201–1271.

Lanata, C. (2001) Children's health in developing countries. Issues of coping, child neglect, and marginalization. In: *Poverty, Inequality and Health. An International Perspective* (eds D. Leon & G. Walt), pp. 137–158. Oxford University Press, Oxford.

Larson, S., Lakin, K.C., Anderson, L., Kwak, N. & Lee, J.H. (2000) Prevalence of mental retardation or developmental disabilities. Analysis of the 1994/1995 NHIS-D. *MR/DD Data Brief 1* (2). Research and Training Center, Minneapolis, MN.

Leventhal, J. M. (2001) The prevention of child abuse and neglect. Successfully out of the blocks. *Child Abuse and Neglect*, **25**, 431–439.

Levesque, R.J.R. (1996) Maintaining children's relations with mentally disabled parents. Recognizing difference and the difference that it makes. *Children's Legal Rights Journal*, **16**, 14–22.

Llewellyn, G. (1995) Relationships and social support. Views of parents with mental retardation/intellectual disability. *Mental Retardation*, **33**, 349–363.

Mashaw, J. (2000) *The Crucial but Bounded Role of Disability Income Policy*. Paper presented at the National Academy of Social Insurance conference, Disability income policy, Opportunities and challenges in the next decade, 15 December. Washington, DC.

Mitchell, L.M. & Buchele-Ash, A. (2000) Abuse and neglect of individuals with disabilities. *Journal of Disability Policy Studies*, **10**, 225–243.

National Center on Child Abuse and Neglect (1993) *A Report on the Maltreatment of Children with Disabilities*. US Department of Health and Human Services, Administration on Children, Youth and Families, Washington, DC.

O'Neill, A.M. (1995) Normal and bright children of mentally retarded parents. The Huck Finn syndrome. *Child Psychiatry and Human Development*, **15**, 255–268.

Pagelow, M.D. (1984) *Family Violence*. Praeger, New York.

Parish, S.L. & Braddock, D. (2001) *The Social Security Administration and Mental Retardation Eligibility Determinations. Understanding the Context*. Paper commissioned by the National Academy of Sciences, Committee on Mental Retardation Eligibility Determination. University of Illinois at Chicago, Department of Disability and Human Development, Chicago.

Public Law 96-272 (1980) Adoption Assistance and Child Welfare Act (United States of America).

Ramey, C.T., Campbell, F.A., Burchinal, M., Skinner, M.L., Gardner, D.M. & Ramey, S.L. (2000) Persistent effects of early childhood education on high-risk children and their mothers. *Applied Developmental Science*, **4**, 2–14.

Reiss, S. (1994) *Handbook of Challenging Behavior. Mental Health Aspects of Mental Retardation*. IDS, Worthington, OH.

Reynolds, A.J., Temple, J.A., Robertson, D.L., & Mann, E.A. (2001) Long-term effects of an early childhood intervention on educational achievement and juvenile arrest. A 15-year follow-up of low-income children in public schools. *Journal of the American Medical Association*, **285**, 2339–2346.

Seagull, E.A.N. & Scheurer, S.L. (1986) Neglected and abused children of mentally retarded parents. *Child Abuse and Neglect*, **10**, 493–500.

Sobsey, D. (1994) *Violence and Abuse in the Lives of People with Disabilities. The End of Silent Acceptance?* Brookes Publishing, Baltimore, MD.

Sobsey, D., Randall, W. & Parrila, R.K. (1997) Gender differences in abused children with and without disabilities. *Child Abuse and Neglect*, **21**, 707–720.

Social Security Administration (2000a) Supplemental Security Income. Determining disability for a child under 18. Final rules. *Federal Register*, **65** (11 September), 54747–54790.

Social Security Administration (2000b) Final Rules. Old-Age, Survivors, and Disability Insurance and Supplemental Security Income for the aged, blind, and disabled; substantial gainful activity amounts; 'Services'' for trial work period purposes – monthly amounts; student child earned income exclusion. *Federal Register*, **65** (29 December), 82905–82912.

Tharinger, D., Horton, C.B. & Millea, S. (1990) Sexual abuse and exploitation of children and adults with mental retardation and other handicaps. *Child Abuse & Neglect*, **14**, 301–312.

Tucker, M.B. & Johnson, O. (1989) Competence promoting vs. competence inhibiting social support for mentally retarded mothers. *Human Organization*, **48**, 95–107.

Tymchuk, A.J. (1990) Parents with mental retardation. A national strategy. *Journal of Disability Policy Studies*, 1, 43–55.

Tymchuk, A.J. (1991) Self-concepts of mothers who show mental retardation. *Psychological Reports*, **68**, 503–510.

Tymchuk, A.J. (1994) Depression symptomatology in mothers with mild intellectual disability. An exploratory study. *Australia and New Zealand Journal of Developmental Disabilities*, **19**, 111–119.

Tymchuk, A.J. & Andron, L. (1990) Mothers with mental retardation who do or do not abuse or neglect their children. *Child Abuse and Neglect*, **14**, 313–333.

Tymchuk, A.J. & Feldman, M.A. (1991) Parents with mental retardation and their children. Review of research relevant to professional practice. *Canadian Psychology*, **32**, 486–494.

Tymchuk, A.J., Yokota, A. & Rahbar, B. (1990) Decision-making abilities of mothers with mental retardation. *Research in Developmental Disabilities*, **11**, 97–108.

Tymchuk, A.J., Lakin, K.C. & Luckasson, R. (2001) Life at the margins. Intellectual, demographic, economic, and social circumstances of adults with mild cognitive limitations. In: *The Forgotten Generation: The Status and Challenges of Adults with Mild Cognitive Limitations* (eds A.J. Tymchuk, K.C. Lakin, & R. Luckasson), pp. 21–38. Brookes Publishing, Baltimore, MD.

US Census Bureau (2001) *Poverty 2000*. US Census Bureau, Washington, DC.

Verdugo, M.A., Bermejo, B.G., & Fuertes, J. (1995) The maltreatment of intellectually handicapped children and adolescents. *Child Abuse & Neglect*, **19**, 205–215.

Watkins, C. (1995) Beyond status. The Americans with Disabilities Act and the parental rights of people labeled developmentally disabled or mentally retarded. *California Law Review*, **83**, 1417–1475.

Whitman, B.Y., Graves, B. & Accardo, P. (1989) Training in parenting skills for adults with mental retardation. *Social Work*, **34**, 431–434.

Yamaki, K. (1999) *Employment and Income Status of Adults with Developmental Disabilities Living in the Community*. PhD thesis, University of Illinois at Chicago.

Zigler, E., Taussig, C. & Black, K. (1992) Early childhood intervention. A promising preventative for juvenile delinquency. *American Psychologist*, **47**, 997–1006.

8 Social Roles and Informal Support Networks in Mid Life and Beyond

Christine Bigby

Introduction

Strong informal support networks are fundamentally important to well-being. This chapter considers why informal networks are important to women with intellectual disability, factors that impact on the nature of their networks and the various functions fulfilled by network members. It examines the gulf between aspirations and the reality that informal networks of many women with intellectual disabilities are small, dense, dominated by family members, contain few friends and perhaps insulate them from the broader community. A particular focus is on mid-life and beyond, and the challenges these life stages pose for sustaining valued roles and robust social networks. Finally, innovative models for building and maintaining informal support are discussed.

Importance of informal support networks

The acquisition of valued social roles and the development of strong networks of informal relationships are regarded as fundamentally important to the social, psychological and physical well-being of people, particularly older people and those with intellectual disabilities. Social gerontology has accumulated considerable evidence as to the association between informal support and the well-being of older people. As Wenger suggests, 'the importance of adequate social support or strong networks as correlates of positive outcomes has become almost part of received wisdom for those working in a professional capacity with older people' (1996: 60). The benefits of social support for older people appear to be related to 'higher morale, less loneliness and worry, feelings of usefulness, a sense of individual respect within the community and a zest for life' (Hooyman, 1983: 139).

The protective aspects of social network ties extend to mortality, health, survival and recovery following acute medical conditions and reduced risks of institutionalization (Mendes del Leon *et al.*, 1999). Community membership and opportunities to be a contributing member of society are integral to conceptualizations of healthy aging, for both the general population and those with intellectual disabilities (Hawkins, 1999; Rowe & Kahn, 1998).

Normalization and its reconceptualization by Wolfensberger (1992) as social role valorization emphasized social roles for people with intellectual disabilities: 'the most explicit and highest goal of normalization must be the creation, support and defense of valued social roles for people at risk of devaluation' (Garvey & Kroese, 1991). However, this approach is not without its critics who suggest it placed the locus of change on the individual rather than society, and that the focus on valued social roles ignored issues of diversity of cultural norms and values (Brown & Smith, 1992). Thus, opportunities for women with intellectual disabilities to acquire social roles and develop relationships may be unduly restricted to those considered 'normative' by middle-class white societies.

Social and physical integration have been key goals of the disability field since the 1970s. Social relationships between people with intellectual disabilities and other community members are used as both indicators and prerequisites of integration (Traustadottir, 1993). For example, Nirje (1976) defined integration as referring to 'relationships between individuals that are based on recognition of each other's integrity, shared basic values and rights'. One of O'Brien's (1987) influential five accomplishments, used as guiding principles for service development and outcomes sought for people with intellectual disabilities, is 'participation in the social life of the community'. This was to be achieved through people with intellectual disabilities developing a network of personal relationships with other community members (Myers *et al.*, 1998).

The focus on social relationships gathered momentum in the 1990s, which Perske suggests, witnessed a wealth of new ideas subsumed under the term inclusion and meant, 'it is not enough merely to place persons with disabilities in a neighborhood – they must be connected to it socially. Their lives must interweave emotionally with the lives of others' (1993: 2). The new paradigm of community membership with its focus on participation and inclusion places a more explicit emphasis on social relationships than the previous paradigm of de-institutionalization which was often more concerned with physical presence than social connectedness (Bradley, 1994). The focus on relationships is further strengthened by framing social well-being as a key domain in the burgeoning quality of the life perspective (Brown, 2000). Using this perspective, social well-being encompasses personal relationships with friends, family and relatives, community involvement, and acceptance and support.

Human rights movements in Australia, the UK and the US have achieved citizenship rights for people with disabilities, creating social space for them to occupy formal roles such as worker or consumer. But rights alone will not achieve inclusion or human fulfillment for people with intellectual disabilities (Reinders, 2001, 2002). For this to occur he considers they must be included in the informal social sphere, one of 'civic friendship'. This depends not on the existence or exercise of formal rights alone but also on the development of relationships between people with and without disabilities. This requires significant moral and cultural change in societies.

Understanding informal networks

The term 'informal support' lacks precision and is often interchangeable with informal care, social support, support networks and social relationships. The distinguishing characteristic, however, is that informal support and relationships develop on the basis of personal ties between individuals as individuals. These may stem from membership of a common kinship system in the case of family members, personal affinity as occurs between friends, or geographic propinquity or use of common spaces by neighbors or acquaintances.

The concept of networks is a framework for the analysis of informal relationships, and a vehicle through which support is exchanged. A social network approach draws attention to the structure of relationships that exist between network members, the specific exchanges that take place and the roles they play in relation to one another. The structural characteristics of informal networks often predict the nature of support provided informally (Wenger, 1996). Thus, an understanding of networks is useful for considering how they may be complemented by formal services. Details of individuals in a network – such as age, gender and life cycle status, the nature of the relationship, its origin, duration, affectional content and interactional contexts, and structural properties such as size and density – are used to describe the properties of social networks.

Social networks are dynamic, determined by a combination of personal characteristics, social and economic context and the pattern of opportunities available. A useful concept is that of a convoy of social support which suggests that the history of supportive networks is central to understanding present relationships, and that people move through life surrounded by a convoy of others which varies across time and situations (Antonucci & Akiyama, 1987). People with intellectual disabilities are particularly dependent on externally provided support and opportunities to develop social networks (Myers et al., 1998; Hawkins, 1999), which are too often mediated by the limiting factor of resources and the low expectations of others.

Network functions

Informal support is a multidimensional concept that operates at different levels of intensity and is conceptualized in various ways. One of the most common is in terms of 'caring about' and 'caring for'. The latter involves direct hands-on, day-to-day caring tasks, while the former involves feelings of concern or anxiety and more indirect negotiation of care (Dalley, 1988). Horowitz (1985) divides informal support into four components:

(1) Emotional support
(2) Direct instrumental support
(3) Financial assistance
(4) Management of relationships with formal organizations.

Refining this further, ten distinct types of instrumental support for older people with intellectual disabilities from family and friends are identified:

(1) Decision-making
(2) Financial management
(3) Adoption of formal or legal roles
(4) Mediating, negotiating and advocating with service systems
(5) Monitoring service quality
(6) Provision of primary care
(7) Supervision of medical needs
(8) Co-ordinating support from other network members
(9) Provision of back-up or short-term replacement of other members
(10) Skills development

(Bigby, 2000a)

The bulk of care for older people living in the community is provided through informal networks (Hooyman & Kiyak, 1999). This hands-on care and the 'carers', predominantly women, who provide it were recognized explicitly in social policies from the mid-1980s (Baldock & Evers, 1991). A focus on carers has detracted attention from the intangible roles fulfilled by other informal network members and the continued salience of informal support for people who do not live at home.

From a psychological rather than functional perspective the essence of informal relationships is the sense of identity, value, belonging and self-esteem they provide. Conversely, an absence of relationships causes loneliness, exclusion and a sense of social failure (Chappell, 1994). The individual's interaction with their social environment, their social roles and accomplishments may confirm or force revision of self-image (Hooyman & Kiyak, 1999).

Different members of informal networks may fulfill different functions. The various relational ties people have bring different limitations and strengths to an informal network. Litwak's (1985) theory of task specificity argues that family, friends and neighbors each have particular characteristics that differentiate the type of support they are best able to provide. For example, neighbors are characterized by close proximity but loose or non-affective ties, and thus are well suited to support that requires low commitment but either speedy response or proximity, such as emergency assistance, monitoring an empty house or feeding the cat. By contrast, relationships with spouses or other close family members are characterized by proximity, face-to-face contact on a daily basis, and high degree of commitment. They are often the only network members in a position to provide support with primary care tasks. Other family members may not be geographically close but may still have a strong commitment and may be suited to tasks that do not require frequent day-to-day contact such as administering financial affairs, advocacy or negotiation with formal organizations. Friendships are characterized by affective ties but often not by proximity or long-term commitment and may be better suited to tasks such as emotional support, companionship or shared activities that require intermittent contact with a low level of commitment.

Clearly, this delineation of characteristics of primary groups is based on ideal types. Both relationships and the tasks fulfilled by informal network members are mediated by factors such as gender, social context, individual resources, personal histories, life course stage and negotiated commitments. Nevertheless, Litwak's ideas provide a basis for considering the varied tasks undertaken by informal support and thus indicate which functions may not be well performed by a person's network. In addition, this perspective can help ensure that tasks are not expected from network members that do not match their characteristics, which may therefore place too great a strain on the relationship or may be impossible to fulfill.

Bayley (1997) discusses the cognitive and emotional needs met by various types of friendships. These include:

- Attachment and intimacy where friendships allow individuals to express feelings freely and without which they may experience loneliness as distinct from social isolation
- Social integration where common concerns and interests are shared by friends, often by means of joint activities
- Opportunities for nurturance, whereby friendships provide an opportunity to give back and achieve a sense of being needed
- Reassurance of worth where friends affirm a person's competence in a social role either at work or in the family
- Reliable assistance where friends provide direct assistance
- Obtaining guidance from respected others to assist in life decisions

■ The exercise of choice, which is fundamental to a sense of autonomy, human worth and dignity.

In a similar vein to Litwak, Bayley suggests that a single friendship is unlikely to meet this range of needs and further that inappropriate behavior and strain on relationships may occur if too much is expected of any one friendship. Thus, people require various friendships of different styles and intensities to fulfill their range of needs.

The relative value of friendships between people with intellectual disabilities and those with people without intellectual disabilities is a source of debate. Arguably, the relations between people with and without disabilities are of more value as they provide avenues to inclusion, access to more valued roles and to instrumental tasks (Chappell, 1994). However, such a position devalues the social connections that arise from friendships between people with disabilities, and ignores the aspects of solidarity in such relationships that have the potential to bring about social change. The fundamental question should be whether friendships between peers with disabilities are based on common affiliations and choice, and therefore quite different from enforced segregation solely on the basis of a shared disability. Indeed, relationships between people with disabilities are too often devalued or ignored by family (Bigby, 2000a), leading to unforeseen losses and social disruption of people's networks. Ethnographic research that has tapped the views of older people with intellectual disabilities suggests that they often do not distinguish between friends on the basis of their disability, but value friendships from both sources (Mahon & Mactavish, 2000).

Informal support and women with intellectual disabilities

Much of the research literature in the field of disability is not gendered. Women's experiences and the characteristics of their networks are rarely delineated separately from those of men (Traustadottir & Johnson, 2000; Lunsky & Benson, 1999). However, evidence suggests that among the general population, gender helps to determine both who gives and who receives informal support, providing a basis from which to consider the effect of gender on informal networks of women with intellectual disabilities (Gibson, 1998).

Women dominate the pool of informal carers in both the general population and, as reflected in the available research, in that of people with disabilities (Gibson, 1998; Grant, 1993). For adults with intellectual disabilities living at home, mothers provide the bulk of informal care and parents are more likely to expect their daughters than sons to take over this primary care role (Griffith & Unger, 1994; Orsmond & Seltzer, 2000). It seems that such expectations are fulfilled: sisters rather than brothers do replace mothers as primary carers, although this may only be a short-term arrangement (Prosser & Moss, 1996). Grant (1993) found the operation of a gender hierarchy in changes occurring in the provision of primary support for adults living at home, with a progression from mother to father (if he had outlived his wife), to daughter, to daughter-in-law, to son and son-in-law.

The importance of having sisters and other female relatives and friends is demonstrated by the dominance of females in the networks of adults with intellectual disabilities living at home. Support is found for the 'femaleness principle', that sisters are more likely to give and receive help and have more active ties with siblings than do brothers (Akiyma et al., 1996). For example, the most involved siblings in a network are likely to be sisters, and sister-sister dyads have closer bonds than other sibling dyads (Krauss et al., 1992; Seltzer et al., 1991; Cicirelli, 1980). Orsmond and Seltzer (2000) found that sisters were more knowledgeable about the skills and needs of their sibling with intellectual disability, had more frequent contact, felt closer and provided more care and companionship than did brothers. Compared to brother-brother dyads, the brothers of sisters with intellectual disabilities feel the fewest positive and most negative feelings towards their sibling and are more worried about their future (Orsmond & Seltzer, 2000). Thus, women with intellectual disabilities whose most involved or only sibling is a brother may be at particular risk of limited family support after the death of their parents.

A dismal picture emerges when the aspirations of people with disabilities and policy aims are contrasted with research findings. In the aftermath of de-institutionalization, many more people than in previous decades have a physical presence in the community. But few who live in shared supported accommodation have relationships with members of the community (Mansell & Ericsson, 1996; Bayley, 1997; Chappell, 1994). Most 'lead lives isolated from the larger community with personal contacts limited to service providers and family members' (MacEachen & Munby, 1996: 71). People with intellectual disabilities increasingly visit or use community facilities but their interactions with others remain at an anonymous or impersonal level rather than being part of the rich social relationships found within the numerous voluntary, cultural or sporting organizations that make up the fabric of civic society (Walker, 1995). In Australia, a recent audit of intellectual disability services stated:

'Overall we conclude that service sites visited had a satisfactory level of basic care, but beyond that there were wide variations in the extent to which the legislative principles and standards were met in relation to the provision of developmental opportunities and integration into the community.'

(Victoria Auditor General, 2000: 68)

The picture is little different for people with intellectual disabilities who remain at home in the community. Their networks are small and dominated by family members. Friends are often shared with the rest of the family. While such networks serve to nurture and provide security for adults with intellectual disabilities, they also insulate them from the communities in which they live (Grant, 2001). However, women with intellectual disabilities living at home have more friends in their social networks than do men in the same situation (Krauss *et al.*, 1992).

As they age, women have more robust informal support networks and are at less risk of social isolation than men. Women are more likely to receive both instrumental and affective support and have closer ties and more expressive social bonds than men are (Davey *et al.*, 1999; Campbell *et al.*, 1999). However, these advantages may be counterbalanced by the more protective stance of parents towards daughters, a phenomenon found both in the general population and among parents whose adult child has an intellectual disability (Fullmer *et al.*, 1997). Contrary to the positive picture for women suggested by the aging literature, these authors show that women with intellectual disabilities living with mothers may have limited opportunities to acquire social roles and develop relationships. Compared to men, women with intellectual disabilities are less likely to attend day programs, and play a greater role in undertaking daily household tasks and are subject to greater vigilance by mothers.

For adults with intellectual disabilities living in residential settings, gender, together with age, level of disability and type of residence, have been shown to predict the size of a person's total support network, with women having larger networks than men (Lunsky & Benson, 1999). However, a larger study of adults in three types of residential settings in the UK did not identify gender as an important variable in determining network size. Important factors here were age, autism, ability, challenging behavior, type of current and previous accommodation, staffing ratios, institutional climate and the implementation of active support (Robertson *et al.*, 2001).

Vulnerability of networks

Despite their anxiety about the future, many older parents of adults with intellectual disabilities continue to provide care at home for as long as they are able; some do so from choice, and some because there are no other options available (Bigby *et al.*, in press). The lifestyle of the adult with a disability may become restricted by the care needs and decreased mobility and stamina of their parent. In some households a fine balance of interdependence between an adult child with intellectual disability and aged parent develops, as the adult child provides care for their elderly parent (Bigby, 2000a; Grant, 2001; Walmsley, 1996).

This new role may be unwelcome or restrictive for an adult with intellectual disability. For example, Bronwyn's mother had developed Alzheimer's disease. Her mother's incapacity significantly increased Bronwyn's caring role and placed further restrictions on her. Bronwyn said:

> 'I used to look after mum. I couldn't do a thing with her. I couldn't get her to wash her hair and she wouldn't eat. I wasn't getting any rest, she was getting me up at half past 12 in the morning so my brother decided to find a place to put her. I didn't go out because I couldn't go out and leave her.'

> (Bigby, 2000b: 75)

Yet for women such as Bronwyn, who are supported to remain in the family home after the death of their parent, later life can be a time when their social worlds expand and, freed from the restrictions imposed by parents, they can exploit opportunities to build new relationships in their neighborhood and as participants in community activities. With the cessation of the role of daughter, some older women even develop intimate friendships and are treated as adults for the first time in their lives. Ada's story, told in the case study, illustrates the expansion of her social world after the death of her parents, but also the vulnerability of her informal social support network as she ages.

Case study: Ada

Ada is 55 years old. An only child, she spent most of her life living at home with her parents. Her father died 20 years ago, and her mother two years ago. Since then Ada has shared the family home with her aunt Letty, who is aged 90 years. Letty had lived in a flat attached to the family home since 1964 and has a close relationship with Ada. They share the household tasks, and Letty provides support for Ada with personal care and supervises her affairs. Letty's view was 'we couldn't live without one another now'.

Both Ada and Letty are quite fit and spend a lot of time together visiting Letty's circle of friends, many of whom are connected to the local church. Ada has no real friends of her own but shares Letty's friends, many of whom were also friends of her parents. Letty encourages Ada to be more independent and recently she has begun to attend a social group for people with disabilities at the local community center. Here she has met several other women with disabilities but she doesn't see any of them outside the group. She has also begun to do her own banking and is learning how to use public transport to get to the local shopping center. Letty feels strongly that Ada's mother doted on her too much and that she was never given the opportunity to develop as much as she could have done. Letty and Ada started using community support services when Ada's mother was sick, and were subsequently referred to the local disability services office. They were offered various services, but a weekend in a respite house was the only one they took up. Ada enjoyed this stay but was very nervous of staying away overnight.

Ada has another aunt, who is widowed and lives several suburbs away. Ada and Letty visit her for tea every week. Ada has five cousins who are all married and have young families of their own. One cousin, Gayle, lives locally and usually drops in every couple of weeks. The others are all male and live in various country towns across the state. They stay in touch by phone and drop in occasionally when they come to Melbourne. Letty's two favorite great-nephews, Ada's cousins, are executors of Letty's will and as Letty says, 'I have mentioned it to them occasionally, they would have to see to everything and find a place for Ada'. She is also clear that if anything should happen to her, Ada's other aunt will step in. However, she would not be able to care for Ada in the long term as she has her own family and grandchildren.

Few women with intellectual disabilities marry or have children and thus the two key providers of informal support in later life – children and spouses – are missing from their support networks as they age (Walsh *et al.*, 2000). The absence of these relationships means new roles typically acquired in later life, such as grandparent or mother-in-law, will not emerge to replace lost roles such as that of daughter. This may be compensated by increased importance being attached to the role of aunt or great-aunt. Social interaction with extended family members is often incidental for adults with disabilities living at home, as parents rather than the adult are the prime reason for visits. Incidental social interaction arising from family visits is liable to be lost after the death of the parent unless extraordinary efforts are made by other relatives to continue the involvement of the adult with a disability in family events (Bigby, 2000a).

As parents die or become incapacitated, relationships between people with intellectual disabilities and one or more of their siblings change from being primarily affective to ones that fulfill instrumental tasks, as siblings replace some of the functions previously fulfilled by their parents. In the long term, while few siblings replace parents as primary carers many play a continuing vital role in their sister's informal support network. For example, siblings occupied a key role in the social network of 73% of older adults in Australia who had siblings (Bigby, 1997b). Their role involves companionship and shared activities as well as a range of instrumental tasks that amount to general oversight and monitoring of the well-being of their sibling with intellectual disability. Sibling relationships are often the longest of all family ties and tend to increase in salience with age (Campbell *et al.*, 1999). For people with intellectual disabilities, siblings are often their closest family members after the death of parents and most siblings maintain at least a minimum of twice-yearly social contact with their sister with intellectual disability (Bigby, 1997b).

Findings show that women with intellectual disabilities had better relationships with their brother or sister without a disability than men did in the same situation, suggesting that gender may play a role in the strength of sibling relationships (Pruchno *et al.*, 1996). Relationships between women with intellectual disabilities and their siblings were also more likely to provide functional assistance than those between men with intellectual disabilities and their brothers.

Despite assumptions to the contrary, informal support particularly from kin continues to play a significant part in the lives of older adults with intellectual disabilities after the loss of their parents (Bigby, 1997a). One mechanism by which this is achieved is through parental planning. A central focus of both formal and informal parental plans is to nominate a family member or friend to oversee the well-being of the adult with intellectual disability. Choice of this key person is based on strength of their prior relationship with the adult with a disability, rather than following genealogical lines. For example, where there are no siblings or none with a close relationship to the adult with a disability, parents will nominate another person. Plans of this nature are usually successfully implemented, and while they do not always achieve stability in the provision of primary care, they do guarantee that an informal network member is available to negotiate, monitor and oversee the well-being of adults with intellectual disabilities and their relationship with the formal service system (Bigby, 2000c). The planning process is often continued by this next generation of key network members who in turn nominate a successor to themselves to undertake the 'caring about' role. However, the likelihood of the key person being replaced decreases with age. Thus, older people with intellectual disabilities are less likely to have a key informal network member.

Older people with intellectual disabilities have few friends and are more likely to have acquaintances. As they age, their relationships are vulnerable to disruption and loss stemming from retirement, mobility and attitudes that impose age stereotypes or fail to recognize or value their friendships (Grant, 2001; Bigby, 2000a). People may experience several residential moves after the death of parents, often resulting in loss of local neighborhood acquaintances and relationships with co-residents. For older people, friendships are contextual: they tend not to see friends out of hours and invariably lose contact if they move out of a particular locality. Thus, retirement from work or a specialist disability day center is likely to involve loss of friendships if, as too often occurs, no support is provided to retain contact. It is little wonder that older people themselves seldom talk about retiring from day centers and when they do, they express substantial reservations about its impact on their lives (Bigby et al., 2001; Mahon & Mactavish, 2000).

Informal relationships have unique value: formal organizations cannot replicate all the tasks they perform. In middle age and beyond, formal services increasingly replace parents as primary carers, providing direct 'care for' tasks for people with intellectual disabilities. However, informal support, primarily family, continues to fulfill the 'caring about' tasks, providing affective support, managing and mediating relations with formal services and providing significant advocacy. These latter functions are crucial to the quality of life, particularly for people who live in shared supported accommodation, and are those not easily replicated by formal services. For example, formal organizations find it difficult to take into account idiosyncratic needs and perform non-routine tasks. Nor can they adequately fulfill tasks that require long-term commitment, advocacy or an affective relationship such as emotional support, financial or personal affairs management and monitoring and negotiation of services quality (Litwak, 1985). Formal services cannot provide a continuing comprehensive oversight of an individual's well-being (Bigby, 2000a).

Summary

Formal services are no substitute for roles fulfilled by informal network members: those who lack strong networks are especially vulnerable. Thus it is important to acknowledge and maintain informal supportive ties and to find ways to foster the development of informal sources of support. To do so, attention must be paid to the everyday structures that govern women's lives to ensure that they support and develop rather than rupture and ignore social relations (Bayley, 1997). Examples of innovative models of support – PLAN (Planned Lifetime Advocacy Network), circles of support, citizen advocacy and community builders – are found in many countries (Gold, 1994; Etmanski, 2000; Kultgen et al., 2000; Ramcharan, 1995). Each demonstrates intensive, lengthy processes for building networks successfully. Building networks is not an easy task. On the contrary, doing so requires commitment, resources and, perhaps fundamentally, recognition of the value and importance of informal social relationships for the quality of life and well-being of women with intellectual disabilities.

References

Akiyama, H., Elliot, K., & Antonucci, T. (1996) Same-sex and cross-sex relationships. *Journal of Gerontology: Psychological Sciences*, 51 B, 374–382.

Antonucci, T. & Akiyama, H. (1987) Social networks in adult life and a preliminary examination of the convoy model. *Journal of Gerontology*, **42**, 519-527.

Baldock, J. & Evers, A. (1991) Innovations and care of the elderly: the frontline of change in social welfare services. *Aging International*, June, 8–21

Bayley, M. (1997) Empowering and relationships. In: *Empowerment in Everyday Life* (eds P. Ramcharan, G. Roberts, G. Grant & J. Borland), pp. 15–34. Jessica Kingsley, London.

Bigby, C. (1997a) When parents relinquish care. The informal support networks of older people with intellectual disability. *Journal of Applied Intellectual Disability Research*, **10** (4), 333–344.

Bigby, C. (1997b) In place of parents? The sibling relationships of older people with intellectual disability. *Journal of Gerontological Social Work*, **29** (1), 3–22.

Bigby, C. (2000a) *Moving on without Parents: Planning, Transitions and Sources of Support for Older Adults with Intellectual Disabilities*. McLennan + Petty/P.H. Brookes, New South Wales/Baltimore.

Bigby, C. (2000b) Life without parents: the experiences of older women with intellectual disabilities. In: *Women with Intellectual Disabilities: Finding a Place in the World* (eds R. Traustadottir & K. Johnson), pp. 69–85. Jessica Kingsley, London.

Bigby, C. (2000c) Models of parental planning. In: *Community Supports for Aging Adults with Lifelong Disabilities* (eds M. Janicki & E. Ansello), pp. 81–96. Paul H Brookes, Baltimore.

Bigby, C., Fyffe, C., Balandin, S., Gordon, M. & McCubbery, J. (2001) *Day Support Services Options for Older Adults with a Disability*. A report commissioned by the National Disability Administrators Group, Melbourne.

Bigby, C., Ozanne, E. & Gordon, M. (in press) Facilitating transition: elements of successful case management practice for older parents of adults with intellectual disability. *Journal of Gerontological Social Work*, in press.

Bradley, V. (1994) Introduction. In: *Creating Individual Supports for People with Developmental Disabilities: A Mandate for Change at Many Levels* (eds V. Bradley, J. Ashbaugh & B. Blaney), pp. 3–9. Brookes, Baltimore.

Brown, R. (2000) Learning from quality of life models. In: *Community Supports for Aging Adults with Lifelong Disabilities* (eds M. Janicki & E. Ansello), pp. 19–40. Brookes, Baltimore.

Brown, H. & Smith, H. (1992) *Normalization: A Reader for the Nineties*. Routledge, London.

Campbell, L., Connidis, I.A. & Davies, L. (1999) Sibling ties in later life – a social network analysis. *Journal of Family Issues*, **20** (1), 114–148.

Chappell, A. (1994) A question of friendship: community care and the relationships of people with learning difficulties. *Disability and Society*, **9** (4), 419–433.

Cicirelli, V. (1980) Sibling relationships in adulthood: a lifespan perspective. In: *Aging in the 1980s: Psychological Issues* (ed. L. Poon), pp. 455–462. APA, Washington, DC.

Dalley, G. (1988) *Ideologies of Caring: Rethinking Community and Collectivism.* Mac-Millan, Basingstoke.

Davey, A., Femia, E.E., Shea, D.G., Zarit, S.H., Sundstrom, G. & Berg, S. (1999) How many elders receive assistance? A cross-national comparison. *Journal of Aging and Health,* **11** (2), 199–220.

Etmanski, A. (2000) *A Good Life for You and Your Relative with a Disability.* Orwell Cove and Planned Lifetime Advocacy Network, British Columbia.

Fullmer, E., Tobin, S. & Smith, G. (1997) The effects of offspring gender on older mothers caring for their sons and daughters with mental retardation. *The Gerontologist,* **37** (6), 795–803.

Garvey, K. & Kroese, B. (1991) Social participation and friendships of people with learning difficulties: A review. *The British Journal of Mental Subnormality,* **36** (1), 17–24.

Gibson, D. (1998) *Aged Care: Old Policies, New Problems.* Cambridge University Press, Melbourne.

Gold, D. (1994) We don't call it a 'Circle': The ethos of a support group. *Disability and Society,* **9** (4), 435–452.

Grant, G. (1993). Support networks and transitions over two years among adults with mental handicap. *Mental Handicap Research,* **6**, 36–55.

Grant, G. (2001) Older people with learning disabilities: health, community inclusion and family care giving. In: *Working with Older People and their Families: Key Issues in Policy and Practice* (eds M. Nolan, S. Davies & G. Grant), pp. 151–174. Open University Press, Basingstoke.

Griffith, D. & Unger, D. (1994) Views about planning for the future among parents and siblings of adults with mental retardation. *Family Relations,* **43** (2), 221–227.

Hawkins, B. (1999) Rights, place of residence and retirement: lessons from case studies on aging. In: *Aging, Rights and Quality of Life* (eds S. Herr & G. Weber), pp. 93–108. Brookes, Baltimore.

Hooyman, N. (1983) Social support networks in services to the elderly. In: *Social Support Networks: Informal Helping in Human Services* (eds J. Whittaker & J. Garbarino), pp. 133–164. Aldine, New York.

Hooyman, N. & Kiyak, H. (1999) *Social Gerontology: A Multidisciplinary Perspective,* 5th edition. Allyn & Bacon, Mass.

Horowitz, A. (1985) Family caregiving to the frail elderly. In: *Annual Review of Gerontology and Geriatrics* (ed. D. Maddox), pp. 174–246. Springer, New York.

Krauss, M., Seltzer, M. & Goodman, S. (1992) Social support networks of adults with mental retardation who live at home. *American Journal on Mental Retardation,* **96**, 432–441.

Kultgen, P., Harlan-Simmons, J. & Todd, J. (2000) Community membership. In: *Community Supports for Aging Adults with Lifelong Disabilities* (eds M. Janicki & E. Ansello), pp. 153–166. Brookes, Baltimore.

Litwak, E. (1985) *Helping the Elderly.* The Guildford Press, New York.

Lunsky, Y. & Benson, B. (1999) The social circles of adults with mental retardation, as viewed by their caregivers. *Journal of Developmental and Physical Disabilities,* **11**, 115–129.

MacEachen, E. & Munby, H. (1996) Developmentally disabled adults in community living: the significance of person control. *Qualitative Health Research*, **6** (1), 71–83.

Mahon, M. & Mactavish, J. (2000) A sense of belonging. In: *Community Supports for Aging Adults with Lifelong Disabilities* (eds M. Janicki & E. Ansello), pp. 41–53. Brookes, Baltimore.

Mansell, J., & Ericsson, K. (1996) *De-institutionalization and Community Living: Intellectual Disability Services in Britain, Scandinavia and United States*. Chapman and Hall, London.

Mendes del Leon, C., Glass, T., Beckett, L., Seeman, T., Evans E. & Berkman, L. (1999) Social networks and transition across eight intervals of yearly data in the New Haven EPESE. *Journal of Gerontology*, **54** (3), 162–172.

Myers, F., Ager, A., Kerr, P. & Myles, S. (1998) Outside looking in: studies of the community integration of people with learning disabilities. *Disability and Society*, **13**, 389–414.

Nirje, B. (1976) The normalization principle and its human management implications. In: *The History of Mental Retardation: Collected Papers*, vol. 2 (eds M. Rosen, C.R. Clark & M.S. Kivitz), pp. 363–376. University Park Press, Baltimore. As cited in Mahon, M. & Mactavish, J. (2000) A sense of belonging. In: *Community Supports for Aging Adults with Lifelong Disabilities* (eds M. Janicki & E. Ansello), pp. 41–53. Brookes, Baltimore.

O'Brien, J. (1987) A guide to lifestyle planning: using the Activity Catalog to integrate service and natural support systems. In: *A Comprehensive Guide to the Activities Catalog: An Alternative Curriculum for Youth and Young Adults with Severe Disabilities* (eds G. Bellamy and B. Wilcox), pp. 175–189. Brooks, Baltimore.

Orsmond, G. & Seltzer, M. (2000) Brothers and sisters of adults with mental retardation: gendered nature of sibling relationships. *American Journal on Mental Retardation*, **105**, 486–508.

Perske, R. (1993) Introduction. In: *Friendships and Community Connections between People with and without Developmental Disabilities* (ed. A. Novak Amado), pp. 1–6. Paul H. Brookes, Baltimore, MD.

Prosser, H. & Moss, S. (1996) Informal care networks of older adults with intellectual disability. *Journal of Applied Research in Intellectual Disabilities*, **9**, 17–30.

Pruchno, R., Patrick, J. & Burant, C. (1996) Aging women and their children with chronic disabilities: perceptions of sibling involvement and effects of well being. *Family Relations*, **45**, 318–326.

Ramcharan, P. (1995) Citizen advocacy and people with learning disabilities in Wales. In: *Empowerment in Community Care* (ed. R. Jack), pp. 222–242. Chapman and Hall, London.

Reinders, H. (2001) *The Good Life for Citizens with Intellectual Disabilities*. Keynote address to the annual conference of the Council on Intellectual Disability Agencies (CIDA), Melbourne, 10 May 2001.

Reinders, J. (2002) Guest editorial: The good life for citizens with intellectual disability. *Journal of Intellectual Disability Research*, **46**, 1–5.

Robertson, J., Emerson, E., Gregory, N., Hatton, C., Kessissoglou, S., Hallam, A. & Linehan, C. (2001) Social networks of people with mental retardation in residential settings. *Mental Retardation*, **39**, 201–214.

Rowe, J. & Kahn, R. (1998) *Successful Aging*. Dell Publishing, New York.

Seltzer, G., Begun, A., Seltzer, M. & Krauss, M. (1991) Adults with mental retardation and their aging mothers: impacts of siblings. *Family Relations*, **40**, 310–317.

Traustadottir, R. (1993) The gendered context of friendship. In: *Friendships and Community Connections between People with and without Developmental Disabilities* (ed. A. Novak Amado), pp. 109–128. Brookes, Baltimore.

Traustadottir, R. & Johnson, K. (2000) *Women with Intellectual Disabilities: Finding a Place in the World*. Jessica Kingsley, London.

Victoria Auditor General (2000) *Services for People with an Intellectual Disability*. Government Printer, Melbourne.

Walker, P. (1995) Community-based is not community: the social geography of disability. In: *The Variety of Community Experience. Qualitative Studies of Family and Community Life* (eds S. Taylor, R. Bogdan & Z. Lutfuyya), pp. 175–192. Brookes, Baltimore.

Walmsley, J. (1996) Doing what mum wants me to do: looking at family relationships from the point of view of adults with learning disabilities. *Journal of Applied Research in Intellectual Disabilities*, **9** (4), 324–341.

Walsh, P., Heller, T., Schupf, N. & van Schrojenstein Lantman-de Valk, H. (2000) *Healthy Aging – Adults with Intellectual Disabilities: Women's Health Issues*. World Health Organization, Geneva.

Wenger, C. (1996) Social network research in gerontology: how did we get here and where do we go next? In: *Sociology of Aging: International Perspectives* (eds V. Minichiello, N. Chappell, H. Kendig & A. Walker), pp. 60–81. International Sociological Association, Research Committee on Aging, Melbourne.

Wolfensberger, W. (1992) *A Brief Introduction to Social Role Valorization as a High-order Concept for Structuring Human Services*, revised edition. Training Institute for Human Service Planning, Leadership and Change Agentry, Syracuse University, New York.

Part 3
Promoting Health

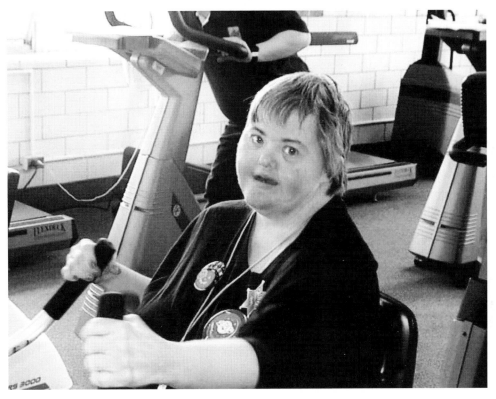

Woman exercising in the University of Illinois at Chicago Center for Health Promotion Research for Persons with Disabilities.

9 Health and Aging Issues for Women in Their Own Voices

Carol J. Gill and Allison A. Brown

Introduction

The population of older women with disabilities is expanding rapidly. Advances in medical care and community services have undeniably contributed to longer and healthier lives for this population. Unfortunately, they still confront multiple barriers to options for healthy aging (Jans & Stoddard, 1999). Until quite recently, disability research tended to focus on 'people with disabilities' as an undifferentiated aggregate, neglecting both gender-related and age-related differences (Fine & Asch, 1988). In the last decade of the twentieth century, studies documenting the distinct characteristics and experiences of girls and women with disabilities began in earnest, but much of this research has focused on physical, not cognitive or intellectual disability (Krotoski *et al.*, 1996).

The research literature on aging and health in women with intellectual disabilities is nascent, at best (Gill & Brown, 2000; Lunsky & Reiss, 1998; McCarthy 1998b; Sank & Lafleche, 1981). Yet as women with intellectual disabilities grow empowered through policies that support greater community integration and longevity, they and their advocates, including health professionals, need more accurate information about their health concerns to promote genuine options (Ridenour & Norton, 1997; Sulpizi, 1996). In this chapter, we will present a brief overview of salient topics emerging from research on health and aging in women with intellectual disabilities. This will be followed by a discussion of innovative directions for future health service provision and research. The remainder of the chapter will focus on promising work that incorporates the perspectives and voices of the women themselves.

Salient health issues of older women with intellectual disabilities

General health

It has been hypothesized that older persons with intellectual disabilities experience more health problems and a faster rate of physical decline than age-matched persons in the general population, but the extent of this is unclear (Cooper, 1999; Evenhuis, 1997; Kapell *et al.*, 1998; Martin *et al.*, 1997; Ridenour & Norton, 1997). Also unclear is the pattern of differences between women and men with intellectual disabilities regarding the types and rates of health problems that they encounter as they grow older. Depending on the study method, the particular health condition under investigation, and the residential circumstances of the subjects, results vary as to whether women in this population are less or more 'at risk' than male peers for such life-threatening conditions as cancer, stroke and heart disease (Anderson *et al.*, 1987; Janicki *et al.*, 1999; Rimmer *et al.*, 1992). Data from multiple sources, however, suggests that obesity and nutritional disorders may be particular problems for older women with intellectual disabilities (Chicoine *et al.*, 1997; Ridenour & Norton, 1997; Rimmer *et al.*, 1993).

Reproductive health

In general, except for genetic conditions that directly affect the repro-ductive system, women with intellectual disabilities parallel women in the general population with respect to age of onset and regularity of menstruation (e.g. Scola & Pueschel, 1992). However, the use of psycho-tropic and anti-seizure medication is common in this population and may be associated with menstrual irregularity, infertility and age-related dis-orders linked to reduced estrogen levels. Unfortunately, little formal research has systematically examined the effects of such medications on the health of women with intellectual disabilities.

Several studies have discovered an earlier onset of menopause for women with Down syndrome compared to women with other intellectual disabilities and women in the general population (Carr & Hollins, 1995; Schupf *et al.*, 1997; Seltzer *et al.*, 2001). For example, Schupf *et al.* (1997) determined that the age-adjusted likelihood of menopause was twice as high in women with Down syndrome as in women with other intellectual disabilities. For some women with epilepsy, menopause is associated with changes in seizure activity and may be related to the onset of seizures (Abbasi *et al.*, 1999).

Some studies on persons with physical and specific developmental disabilities suggest that disability status and related treatments can sig-nificantly affect the process of aging for women. For example, preliminary reports on women with intellectual disabilities and women with physical disabilities suggest that osteoporosis may occur earlier than in the population without disabilities (Ehrenkranz & May, 1993; Turk *et al.*, 1995), leading to an increased risk of fractures. Although the longtime use of anti-convulsive medication is a known risk factor for osteoporosis for both sexes, Jancar and Jancar (1998) found that women with intellectual disabilities and epilepsy were more likely to sustain fractures than their male counterparts. Hormone replacement therapy has been used in the general population as a primary prevention for heart disease and osteoporosis, but it has not been studied systematically in this group. Many women with intellectual disabilities undergo hysterectomy or long-term contraception, such as Norplant or hormone injections for menstrual management or pregnancy prevention, further complicating the role of hormones in their aging process.

Mental health

It is commonly believed that persons with intellectual disabilities are at increased risk for mental health problems compared to the general population (Cooper, 1999; Holland & Koot, 1998), although direct comparisons between the two groups have not been adequately studied. Because of communication limitations, emotional problems of older women with intellectual disabilities may be difficult to diagnose until a significant behavior change occurs. A variety of factors can account for such change, including underlying depression, anxiety and other psychiatric illness as well as reactions to physical illness, pain and hormonal fluctuations (Ridenour & Norton, 1997). It should also be noted that dementia appears to be common in older persons with intellectual disabilities, occurring at a significantly accelerated rate compared to the age-matched general population (Cooper, 1999).

Two additional sources of emotional distress deserve attention when considering the mental health needs of older women with intellectual disabilities: feelings of grief following the loss of significant relationships, and effects of abuse. Since women with intellectual disabilities, like women in general, are likely to live longer than their male counterparts, they may be more likely to experience the loss of family members and other key supporters as they age. These losses can be particularly devastating for women who have learned to depend on key persons throughout their lives for guidance as well as emotional intimacy (Gill, 1991). The loss may be exacerbated by the woman's social isolation, lack of expressive outlets or activities to offset her grief, and the absence of children or grandchildren to offer a sense of familial continuity.

Varied sources indicate that women with intellectual disabilities experience high rates of physical and sexual abuse (Furey, 1994; McCarthy & Thompson, 1997; Sobsey & Doe, 1991; Sundram & Stavis, 1994), a risk factor for the development of depression, anxiety and other psychiatric disorders. Typically, the perpetrators are known by the women and are frequently relatives or others who provide assistance or services, such as direct care staff or attendants (Furey, 1994; Lumley & Miltenberger, 1997). Another category of perpetrator is men with intellectual disabilities who may be co-residents in settings where the women live or peer participants in programs that the women attend (Furey, 1994; McCarthy, 1998a). Factors thought to increase risk for this population include difficulty communicating, others' doubts about the credibility of their reports, lack of adequate sex education, conditioned acquiescence and inadequate social skills training. Additionally, health care providers and other staff may lack sensitivity to the risk of abuse for women with intellectual disabilities. For example, Kopac *et al.* (1998) reported that over a third of service provider agencies included in their study indicated that questions related to the identification and treatment of sexual abuse for women with developmental disabilities were not applicable to their agencies.

Access to health services

Access to routine health exams, particularly reproductive health exams, for older women with intellectual disabilities is complicated by several factors. Health care professionals, family members and legal guardians may fail to prioritize the sexuality and gender-related needs of this group in relation to their other day-to-day needs (McCarthy, 1998b; Sundram & Stavis, 1994). Another set of challenges involves the extra time and logistical considerations that some women may need in the health service setting. For example, informed consent for health services can be complicated by low comprehension of some women with intellectual disabilities. The pressures of managed care funding for health services may severely compromise the time needed for sensitive and respectful procedures and health education. Transportation problems can be a barrier to getting to appointments at all. Insurance coverage may not include all the health care visits, screening procedures or supportive services needed to ensure adequate health maintenance. Furthermore, women with intellectual disabilities often have related physical disabilities that are not well accommodated in inaccessible medical service settings.

Data on access to health services for older women with intellectual disabilities is limited, but extant findings are discouraging. The National Medical Expenditure Survey (Anderson *et al.*, 1987) in the US included a very small sample (19) of women with intellectual disabilities age 40 and above. Only 20% had received a Pap smear within the past year, an additional 26% had received one within two years, 58% had received one more than two years ago, and 16% had never had one. Approximately one-quarter had never received a breast examination. Only 15% had ever had a mammogram (Anderson, 1996). Edgerton *et al.* (1994) found that very few of the women in their five year ethnographic study had received a mammogram or Pap smear. Stein and Allen (1999) reported that in their study of 389 women with intellectual disabilities, cervical cancer screening was significantly lower than for the general female population.

Unfortunately, few physicians and other health professionals receive adequate training regarding the health issues of women with intellectual disabilities, including ways to facilitate medical examinations, and may therefore avoid providing services to this population. A survey of attitudes of primary physicians in the UK indicated that although they tended to agree that they were responsible for the medical care of people with intellectual disabilities in the community, they did not welcome a primary role in health promotion and health screening initiatives for people with intellectual disabilities (Bond *et al.*, 1997). Similarly, Goodenough and Hole-Goodenough (1997) distributed a questionnaire to family practice residency programs in the US asking about didactic teaching, clinical activities and faculty and curriculum planning related to care of the persons with intellectual disabilities. Results revealed that only 32% of respondents teach didactic sessions on such care and fewer than a quarter of their programs plan clinic patient care for this population. The authors conclude that there is little enthusiasm among residency directors for training in care of patients with intellectual disabilities.

In addition to difficulties with basic access to health care, many women express negative feelings about the services they do receive. In general, women with intellectual disabilities associate pelvic examinations with significant pain, fear and difficulty (Broughton & Thomson, 2000). In research interviews, they commonly express fears of medical procedures that they do not understand. Many report having to endure encounters with health professionals who handle their bodies without asking permission or offering any explanation of procedures or of medical equipment (Broughton & Thomson, 2000; Martin *et al.*, 1997). Available data suggests that women with intellectual disabilities continue to lack adequate education about reproductive health, sexuality and gynecological services (Kopac *et al.*, 1998; McRae, 1997). It is still quite common to find sedation and even general anesthesia used routinely to conduct reproductive health exams in women who fear them, even before educational and supportive measures have been exhausted. Although such approaches may be necessary as a last resort for some individuals, premature adoption of pharmacological strategies merely reinforces the women's fears and loss of control in the medical setting.

Promising directions

Although it is possible to find many instances of health service programs and research that exclude the perspectives of women with intellectual disabilities, there are encouraging trends to the contrary. Increasingly, the rights and competence of the women to express their views and to receive information are recognized in innovative service models and qualitative research approaches.

Health services

Several authors have described various approaches, strategies and models for the provision of health services, particularly reproductive health services, to women with intellectual disabilities. McRae (1997) describes a 'comprehensive family planning and well-woman service' clinic initiated in 1994 in Scotland that supports the right of women with intellectual disabilities to make informed choices about their health needs. Strategies include longer and multiple appointments to allow for counseling and relaxation sessions before exams. An interdisciplinary 'model clinic' established by Elkins *et al.* (1986) has stressed the ethical provision of reproductive health services to people with intellectual disabilities in the context of least restrictive and least harmful options. Strategies include group counseling, organized separately for consumers and family members, and behavioral training in combination with medication. Prevatt (1998) describes a gynecology program at a Florida residential facility for people with intellectual disabilities that relies on nurses to provide education and desensitization through a training film, discussion and demonstration of medical equipment.

There are also a growing number of education and support programs that acknowledge and utilize the abilities of women with intellectual disabilities to interact meaningfully with educators, counselors and each other to explore critical concerns, such as sexuality, reproductive choice and abuse. For example, the Women's Health Issues Group (WHIG) was organized in Scotland in 1991 (reported in McRae, 1997) to address the health education needs of this population. The group gathered information directly from women with intellectual disabilities about their health knowledge and needs through interviews and questionnaires. Results indicated that a large proportion of women lacked basic gynecological information or services. This information-gathering project led to the development of a joint venture between WHIG and community women's health programs to provide accessible health services in an informal, friendly environment. In the domain of abuse and mental health, psychologists Barber, Jenkins and Jones (2000) report on their group therapy work with young women with intellectual disabilities who have survived sexual assault. They describe a ten-week long collaborative process in which the counselors invited participants to shape the content of weekly group counseling sessions. Participants were also encouraged to develop the group's goals and ground rules. Through a combination of discussion, role-play, and structured activities such as painting, a supportive and interactive group atmosphere was established, leading to increases in self-esteem and assertiveness.

Qualitative research

One of the most gratifying developments involving the health and well-being of women with intellectual disabilities has been their recent inclusion in qualitative and participatory research. Project investigators, many embracing feminist research principles, have acknowledged that women with intellectual disabilities are the real authorities about their own experiences. Although the women may evidence gaps in knowledge and comprehension of *information*, their grasp of *emotional issues*, insights about relationships, and their ability to express feelings and preferences can be both reliable and enlightening.

Until recent years, adults with intellectual disabilities were rarely asked directly for their opinions in projects about their lives. Because these individuals have often been infantilized and judged incapable of valid self-report, their care providers have acted as decision-makers on their behalf (Rogers *et al.*, 1998). Researchers who compare the subjective reports of persons with intellectual disabilities regarding their life experiences to the proxy reports provided by supporters without disabilities have indeed found disagreement between the two perspectives (Chadsey-Rusch *et al.*, 1997). The divergence between 'insider' and 'outsider' views seems particularly evident when research focuses on participants' feelings rather than objective information (Bramston & Fogarty, 2000). It has been argued that as long as research questions can be made comprehensible to participants with intellectual disabilities, their subjective opinions and personal preferences should be honored as the 'best source of information' (Stancliffe, 1999), since cognitive impairment does not necessarily compromise one's ability to report emotional experience. In fact, several qualitative researchers confirm that their participants with intellectual disabilities have demonstrated a high level of competence in grasping and expressing psychosocial issues (Finucane, 1998; Stancliffe, 1999; Waite, 1993).

The importance of inviting, documenting and heeding the voices of people with intellectual disabilities in research about their lives has been increasingly discussed and advocated by investigators in the last few years. Journal articles report the inclusion of participants with intellectual disabilities in various types and levels of collaborations, including grounded theory research that involves people with disabilities as 'expert' partners (Knox et al., 2000), emancipatory research (Stalker, 1998; Walmsley, 2001), feminist research process (Brigham, 1998; Walmsley, 2000), and participatory action research (Sample, 1996). Richardson (2000) provides more examples, in historical context, of participatory qualitative research that privileges the contributions of people with intellectual disabilities and positions them as authorities on their own needs and experiences.

More specifically, in the area of women's health – defined to encompass both medical and psychosocial well-being – a growing strand of qualitative investigation has begun to document the views of women with intellectual disabilities. One of the earliest published examples appeared in the long-running feminist news journal, *Off Our Backs*. In an article addressing the importance of including 'mentally retarded women' in the women's health movement, Sank and Lafleche (1981) reported the results of a discussion group interview they conducted with women with intellectual disabilities. Questions focused on women's reproductive health, sexuality, identity, experience of violence and women's rights. Results indicated that the participants valued their identity as women and that many had experienced verbal and physical assault.

A more recent example of the inclusion of the perspectives of this population in health research is a study of the experiences and views of women with intellectual disabilities regarding cervical smear tests (Broughton & Thomson, 2000). Fifty-two women aged 20–64 were interviewed about their background, sexual history and experience of the smear test. Emergent themes included anxiety about the procedure, pain experienced during the test, preferences for a female clinician, and the helpfulness of support from others.

Projects utilizing various qualitative approaches, including interviews, group discussion, writing and art work, have been conducted to help women with intellectual disabilities articulate their personal life stories within a feminist framework (Brigham, 1998; Walmsley, 2000). McCarthy (see Chapter 9) has conducted a series of important qualitative investigations of reproductive health, sexuality, abuse and body image of women with intellectual disabilities. She conducted intensive interviews with 17 women, age 19–55 with mild to moderate intellectual disabilities, over a three year period about their experiences of sexuality, abuse and their bodies (McCarthy, 1998b). In addition to documenting the prevalence of abuse by men in their environment, this work has addressed the women's feelings about their body and appearance as well as related issues of power and control. Results suggest that, like many other women, most women with intellectual disabilities in this study feel the pressure of society's gender prescriptions regarding weight, body shape and norms of femininity.

An international effort to report the major health issues of women with intellectual disabilities as they grow older, conducted by the Aging Special Interest Group of the International Association for the Scientific Study of Intellectual Disabilities (IASSID) in collaboration with the World Health Organization (Walsh *et al.*, 2000) included a key qualitative data gathering phase. Several researchers, including the present authors, conducted focus groups at various sites, composed of women with intellectual disabilities, family members and/or other supporters. Common themes suggested that most of the women had inadequate information about physical changes associated with aging and related health issues. Many saw aging in exclusively negative terms. Their experiences in health care settings were often confusing, frightening and uncomfortable. Their ability to practice preventive health behaviors was compromised by lack of support, information and options. Their health professionals often seemed inattentive to the women's issues regarding sexuality, abuse and reproductive health choices.

Conclusions and recommendations

The clinical work and research represented in this chapter have begun to construct a long-absent health profile of older women with intellectual disabilities. We now know that as she ages, a woman in this population is likely to have inadequate information to prepare her for the physical and social changes awaiting her. Because her prior health service visits have been confusing at best and hurtful at worst, she is likely to approach health screening tests with fear. Because of environmental barriers and lack of health professional training about her needs, adequate health services may not even be accessible to her. She is likely to have received little formal education about sexuality, women's health options and health promotion. Menstruation, menopause, pregnancy and sexually transmitted diseases may be mysterious phenomena to her. Nutritional problems and excess weight may undermine her physical well-being, activity level and body image. She is very likely to have experienced abuse once or several times from persons with whom she lives or from whom she receives services. She may be dealing with depression secondary to abuse, social isolation, loss of relationships or other causes, yet her distress may go unrecognized and unaddressed for years. She may find both value and pressure associated with her gender role, yet receive little acknowledgment from others of her needs and rights as a woman.

As women with intellectual disabilities increasingly find their place in the community, researchers and health service providers have unprecedented opportunities to meet them and forge partnerships with them to articulate and address their needs. The following recommendations are offered to encourage the expansion of positive trends noted in this chapter:

(1) Women with intellectual disabilities must be appreciated in their full complexity, both as women and as adults with lifelong disabilities. As women, the needs and experiences they have in common with other women should be better acknowledged. Yet their disability-related health risks and complications of aging must not be overlooked when designing safe and effective health promotion programs and medical services. Many women with intellectual disabilities also belong to other social minority groups defined by race, ethnicity, sexual orientation, class and religion. These identities introduce additional social, political, cultural, economic and physical variables that must be considered in assessing each woman's access to health information, resources and services.

(2) More research is needed on prevalence of physical and mental health conditions, including comparisons with the general population and with both men and younger women with intellectual disabilities. Preventive health care programs need to be developed and tested for effectiveness. Abuse and mental health problems must be acknowledged as issues that are equal to physical problems in importance. Educational programs on health, sexuality and abuse must be designed for the women themselves and for their families. Effective materials and curricula for training health professionals about issues affecting older women with intellectual disabilities are critically needed.

(3) The lack of communication and education about health that many older women with disabilities still grapple with, is a source of distress that can and should be addressed by educational efforts responsive to each woman's level of interest and comprehension. Women with intellectual disabilities generally want to know more about their bodies and their health services. Better knowledge can help them feel less threatened and more in control in health service settings and may lead to more positive health maintenance behaviors in everyday life. The elements of model clinical programs that have been helpful to women with intellectual disabilities, such as desensitization, demonstration of equipment and procedures before

exams, relaxation and staff support, should be more widely adopted. In view of studies suggesting that women with intellectual disabilities identify with other women, the use of peer support and mentoring should be better explored in health education and clinical services.

(4) The views and preferences of older women with intellectual disabilities have been routinely underestimated as resources for guiding health services and health research. Fortunately, several influential developments – community integration, consumer empowerment, research focusing on the social determinants of disability, and qualitative studies that honor the typically marginalized voice – are countering this neglect, and women with intellectual disabilities are increasingly recognized as valuable informants with a right to express their views. Researchers and health program developers should continue to seek equitable collaborations with this community. Particular attention should be paid to making questions and information accessible and easy to understand and to ensuring that the conditions of informed consent are met.

(5) Although there have been some promising efforts to make research and program development more inclusive, there are many areas for improvement. Participatory approaches should engage women with intellectual disabilities in project activities beyond the often token role of advisory board member or the often exploitative role of research subject. More creativity and effort should be invested in tailoring communications to the comprehension needs of the women so they can participate meaningfully in selecting and framing research problems or program goals that are relevant to their lives, interpreting data, and disseminating results to audiences that need the information.

Note

A more detailed presentation of the literature on health and aging in women with intellectual disabilities can be found in the authors' earlier review article (Gill & Brown, 2000).

References

Abbasi, F., Krumholz, A., Kittner, S.J. & Langenberg, P. (1999) Effects of menopause on seizures in women with epilepsy. *Epilepsia*, **40** (2), 205–210.
Anderson, D. J. (1996) *Health-related Needs and Services for Older Adults with MR/DD*.

Symposium presented at American Association on Mental Retardation, San Antonio, Texas.

Anderson, D., Lakin, K., Bruininks, R. & Hill, B. (1987) *A National Study of Residential and Support Services for Elderly Persons with Mental Retardation.* University of Minnesota, Minneapolis, MN.

Barber, M., Jenkins, R. & Jones, C. (2000) A survivors group for women who have a learning disability. *British Journal of Developmental Disabilities,* **46** (90, Part 1), 31–41.

Bond, L., Kerr, M., Dunstan, F. & Thapar, A. (1997) Attitudes of general practitioners towards health care for people with intellectual disability and the factors underlying these attitudes. *Journal of Intellectual Disability Research,* **41** (5), 391–400.

Bramston, P. & Fogarty, G. (2000) The assessment of emotional distress experienced by people with an intellectual disability: a study of different methodologies. *Research in Developmental Disabilities,* **21** (6), 487–500.

Brigham, L. (1998) Representing the lives of women with learning difficulties: ethical dilemmas in the research process. *Mental Handicap,* **26** (4), 146–150.

Broughton, S. & Thomson, K. (2000) Women with learning disabilities: risk behaviours and experiences of the cervical smear test. *Journal of Intellectual Disability Research,* **44** (3&4), 220.

Carr, J. & Hollins, S. (1995) Menopause in women with learning disabilities. *Journal of Intellectual Disability Research,* **39** (2), 137–139.

Chadsey-Rusch, J., Linneman, D. & Rylance, B.J. (1997) Beliefs about social integration from the perspectives of persons with mental retardation, job coaches, and employers. *American Journal on Mental Retardation,* **102** (1), 1–12.

Chicoine, B., Rubin, S. & McGuire, D. (1997) *Health and Psychosocial Findings of the Adult Mental Retardation Center.* Presentation at the IASSID International Roundtable on Aging and Intellectual Disability, Chicago, IL.

Cooper, S.A. (1999) The relationship between psychiatric and physical health in elderly people with intellectual disability. *Journal of Intellectual Disability Research,* **43**, 54–60.

Edgerton, R.B., Gaston, M.A., Kelly, H. & Ward, T.W. (1994) Health care for aging people with mental retardation. *Mental Retardation,* **32** (2), 146–50.

Ehrenkranz, J.R.L. & May, P.B. (1993) Oligomenorrhea and osteoporosis in women with mental retardation. *The Endocrine Society Abstracts,* **1032**, 308.

Elkins, T.E., Gafford, L.S., Wilks, C.S. Muram, D. & Golden, G. (1986) A model clinic approach to the reproductive health concerns of the mentally handicapped. *Obstetrics & Gynecology,* **68** (2), 185–188.

Evenhuis, H.M. (1997) Medical aspects of ageing in a population with intellectual disability: III. Mobility, internal conditions and cancer. *Journal of Intellectual Disability Research,* **41** (1), 8–18.

Fine, M. & Asch, A. (1988) Disability beyond stigma: social interaction, discrimination, and activism. *Journal of Social Issues,* **44**, 3–21.

Finucane, B. (1998) Acculturation in women with mental retardation and its impact on genetic counseling. *Journal of Genetic Counseling,* **7** (1), 31–47.

Furey, E.M. (1994) Sexual abuse of adults with mental retardation. Who and where. *Mental Retardation,* **32**, 173–180.

Gill, C.J. (1991) Parents: why their death affects us more. *Mainstream*, **15** (7), 46–48.

Gill, C.J. & Brown, A.A. (2000) Overview of health issues of older women with intellectual disabilities. *Physical & Occupational Therapy in Geriatrics*, **18** (1), 23–36.

Goodenough, G.K. & Hole-Goodenough, J. (1997) Training for primary care of mentally handicapped patients in US family practice residencies. *Journal of the American Board of Family Practice*, **10** (5), 333–336.

Holland, A.J. & Koot, H.M. (1998) Mental health and intellectual disability: an international perspective. *Journal of Intellectual Disability Research*, **42**, 505–512.

Jancar, J. & Jancar, M.P. (1998) Age-related fractures in people with intellectual disability and epilepsy. *Journal of Intellectual Disability Research*, **42** (5), 429–433.

Janicki, M.P., Dalton, A.J., Henderson, C.M. & Davidson, P.W. (1999) Mortality and morbidity among older adults with intellectual disability: health services considerations. *Disability and Rehabilitation*, **21** (5–6), 284–294.

Jans, L. & Stoddard, S. (1999) *Chartbook on Women and Disability in the United States. An InfoUse Report.* US Department of Education, National Institute on Disability and Rehabilitation Research, Washington, DC.

Kapell, D., Nightingale, B., Rodriguez, A., Lee, J.H., Zigman, W.B. & Schupf, N. (1998) Prevalence of chronic medical conditions in adults with mental retardation: comparison with the general population. *Mental Retardation*, **36** (4), 269–279.

Knox, M., Mok, M. & Parmenter, T.R. (2000) Working with the experts: collaborative research with people with an intellectual disability. *Disability & Society*, **15** (1), 49–61.

Kopac, C.A., Fritz J. & Holt R.A. (1998) Gynecologic and reproductive services for women with developmental disabilities. *Clinical Excellence for Nurse Practitioners*, **2** (2), 88–95.

Krotoski, D.M., Nosek, M.A. & Turk, M.A. (eds) (1996) *Women with Physical Disabilities: Achieving and Maintaining Health and Well-being.* Paul H. Brookes, Baltimore, MD.

Lumley, V.A. & Miltenberger, R.G. (1997) Sexual abuse prevention for persons with mental retardation. *American Journal on Mental Retardation*, **101** (5), 459–472.

Lunsky, Y. & Reiss, S. (1998) Health needs of women with mental retardation and developmental disabilities. *American Psychologist*, **53**, 319.

Martin, D.M., Roy, A., Wells, R.B. & Lewis, J. (1997) Health gain through screening – users' and carers' perspectives of health care: developing primary health care services for people with an intellectual disability. *Journal of Intellectual & Developmental Disability*, **22** (4), 241–242.

McCarthy, M. (1998a) Sexual violence against women with learning disabilities. *Feminism and Psychology*, **8** (4), 544–551.

McCarthy, M. (1998b) Whose body is it anyway? Pressures and control for women with learning disabilities. *Disability & Society*, **13**, 557–574.

McCarthy, M. & Thompson, D. (1997) A prevalence study of sexual abuse of adults with intellectual disabilities referred for sex education. *Journal of Applied Research in Intellectual Disabilities*, **10** (2), 105–124.

McRae, D. (1997) Health care for women with learning disabilities. *Nursing Times*, **93** (15), 58–59.

Prevatt, B. (1998) Gynecologic care for women with mental retardation. *Journal of Obstetric, Gynecologic, & Neonatal Nursing,* **7** (3), 2516.

Richardson, M. (2000) How we live: participatory research with six people with learning difficulties. *Journal of Advanced Nursing,* **32** (6), 1383–1395.

Ridenour, N. & Norton, D. (1997) Community-based persons with mental retardation: opportunities for health promotion. *Nurse Practitioner Forum,* **8** (2), 45–49.

Rimmer, J.H., Braddock, D. & Fujiura, G. (1992) Blood lipid and percent body fat levels in Down syndrome versus non-DS persons with mental retardation. *Adapted Physical Activity Quarterly,* **9** (2), 123–129.

Rimmer, J.H., Braddock, D. & Fujiura, G. (1993) Prevalence of obesity in adults with mental retardation: implications for health promotion and disease prevention. *Mental Retardation,* **31** (2), 105–110.

Rogers, N.B., Hawkins, B.A. & Eklund, S.J. (1998) The nature of leisure in the lives of older adults with intellectual disability. *Journal of Intellectual Disability Research,* **42** (2), 122–130.

Sample, P.L. (1996) Beginnings: participatory action research and adults with developmental disabilities. *Disability & Society,* **11** (3), 317–332.

Sank, C. & Lafleche, E. (1981) Special sisters: health issues for mentally retarded women. *Off our Backs: a Women's News Journal,* **11** (5), 26.

Schupf, N., Zigman, W., Kapell, D., Lee, J.H., Kline, J. & Levin, B. (1997) Early menopause in women with Down syndrome. *Journal of Intellectual Disability Research,* **41** (3), 264–247.

Scola, P.S. & Pueschel, S.M. (1992) Menstrual cycles and basal body temperature curves in women with Down syndrome. *Obstetrics and Gynecology,* **79** (1), 91–94.

Seltzer, G.B., Schupf, N. & Wu, H. (2001) A prospective study of menopause in women with Down syndrome. *Journal of Intellectual Disability Research,* **45** (1), 1–7.

Sobsey, D. & Doe, T. (1991) Patterns of sexual abuse and assault. *Disability and Sexuality,* **9**, 243–259.

Stalker, K. (1998) Some ethical and methodological issues in research with people with learning difficulties. *Disability & Society,* **13** (1), 5–19.

Stancliffe, R.J. (1999) Proxy respondents and the reliability of the Quality of Life Questionnaire Empowerment factor. *Journal of Intellectual Disability Research,* **43** (3), 185–193.

Stein, K. & Allen, N. (1999) Cross sectional survey of cervical cancer screening in women with learning disability. *British Medical Journal,* **318**, (7184), 641.

Sulpizi, L.K. (1996) Issues in sexuality and gynecologic care of women with developmental disabilities. *Journal of Obstetric, Gynecologic & Neonatal Nursing,* **25** (7), 609–614.

Sundram, C.J. & Stavis, P.F. (1994) Sexuality and mental retardation: unmet challenges. *Mental Retardation,* **32**, 255–264.

Turk, M.A., Overeynder, J.C. & Janicki, M.P. (eds) (1995) *Uncertain Future: Aging and Cerebral Palsy – Clinical Concerns.* A Report of the Workgroup on Aging and Cerebral Palsy. New York State Developmental Disabilities Planning Council, Albany, New York.

Waite, L.M. (1993) Drama therapy in small groups with the developmentally disabled. *Social Work with Groups,* **16** (4), 95–108.

Walmsley, J.S. (2000) Writing with women with learning difficulties: a reflective account. *Journal of Intellectual Disability Research*, **44** (3&4), 507–508.

Walmsley, J. (2001) Normalisation, emancipatory research and inclusive research in learning disability. *Disability & Society*, **16**, 187–205.

Walsh, P.N., Heller, T., Schupf, N., van Schrojenstein Lantman-de Valk, H. & Working Group (2000) *Healthy Ageing – Adults with Intellectual Disabilities: Women's Health Issues*. World Health Organization, Geneva, Switzerland.

10 Risk and Vulnerability: Dilemmas for Women

Patricia Noonan Walsh and Glynis H. Murphy

Introduction

The current focus on promoting self-determination among people with intellectual disabilities is sharpened by the growing conviction that human rights should extend to all citizens. Increasingly, those charged with providing formal health and social services – chiefly in countries with developed market economies – aim to provide supports so as to achieve valued personal outcomes for individuals who have intellectual disabilities. Good practice assumes that women with intellectual disabilities who require support should be encouraged to make informed choices and exercise personal control over all aspects of their lives – where they live, where they work and with whom they live and spend leisure time.

For them, as for other adults, reciprocal friendships and intimate relationships form a core domain of quality of life. Yet women in this group incur a heightened risk of physical, emotional and sexual abuse. Living an ordinary adult life holds the promise of greater personal satisfaction, but also heightened exposure to risk. Yet to avoid risk at all cost may have a deleterious impact on women's opportunities for social inclusion and well-being. Rights-based principles for supporting people with intellectual disabilities throughout their lives are not yet widespread in either the laws or service systems in many countries. Safeguards may be unreliable, and varied across cultures. Striving for a life of quality may prove to be a difficult ordeal, rather than an accomplishment. Will the risk of abuse thwart women's emerging rights to make personal choices and thus determine the shape of their own lives?

This chapter explores some dilemmas that women with intellectual disabilities are likely to encounter in their adult lives. It presents evidence about sources of risk and the prevalence of physical, emotional and sexual abuse among women in this population. It suggests effective strategies to equip women so that they may achieve a balance between risk and autonomy at all stages of adulthood. Finally, recommendations for practice, policy and further research are outlined.

Rights and risks

An ecological approach to women's social lives helps to tease out the environmental and personal factors giving rise to the risk of abuse – sexual, physical or emotional – or exploitation. Women and men with intellectual disabilities increasingly exercise their rights to choose where to live, what work to do and with whom to live. What happens if the drive towards self-determination (Wehmeyer *et al.*, 1996) meets resistance in the prevailing cultural climate?

Social and cultural contexts

Environmental factors – social, political and economic – may help or hinder women with intellectual disabilities in exercising their rights to determine the shape of their own lives. Until the 1990s, traditional practices removed these women from typical social roles – in the heyday of large residential institutions in the US, UK, Ireland and elsewhere, few experienced marriage, parenting or paid employment. Current policies in many countries have closed the doors of institutions and now promote greater participation in community living. Most adults with ID in the US, for example, live at home with their families (Fujiura, 1998). In Ireland more than one-quarter of those aged over 55 years continue to do so (Health Research Board, 2001). In many developed countries, adults with intellectual disabilities are likely to enter the ordinary labor market. Even so, being an employee may not always augur radical improvement in social status. On the contrary, evidence suggests that women with intellectual disabilities also experience lower levels of income and less favorable job conditions than their male peers (Olson *et al.*, 2000).

The levels at which women have achieved gender equality and visible participation in political and economic life vary widely from region to region (Chapter 1). Women with intellectual disabilities who live in cultures where gender inequality is conspicuous are at special risk of exclusion from a full part in everyday life. Attitudinal and systemic barriers may arise in any realm of society, for example from within the justice system when women with ID must make statements to police (Keilty & Connelly, 2001).

Sources of support

Today's demographic trends may harbor tomorrow's risks. For example, changes in household composition emerge in the greater diversity of what constitutes a family. US data suggests that households in which a member has a developmental disability are more prevalent among single-parent, female-headed households. These demographic changes may give rise to greater risk for children and those with disabilities (Fujiura, 1998). An additional risk emerges as traditional carers – chiefly women – migrate from home duties. People who depend on others will increasingly form new contractual relationships in the public domain, as paid workers supplant traditional, unpaid forms of care. In the future, who will care, and what will enhance the social equality of women with disabilities as well as their carers (Nussbaum, 2001)?

Personal factors

Individual differences also help to determine the sources and impact of risk on the everyday lives of women with ID. The person's circumstances, gender or health status influence life outcomes such as the extent of social relationships – acknowledged as a mainstay of informal support – and exposure to various risks (Chapter 8). A study of more than 500 adults with intellectual disabilities living in both community-based and campus residential settings in the UK underscored the relative social exclusion of adults in this group (Robertson et al., 2001). Overall, they reported few persons on their social networks; almost none provided support to others, or were involved in reciprocal relationships. Being a woman was associated with a heightened risk of a less healthy lifestyle and obesity, while the presence of a mental health problem was associated with greater overall risk, including the risk of having an accident (Emerson et al., 2000). In another study carried out among 331 American adults, no gender differences were apparent in the prevalence of injuries or falls (Hsieh et al., 2001). Evidence available suggests that although important, gender is unlikely to stand alone in accounting for risks encountered by adults in this group.

By contrast, gender differences emerge in evidence about how men and women perceive social events and take risks. Women with ID are more likely to be victimized than are men (Khemka & Hickson, 2000). Also, it seems that women and men differ in decision-making as a response to a perceived risk. For example, motivational factors may play a relevant and especially useful role in skills training for women with ID. Women showed greater vigilance in a task involving decision-making after being given a vignette in which the protagonist had to make a decision with a peer or an authority figure; the difference was even striking among women with ID (Hickson et al., 1998). These findings suggest that women have more experience of risk, and more exposure to guidance and advice about how to avoid typical situations of risk (Khemka, 2000).

In summary, individual women pursuing personal goals may encounter risks presented by the prevailing social and cultural environment. Building competence is a necessary, but not sufficient, step in helping women to protect themselves and to minimize risks. It is also important to alter the environment and examine the attitudes of others. The next section presents evidence for the prevalence of risk and abuse among women with intellectual disabilities.

Abuse and neglect: the evidence

Physical, financial and sexual abuse and neglect are considered to be crimes in most jurisdictions and it is likely that, both now and in the past, a proportion of all crimes committed have involved victims with intellectual disability. Nevertheless, it is difficult to quantify the extent of such abuse against women with intellectual disabilities – or men for that matter – for a number of reasons:

- Reporting rates for abuse are relatively low, even for women without disabilities – for example, some surveys have suggested that between three and ten unreported rapes occur for every reported rape (Sobsey, 1994: 68).
- Reporting rates for abuse are likely to be even lower for women with intellectual disabilities, since they may have language difficulties and are unlikely to enter a police station unsupported.
- Even where abuse against a woman with intellectual disabilities is reported to the police, it may be difficult in some jurisdictions for the case to proceed as far as a court hearing (for example, in the UK there is widespread recognition of this problem – Mencap, 1997; Home Office, 1998).
- Most jurisdictions do not record the presence (or absence) of disability of the victim in their crime statistics, so these cannot be used to inform us of levels of abuse.

Nevertheless, there are a number of sources of evidence about the prevalence of abuse in women with intellectual disabilities and much of the research is of relatively recent origin:

- Anecdotal reports, from newspapers, case studies and inquiries into failing services
- Systematic research conducted with services for people with intellectual disabilities

■ Systematic research conducted at the court level (for example, of cases involving witnesses with intellectual disabilities)
■ Systematic research conducted directly with people with intellectual disabilities

Anecdotal reports

In the UK and US, from the 1970s and 1980s onwards, it was clear that abuse was widespread within hospital provision for people with intellectual disabilities and had been so at various times in the past. Abuse had included serious physical and sexual abuse, neglect, false imprisonment and medical interventions, such as sterilizations, in the absence of consent (e.g. Martin, 1984; Sobsey, 1994; Trent, 1995; Williams, 1995a). Studies examining anecdotal reports of abuse have also noted evidence of widespread abuse of people with intellectual disabilities in the community at the hands of members of the public, both adults and children, including employers, guardians, staff, family members, and other people (mainly men) with intellectual disabilities (e.g. Williams, 1995a). Williams found evidence of unlawful killings, abductions, assault and battery, sexual offences, threatening behavior, false imprisonment, theft and robbery, deception and a number of other crimes committed against people with learning disabilities.

The world has been slow to recognize the pervasiveness of abuse perpetrated against powerless groups, and much of the systematic research has occurred in the last 40 years (particularly the last 20 years). Systematic studies of abuse began with children rather than adults and tended to focus on sexual rather than other kinds of abuse. It is thought that children with intellectual disabilities are at a higher risk of sexual and physical abuse than other children (Sobsey, 1994) and that girls are at a higher risk than boys. One reviewer concluded that between 39% and 68% of girls and 16% and 30% of boys with intellectual disabilities would be sexually abused before the age of 18 years (Senn, 1988).

Research with service agencies

A number of attempts have been made to obtain accurate estimates of the prevalence of sexual abuse of adults with intellectual disabilities by surveying service providers. Early studies (e.g. Buchanen & Wilkins, 1991; Cooke, 1990) included only small samples of staff and concluded that the prevalence of sexual abuse was about 4–9% among people with intellectual disabilities, most of the victims being women.

In one of the most comprehensive incidence surveys in England, Brown *et al.*, 1995 surveyed the South East Thames Regional Health Authority (population about 3.5 million) in 1989–90 and again two years later. Senior managers in health and social services were asked to provide information about new cases of sexual abuse victims who were known to have intellectual disabilities (Brown *et al.*, 1995; Turk & Brown, 1993). They concluded that, by extrapolation, the incidence was probably about 1400 new cases of sexual abuse occurring in the UK each year. In each survey, about 70–75% of the cases notified were considered 'definite' or 'highly suspected' (the remainder were considered to be possible abuse). In the first survey, about three-quarters of the victims were women and one-quarter were men. About one-third were living in the family home, while the remainder were in residential services of one kind or another; and about two-thirds of the cases came to light as a result of the victim's disclosure, even though the majority of victims had severe to moderate degrees of disability. The types of offences were serious, with around two-thirds of incidents including penetration (or attempted penetration) of the victim. Almost all of the alleged perpetrators (98%) were male and almost all (95%) were already known to the victim. Alleged perpetrators included other service users (nearly half of all cases), staff/volunteers (nearly a quarter of all cases) and family members. Yet in about 50% of incidents there were no consequences for the alleged perpetrator and less than a fifth of the cases resulted in a prosecution.

Other studies of service systems in a variety of countries have confirmed most of these data, despite the many different methodologies employed. For example, there is agreement on the overwhelming likelihood of the perpetrator being male (90–98% are male and this is consistently found in all known studies), and the preponderance of women as victims (Allington, 1992; Hard & Plumb, 1987; McCarthy & Thompson, 1997; Sobsey & Varnhagen, 1989). Further, it is probable that the victims themselves were the ones to reveal the abuse (Brown *et al.*, 1995; Buchanen & Wilkins, 1991; Dunne & Power, 1990), and that it was serious in impact (Brown *et al.*, 1995; Buchanen & Wilkins, 1991; Sobsey & Doe, 1991). Frequently, services responded poorly to the disclosures of abuse (Brown *et al.*, 1995; Buchanen & Wilkins, 1991; Sobsey & Doe, 1991; Sobsey & Varnhagen, 1989).

The sexual abuse of people with intellectual disabilities appears to be similar to that in the general population in a number of ways. For example, the majority of perpetrators are men; frequently, perpetrators seem to pick on particularly powerless victims; often the incidents only come to light some years later. There are some notable differences from sexual abuse in the rest of the population, such as a somewhat higher proportion of men among victims (though most victims are women); the possibility of perpetrators having easier access to victims who may have physical dependence; and the lower degree of danger to the perpetrators from victims who cannot talk or who may not be believed. Carmody (1991) found that of 855 cases of sexual assault reported to the New South Wales Department of Health in one six-month period, about 6% of victims had intellectual disabilities. This finding suggests that they were two to three times as vulnerable to sexual abuse as people without intellectual disabilities (assuming a prevalence of intellectual disabilities of 2–3%). Carmody concluded, as did Turk and Brown (1993), that these incidence figures were very likely to be underestimates of the true figures because of the difficulties of detecting sexual abuse in systems where the potential victims are extremely powerless and any abuse may not be recognized, reported, recorded, responded to or remembered.

Establishing prevalence figures for other types of abuse has been even more difficult. Another of Brown and colleagues' studies involved examining all forms of abuse across all adult care groups reported during one year under adult protection procedures in social services departments in two counties in the south of England (Brown & Stein, 1998). The study tracked a total of 397 cases logged as 'alerts' during the year (equivalent to 14 cases per 10 000 population in one county and 26 per 10 000 in the other county). The majority of cases involved older adults but, because of the much lower prevalence of intellectual disabilities than old age, it transpired that the relative rate of 'abuse alerts' for people with intellectual disabilities was actually higher than for any other group of adults. Across care groups, women again appeared to be the most vulnerable; 65% of all victims were women and 70% of all alleged perpetrators were men (rising to 88% men if only sexual abuse alerts were counted).

The most common form of abuse of people with intellectual disabilities was physical abuse (occurring in over half of the 'abuse alerts' in this care group), with sexual abuse coming a close second (financial abuse and neglect were very uncommon). Physical abuse was also the most common form of abuse in older people and people with physical disabilities. While financial abuse was also quite common in these two groups, sexual abuse was rare. Emotional abuse was relatively uncommonly reported in any of the care groups and very rarely reported for people with intellectual disabilities. But it is difficult to be sure to what extent these figures represent the real levels of abuse and to what extent they simply reflect biases in reporting and the general difficulty of ascertaining a definite threshold at which a disturbing event should become an 'abuse alert' (Brown & Stein, 1998). For all care groups, formal sanctions in relation to the alleged perpetrators were again uncommon (such sanctions occurred in only 3% of all cases).

Research in justice systems

Not all of the 'cases' in the various service surveys described above would reach the police or court. Some attempts have been made to examine the evidence for abuse prevalence within the criminal justice system, however. Sanders *et al.* (1997: 3) attempted to survey all police forces, social services departments and health authorities in England and Wales, 'to find out about the nature and prevalence of reported crimes against people with intellectual disabilities and to collect information about the policies and procedures of the agencies when responding to these alleged crimes'. The project achieved an excellent response rate from the police forces (37 of 43 questionnaires returned) but lower response rates from social services departments and health authorities. About one-third of health and social service departments had policy documents relevant to the issue of crimes against people with intellectual disabilities. Hence, it was possible to examine the process of cases involving witnesses with an intellectual disability in a number of cases.

Sanders *et al.* examined 76 cases of people with learning disabilities who were victims of crime (48 collected through three local areas of police, social services departments and Crown Prosecution Service branches and the remaining 28 taken from a national sample). The cases included 47 sexual offences, 20 other offences against the person and 9 property offences (15 of the victims were children). Analysis of the legal outcome in the 74 cases known to the police showed there was no further action on 39, while in 33 cases the perpetrator(s) were charged and of these, 32 were prosecuted and 13 convicted. These prosecution and conviction figures are likely to be higher than most for victims with intellectual disabilities, as the Oxford team was deliberately selecting cases that were going to proceed through court, so that it could examine the whole legal process and the decision-making at each stage.

Research with service users

Abuse research has a long history among groups without disabilities and it is clear from the many studies completed in the general population that by no means all cases of abuse reach the notice of social services departments, and relatively few cases ever get to court. Many researchers have therefore thought it best to interview people directly about their own experience (e.g. Finklehor *et al.*, 1990). However, for people with intellectual disabilities this is difficult, as those most likely to be at the greatest risk are probably those least able to speak. Nevertheless, some anecdotal reports have appeared (Manthorpe, 1999) and a small number of studies have adopted the methodology of service user interviews. Unsurprisingly perhaps, they report the highest prevalence rates for abuse. Hard & Plumb (1987), for example, reported that 58% of the 95 people they interviewed at a day center said they had been sexually abused. Similarly, McCarthy (1999: 210) in her detailed interviews with 17 women reported that 14 (82%) had been sexually abused and Doucette (1986) interviewed 30 women with disabilities about their experience of physical abuse and reported a prevalence rate of 67% (as compared to 34% for the 32 women without disabilities).

Mencap (1999) conducted a national survey in the UK of bullying of people with intellectual disabilities, sending out 5000 questionnaires to group homes, leisure clubs, employment services and self advocacy groups and receiving 904 replies. They reported that nearly nine out of ten people responding had been bullied in the previous year, about a third of these being bullied on a weekly or daily basis. Most (73%) occurred in public places and much of it was of a serious nature, including physical attacks (21% of incidents reported) that would constitute a crime in most jurisdictions (no figures on the gender of victims were given). Nevertheless, of those people who told anyone, few (only 17%) had reported incidents to the police and very few found the police helpful.

In summary, the evidence reviewed here indicates that women with intellectual disabilities are at high risk of a variety of kinds of abuse. Attempts to change this will need to be multilayered and to consider environments, the likely perpetrators and the women with intellectual disabilities themselves. Strategies are proposed in the next section.

Strategies for change

Given the emerging evidence of the pervasiveness of bullying and abuse in public places, a central problem is the attitude of the public (especially, though not exclusively, children and adolescents) to people with intellectual disabilities. This is a long-standing difficulty and it may be that the increasing moves in many countries towards inclusion in childhood (for example, in schools) and in adulthood will assist community members to be more welcoming of women (and men) with intellectual disabilities. Yet we should not be naïve about this; there is ample evidence from school inclusion studies that children with intellectual disabilities are often not preferred as playmates and may be discriminated against in the playground. There is also considerable evidence that the social networks of people with intellectual disabilities remain very small (Robertson *et al.*, 2001) even when they live in the community. Remarkably few studies have examined the possibility of altering these trends. One of the few was an innovative project implemented by McConkey in Ireland in the 1980s. The CARA program was implemented in secondary schools by arranging joint meetings for young people in the community and people with intellectual disabilities, and showed that attitudes could change (McConkey *et al.*, 1983). These kinds of educational programs need to be widespread and carefully managed.

Apparent gender differences in vulnerability – with men more likely to be perpetrators and women more likely to have experienced risk – may be rooted in the socialization process through which children acquire social roles. If so, it behoves educators to plan strategies aimed at specific learning needs of developing children. Accordingly, boys and young men should have the opportunity to achieve competence in personal and social skills likely to lessen their risk of becoming perpetrators.

The likelihood is that, if abuse does occur, it will be the service users themselves who will voice their concerns. This means that support and training for service users are of crucial importance. A number of sex education packs (e.g. Hinsburger, 1995; Kempton, 1988; McCarthy & Thompson, 1998), abuse awareness materials (Hollins *et al.*, 1992; 1993), assertiveness training packs and crime education packs (e.g. VOICE UK and Change, 2000; Williams, 1995b) and video training materials (South East London Health Promotion Services, 1992) have been produced. Some have been prepared by women with intellectual disabilities themselves (Walsall Women's Group, 1994). There have been very few evaluations of the effectiveness of this kind of training, however (Haseltine & Miltenberger, 1990; Mazzucchelli, 2001) and further evaluation is needed.

It seems that service users, when they voice concerns or disclose abuse, are most likely to tell staff in services, family members or the police, so that service responses to abuse are extremely important, both in health and community care systems as well as in the criminal justice system. These responses also need to be multilayered and to include:

- Policies and procedures, at an inter-agency level, for dealing with abuse when 'alerts' occur (Brown *et al.*, 1994)
- Staff who are skilled in communicating with people who have major communication difficulties and are well-trained in the signs of abuse and the content of abuse policies and procedures (Allington, 1992; Brown *et al.*, 1994; Buchanen & Wilkins, 1991)
- Police who have been trained in how to recognize a person with an intellectual disability (Williams, 1995a: 33)
- Police who have been trained to interview people with intellectual disabilities (Brown *et al.*, 1996; Roeher Institute, 1993; Sanders *et al.*, 1997; Williams, 1995a)
- Courts which have procedures designed to equalize access to justice

and staff who have been trained in disabilities (Kebbell *et al.*, 2001; Mencap, 1997; Sobsey, 1994; Williams, 1995a)
■ Laws that allow everyone access to justice and take account of the presence of intellectual disabilities in victims (Cooke & Davies, 2001; Sobsey, 1994)

In many countries, services have been encouraged and supported to develop 'sexuality' and 'vulnerable adult' policies, in order to specify service responses to signs of abuse and abuse disclosures (NAPSAC, 1993 among others). It has been intended that such policies should improve the recognition, recording, reporting and response to high risk and/or suspected abuse situations, and typically policy documents give guidance to staff about what to do in all these situations. In addition, staff training in the use of the policies and in the basic procedures for recognizing, recording, reporting and responding to suspected abuse situations has been widespread. Evaluations of the effects of such work are rare but they have suggested that, while staff readily learn the basic facts about abuse, they seem to find it harder to recall precisely what their policy documents tell them to do about it. Brown *et al.* (1994), for example, found that about half the staff in their research in England had had some training in sexuality/sexual abuse and most knew their agencies had sexuality policies, but very few could remember anything about their guidelines. This suggests that, all too often, abuse guidelines once written tend to gather dust on a shelf, and that it is important for managers to remind staff about the guidelines in supervision. There also need to be easy-to-follow flow charts available for quick reference, as staff find these easier to refer to than lengthy policy documents, especially when faced with an abuse disclosure on a Friday night when the social work department is closed and the managers have gone home.

When someone from the general population makes a complaint to the police that they have been a victim of a crime, it is usual for the police to interview them. Where the victims have an intellectual disability, the police in some jurisdictions forego an interview (Roeher Institute, 1993; Sanders *at al.*, 1997; Williams, 1995a), often presuming that acquiescence, suggestibility or communication problems will prevent the victims from giving useful evidence in court. This can be a real difficulty at times but need not present problems (Clare & Gudjonsson, 1993; Heal & Sigelman, 1995); with appropriate training for police officers in interviewing techniques, such difficulties can often be overcome (Brown *et al.*, 1996; Roeher Institute, 1993).

In court, some jurisdictions make no allowance for the presence of intellectual disabilities in a victim (e.g. Mencap, 1997, though this will be changing soon in the UK – see Cooke & Davies, 2001) and consequently barriers may be erected that prevent someone with an intellectual disability from giving evidence. A number of countries have provisions that make allowances for disabilities, such as replacement of the oath (e.g. in Canada), the use of video-taped testimony and adjustment of questioning techniques for trials (e.g. in the Netherlands), the provision of special sentences where the victim has an intellectual disability (e.g. in the sexual assault laws in New South Wales, Australia – see Rosser, 1990), and the 'hate crime' laws in some states in the US (Sobsey, 1994: 364). In addition, some countries now prepare victims for a court appearance, with visits to see the lay-out of courtrooms, to meet court officials and to learn about court procedures (e.g. Hollins *et al.*, 1994).

Finally, there is a need for direct treatment services for both victims and perpetrators with intellectual disabilities. In most countries, the direct treatment services for victims are located in psychology departments in intellectual disability teams. Treatment for victims is likely to involve careful disclosure work, with information about abuse and recovery from abuse, a great deal of reassurance, and the possibility of survivor groups in due course, as well as a variety of other strategies such as ensuring proper risk management of the perpetrator (Churchill *et al.*, 1997; Moss, 1998; NAPSAC, 1993). Sometimes, where victims have been extremely frightened and traumatized, direct treatment may need to involve relaxation training, desensitization and treatment for post-traumatic stress disorder (Davison *et al.*, 1994; Moss, 1998). For perpetrators, on the other hand, direct treatment will include aspects of risk management (Churchill *et al.*, 1997) and perhaps a legal framework, such as a probation order, as well as cognitive-behavioral treatment methods, such as anger management or sex offender treatment (Benson, 1992; Benson *et al.*, 1986; Clare & Murphy, 1998; Lindsay & Smith, 1998).

Summary

Women with intellectual disabilities incur heightened risk of various kinds of abuse. Interventions on their behalf should consider the climate of the culture and the homes, workplaces and community settings where women live and work as well as their personal characteristics. Interventions should acknowledge the particular needs of women as learners – for example, in addressing motivational factors when offering advice on responding to perceived risks. Professional workers should also take into account the status of women who have experienced abuse as survivors, not merely victims, in order to further enhance their resilience. Optimal levels of security in community settings may be gained through staff training and development, monitoring the outcomes of policies which take women's needs and preferences into account when devising residential and other supports on their behalf. At the same time, women should realistically be able to shape satisfying, ordinary lives alongside their peers. Further research is needed to explore gender differences in expressing personal choices or other aspects of self-determined behavior, and to improve the efficacy of training materials and other interventions aimed at heightening personal competence.

References

Allington, C.L.J. (1992) Sexual abuse within services for people with learning disabilities: staff's perceptions, understandings of and contact with the problems of sexual abuse. *Mental Handicap*, **20**, 59–63.

Benson, B. (1992) *Teaching Anger Management to Persons with Mental Retardation.* International Diagnostic Systems Inc, Worthington, Ohio.

Benson, B., Johnson Rice, C. & Miranti, S.V. (1986) Effects of anger management training with mentally retarded adults in group treatment. *Journal of Consulting and Clinical Psychology*, **54**, 728–729.

Brown, H. & Stein, J. (1998) Implementing adult protection policies in Kent and East Sussex. *Journal of Social Policy*, **27**, 371–396.

Brown, H., Stein, J. & Turk, V. (1995) The sexual abuse of adults with learning disabilities: a second incidence study. *Mental Handicap Research*, **8**, 3–24.

Brown, H., Hunt, N. & Stein, J. (1994) 'Alarming but very necessary': working with staff groups around the sexual abuse of adults with learning disabilities. *Journal of Intellectual Disability Research*, **38**, 393–412.

Brown, H., Egan-Sage, E., Barry, G. & McKay, C. (1996) *Towards Better Interviewing: A Handbook for Police Officers and Social Workers on the Sexual Abuse of Adults with Learning Disabilities.* National Association for the Protection from Sexual Abuse of Adults and Children with Learning Disabilities, Nottingham.

Buchanen, A.H. & Wilkins, R. (1991) Sexual abuse of the mentally handicapped: difficulties in establishing prevalence. *Psychiatric Bulletin*, **15**, 601–605.

Carmody, M. (1991) Invisible victims: sexual assault of people with an intellectual disability. *Australia & New Zealand Journal of Developmental Disabilities*, **17**, 229–236.

Churchill, J., Brown, H., Craft, A. & Horrocks, C. (1997) *There Are No Easy Answers: the provision of continuing care and treatment to adults with learning disabilities who sexually abuse others.* Association for Residential Care and National Association for the Protection from Sexual Abuse of Adults and Children with Learning Disabilities, Nottingham.

Clare, I.C.H. & Gudjonsson, G.H. (1993) Interrogative suggestibility, confabulation, and acquiescence in people with mild learning disabilities (mental handicap): implications for reliability during police interview. *British Journal of Clinical Psychology*, **32**, 295–301.

Clare, I.C.H. & Murphy, G. (1998) Working with offenders or alleged offenders with intellectual disabilities. In: *Clinical Psychology and People with Intellectual Disabilities* (eds E. Emerson, A. Caine, J. Bromley & C. Hatton), pp. 154–176. John Wiley and Sons, Chichester.

Cooke, L. (1990) Abuse of mentally handicapped adults. *Psychiatric Bulletin*, **14**, 608–609.

Cooke, P. & Davies, G. (2001) Achieving best evidence from witnesses with learning disabilities: new guidance. *British Journal of Learning Disabilities*, **29**, 84–87.

Davison, F.M., Clare, I.C.H., Georgiades, S., Divall, J. & Holland, A.J. (1994) Treatment of a man with mild learning disabilities who was sexually assaulted whilst in prison. *Medicine, Science and the Law*, **34**, 346–353.

Doucette J. (1986) *Violent Acts Against Disabled Women*. Disabled Women's Network Canada, Toronto, Ontario.

Dunne, T.P. & Power, A. (1990) Sexual abuse and mental handicap: preliminary findings of a community-based study. *Mental Handicap Research*, **3**, 111–125.

Emerson, E., Robertson, J., Gregory, N., Hatton, C., Kessissoglou, S., Hallam, A., Knapp, M., Jaerbrink, K., Netten, A. & Walsh, P.N. (2000) The quality and costs of village communities, residential campuses and community-based residential supports for people with learning disabilities. *Tizard Learning Disability Review*, **5**, 5–16.

Finklehor, D., Hotaling, G., Lewis, I.A. & Simth, C. (1990) Sexual abuse in a national survey of adult men and women: prevalence, characteristics and risk factors. *Child Abuse & Neglect*, **14**, 19–28.

Fujiura, G.T. (1998) Demography of family households. *American Journal on Mental Retardation*, **103**, 225–235.

Hard, S. & Plumb, W. (1987) Sexual abuse of persons with developmental disabilities: a case study. Unpublished manuscript, available from the authors, Tizard Centre, University of Kent.

Haseltine, B. & Miltenberger, R. (1990) Teaching self-protection skills to persons with mental retardation. *American Journal on Mental Retardation*, **95**, 188–197.

Heal, L.W. & Sigelman, C.K. (1995) Response biases in interviews of individuals with limited mental ability. *Journal of Intellectual Disability Research*, **39**, 331–340.

Health Research Board (2001) *National Intellectual Disability Database Report*. Health Research Board, 73 Lower Baggot Street, Dublin 2.

Hickson, L., Golden, H., Khemka, I., Urw, T. & Yamusah, S. (1998) A closer look at interpersonal decision-making in adults with and without mental retardation. *American Journal on Mental Retardation*, **103**, 209–224.

Hinsburger, D. (1995) *Just Say Know!* Diverse City Press, Quebec.

Hollins, S., Sinason, V. & Webb, B. (1992) *Jenny Speaks Out*. St. George's Mental Health Library, London.

Hollins, S., Sinason, V. & Webb, B. (1993) *Bob Tells All*. St. George's Mental Health Library, London.

Hollins, S., Sinason, V., Boniface, J. & Webb, B. (1994) *Going to Court*. St. George's Mental Health Library, London.

Home Office (1998) *Speaking Up For Justice*. The Stationery Office, London.

Hsieh, K., Heller, T. & Miller, A. B. (2001) Risk factors for injuries and falls among adults with developmental disabilities. *Journal of Intellectual Disability Research*, **35** (1), 76–82.

Kebbell, M., Hatton, C., Johnson, S.D. & O'Kelly, C.M.E. (2001) People with learning disabilities: what questions should lawyers ask? *British Journal of Learning Disabilities*, **29**, 98–102.

Keilty, J. & Connelly, G. (2001) Making a statement: an exploratory study of barriers facing women with an intellectual disability when making a statement about sexual assault to police. *Disability & Society*, **16**, 273–291.

Kempton, W. (1988) *Life Horizons, I & II*. James Stanfield & Co., Santa Monica.

Khemka, I. (2000) Increasing independent decision-making skills of women with mental retardation in simulated interpersonal situations of abuse. *American Journal on Mental Retardation*, **105**, 387–401.

Khemka, I. & Hickson, L. (2000) Decision-making by adults with mental retardation in simulated situations of abuse. *Mental Retardation*, **38**, 15–26.

Lindsay, W.R. & Smith, A.H.W. (1998) Responses to treatment for sex offenders with intellectual disability: a comparison of men with 1 and 2 year probation sentences. *Journal of Intellectual Disability Research*, **42**, 346–353.

Manthorpe, J. (1999) Users' perceptions: searching for the views of users with learning disabilities. In: *Institutional Abuse: Perspectives Across the Life Course* (eds N. Stanley, J. Manthorpe & B. Penhale), pp. 110–129. Routledge, London.

Martin, J.P. (1984) *Hospitals in Trouble*. Blackwell, Oxford.

Mazzucchelli, T.G. (2001) Feel safe: a pilot study of a protective behaviours programme for people with intellectual disability. *Journal of Intellectual & Developmental Disability*, **26**, 115–126.

McCarthy, M. (1999) *Sexuality and Women with Learning Disabilities*. Jessica Kingsley, London.

McCarthy, M. & Thompson, D. (1997) A prevalence study of sexual abuse of adults with intellectual disabilities referred for sex education. *Journal of Applied Research in Intellectual Disabilities*, **10**, 105–124.

McCarthy, M. & Thompson, D. (1998) *Sex and the 3Rs: Right, Responsibilities and Risks*, 2nd edition. Pavilion Publishing, Brighton.

McConkey, R., McCormack, B. & Naughton, M. (1983) Changing young people's perceptions of mentally handicapped adults. *Journal of Mental Deficiency Research*, **27**, 279–290.

Mencap (1997) *Barriers to Justice*. Mencap, London.

Mencap (1999) *Living in Fear*. Mencap, London.

Moss, J. (1998) Working with issues of sexual abuse. In: *Clinical Psychology and People with Intellectual Disabilities* (eds E. Emerson, A. Caine, J. Bromley & C. Hatton), pp. 177–192. John Wiley and Sons, Chichester.

NAPSAC (1993) *It Could Never Happen Here*. Association of Residential Care/National Association for the Protection from Sexual Abuse of Adults and Children with Learning Disabilities, Chesterfield.

Nussbaum, M. (2001) Disabled Lives: Who Cares? In: *The New York Review of Books*, **XLVIII** (1), 34–37.

Olson, D., Cioffi, A., Yovanoff, P. & Mank, D. (2000) Gender differences in supported employment. *Mental Retardation*, **38**, 89–96.

Robertson, J., Emerson, E., Gregory, N., Hatton, C., Kessissoglou, S., Hallam, A. & Linehan, C. (2001) Social networks of people with mental retardation in residential settings. *Mental Retardation*, **39**, 201–214.

Roeher Institute (1993) *Answering the Call: the police response to family and caregiver violence against people with disabilities.* Roeher Institute, Ontario, Canada.

Rosser, K. (1990) A particular vulnerability. *Australian Legal Services Bulletin*, **15** (1), 32–34. Quoted in McCarthy, M. (1999) *Sexuality and Women with Learning Disabilities.* Jessica Kingsley, London.

Sanders, A., Creaton, J., Bird, S. & Weber, L. (1997) *Victims with Learning Disabilities: Negotiating the Criminal Justice System.* Occasional paper no. 17, Centre for Criminological Research, University of Oxford.

Senn, C.Y. (1988) *Vulnerable: Sexual Abuse and People with an Intellectual Handicap.* Roeher Institute, Downsview, Ontario. Quoted in Sobsey, D. (1994) *Violence and Abuse in the Lives of People with Disabilities: The End of Silent Acceptance?* Paul H. Brookes, Baltimore.

Sobsey, D. (1994) *Violence and Abuse in the Lives of People with Disabilities: The End of Silent Acceptance?* Paul H. Brookes, Baltimore.

Sobsey, D. & Doe, T. (1991) Patterns of sexual abuse and assault. *Journal of Sexuality and Disability*, **9**, 243–259.

Sobsey, D. & Varnhagen, C. (1989) Sexual abuse of people with disabilities. In: *Special Education Across Canada: Challenges for the 90s* (eds M. Caspo & L. Gougen), pp. 199–218. Centre for Human Development & Research, Vancouver, Canada.

South East London Health Promotion Services (1992) *My Choice, My Own Choice.* A sex education video for people with learning disabilities.

Trent, J. (1995) *Inverting the Feeble Mind. A History of Mental Retardation in the United States.* University of California Press, Berkeley.

Turk, V. & Brown, H. (1993) The sexual abuse of adults with learning disabilities: results of a two-year incidence survey. *Mental Handicap Research*, **6**, 193–216.

VOICE UK and Change (2000) *No More Abuse.* VOICE UK, Derby.

Walsall Women's Group (1994) *Walsall Women's Group Safety Video – No Means No.* The Women's Group, College of Continuing Education, Walsall.

Wehmeyer, M.L., Kelchner, K. & Richards, S. (1996) Essential characteristics of self-determined behavior of individuals with mental retardation. *American Journal on Mental Retardation*, **100**, 632–642.

Williams, C. (1995a) *Invisible Victims: Crime and Abuse against People with Learning Difficulties.* Jessica Kingsley, London.

Williams, C. (1995b) *Cracking Crime – A Learning Pack.* Pavilion Publishing Company, Brighton.

11 Health Promotion and Women

Tamar Heller and Beth Marks

Health promotion and women with intellectual disabilities

Health care systems are expanding from an emphasis on treatment of diseases to a focus on health promotion through health education, preventive health care and supportive socioenvironmental conditions. A growing body of research data associates successful aging and disease prevention with health behaviors and environmental conditions. Among women with disabilities health promoting activities and settings can lead to enhanced functioning, prevention of chronic conditions related to lifestyle, and an increased quality of life. For women with intellectual disabilities, the current focus on individual rights has expanded their interest in participating in health promoting activities to maintain and/or enhance their quality of life. However, researchers have only recently begun to explore the conditions promoting optimum health among older persons with intellectual disabilities, and even less among women with intellectual disabilities.

Despite the documented significance of health promotion activities to maintain health and control or remove deleterious risk factors, women with intellectual disabilities, for the most part, have not been included in health promotion programs. This is especially critical as mortality rates decrease and the likelihood of developing chronic conditions related to lifestyle and aging increases. While the health care system is usually responsive to acute care needs, such as infections and emergency care, health promotion programs that facilitate active participation to create behavior change and improve health status through modification of lifestyles and living conditions are not readily available.

This chapter will provide a brief overview of the health status of women with intellectual disabilities, discuss the risk factors that predispose women to acquiring chronic conditions, and review key aspects of health promotion programs designed for persons with intellectual disabilities.

Health status of women with intellectual disabilities

The major factors associated with morbidity and mortality among women with intellectual disabilities remain largely unexplored. Moreover, the limited research has not consistently documented a pattern of differences in health conditions between men and women with intellectual disabilities, although some of these studies suggest that women outlive men by as much as eight years, which is similar to the general population. Additional studies have examined the types and magnitude of specific health problems, such as cardiovascular disease (CVD), obesity, osteoporosis, Alzheimer's disease, arthritis, cancer, diabetes, epilepsy, and dental caries and oral conditions. This section will provide a brief overview of the health status in women with intellectual disabilities.

The onset of CVD, a leading cause of death among both men and women, is strongly associated with health-related behaviors – specifically tobacco use, lack of physical activity and poor nutrition. Among adults with intellectual disabilities, CVD and respiratory disease are the two most common causes of death (Janicki et al., 1999). Limited data also reports higher rates of obesity, nutritional problems and cholesterol levels among adults with intellectual disabilities than in the general population (Fujiura et al., 1997). Studies in the US have found high cholesterol and obesity among women and adults living in independent settings (Rimmer et al., 1995) and higher rates of malnutrition or obesity among women with intellectual disabilities living in residential facilities, compared to men.

While the literature concerning the prevalence rates of cancer for women with intellectual disabilities is limited, research suggests that women seem to have the same risk for breast and cervical cancer. Additionally, women with disabilities, especially intellectual disabilities, living in community-based settings are less likely than their peers who do not have disabilities to receive preventive health screenings (e.g. mammography and Pap smear) (Lennox & Kerr, 1997). Osteoporosis is another concern for women due to the tendency to lose more bone density compared to men after menopause. Women with intellectual disabilities may have an even higher risk due to long-term use of medication, such as anti-epileptic medications.

Women in the US have a greater risk compared to men of experiencing three or more psychiatric conditions (National Center for Health Statistics, 1996). While the prevalence rates for women with disabilities have not been systematically explored, women with intellectual disabilities may have an elevated risk for stress-related conditions due to daily stressors related to their disability. Additionally, women with disabilities receive low levels of treatment for mental health conditions due to the lack of physical, economic and communication access at many community-based mental health centers.

The oral health status among persons with disabilities internationally is associated with higher levels of disease and less dental attention compared to the general population, as the treatment and care afforded to them is often minimal (Vignehsa *et al.*, 1991). Individuals with intellectual disabilities who are dependent on assistance in brushing have more plaque and gingivitis (Stiefel *et al.*, 1993). The use of anti-seizure medications among women with intellectual disabilities also makes them increasingly susceptible to gum disease and can lead to nutritional problems.

Although the traditional medical model cannot eliminate chronic universal diseases, postponement of these conditions by removing or modifying the risk factors associated with the acceleration of the process has been well established. The available health status data for women with intellectual disabilities demonstrates the need for expanding research to examine health behaviors and development of health promotion programs that address these women.

Health risks

The decrease in mortality and morbidity rates for adults with intellectual disabilities is prompting greater interest in preventing chronic diseases related to their lifestyle and social environment. Women with disabilities increasingly indicate that social, political and economic barriers, not just the intrinsic limitations of their disability, are a large component of their health concerns. Researchers are just beginning to evaluate the health promotion needs and health behaviors of adults with intellectual disabilities in an attempt to disentangle the socially constructed determinants of their problems (e.g. access to screening tests, risk from violence/abuse, stress-related disease) from those attributable to physiology. For persons with intellectual disabilities, modifying socioeconomic and environmental conditions may maintain or improve physical, mental and social functioning. Additionally, creating supportive environments may enable women to engage in health promoting and prevention behaviors to prevent premature onset of disease and chronic conditions.

Health care services often neglect to address the risk factors associated with developing chronic conditions as a result of lifestyle factors for women with intellectual disabilities. Some of these risk factors include socioeconomic and environmental factors, behavioral risk factors and biological factors.

Socioeconomic and environmental risk factors

In addition to socioeconomic risk factors, environmental factors may include inaccessible health care services and information, negative attitudes from carers regarding the benefits of health promotion, and violence toward women with disabilities. In order to control or remove harmful risk factors, personal choice or social and environmental changes may be required. Health promotion strategies are primarily concerned with creating behavior change through modification of lifestyles and living conditions to increase well-being. Lifestyle changes can be facilitated by a combination of efforts to enhance awareness, change behavior and create environments that support good health practices. However, the influence of lifestyle and living conditions on the state of well-being varies among different socioeconomic levels (WHO, 1988). For example, while personal lifestyles may dramatically affect the development of a state of well-being among the affluent, social and environmental conditions may be larger determinants of well-being among the less affluent. Thus, for many women with intellectual disabilities who are increasingly projected to be living in poverty or low-income settings, the socioeconomic and environmental contexts may be critical determinants.

Economic factors

Inadequate financial resources restrict people with disabilities from obtaining necessary health care services. Even for people who have health insurance, 32% of people with disabilities in the US say they have special needs related to their disability, such as particular therapies, equipment or medicine that are not covered by their health insurance. Insurance is also limited and often restricts or excludes coverage of services that are important for persons with disabilities to achieve independence (e.g. assistive devices and personal assistance) (National Organization on Disability, 1998). Public health insurance programs, like private insurance, may impose requirements and restrictions that limit access to needed services. Thus, they foster a sense of dependency on the 'system'. So, while approximately 90% of adults with disabilities in the US are covered by health insurance, adults with disabilities are more likely than adults without disabilities to report dissatisfaction with health care services, to be denied insurance coverage because of a disability or pre-existing health condition, and to postpone getting health care they thought they needed in the past year because they could not afford it.

Access to health services and health information

Health care delivery systems are constantly changing and have significant implications for health. Currently, many health care systems worldwide are consolidating services, and available resources and funding within health care and health-related programs are increasingly limited. Increased time pressures are especially problematic for women with intellectual disabilities who often need extra time for examinations, tests, procedures and health teaching. They need more information to reduce their fears and to help them make informed health care choices for themselves and their families; for them, access to health promotion services and health information is a critical ingredient. However, major gaps exist in accessing health care services for primary health care and for health preventive and promotive services, such as dental care, home-based medical care and health screening activities. While many people face access barriers to health care services, people with intellectual disabilities are especially vulnerable to the inadequacies of the existing health care system. Access barriers may include lack of adequate preparation of health care providers, lack of health insurance coverage, transportation problems and geographic unavailability of health services.

Rimmer *et al.* (2000) found that women with one or more physical disabilities are interested in becoming more active but barriers prevent their participation. Barriers identified by the women included cost of the exercise program, transportation and lack of information regarding exercise facilities. In a study of adults with Down syndrome, women were significantly more likely than men to report access barriers to exercise. Specifically, they were more likely to report not knowing where to exercise, concern that people might make fun of them or that no one would show them how to exercise, and the high expense of exercising (Heller, Hsieh, & Rimmer, in press).

The understanding and knowledge of women with intellectual disabilities regarding their personal health issues and ways to access services affects their health. They may not understand spoken and/or written information about health-related topics. Informal modes of information exchange through peers, television and radio also may be limited. Use of illustrations can enhance a woman's understanding of the health information. In order to access services adequately, women must be given culturally appropriate health information regarding the availability of such services; and health education training materials and educational programs need to be developed for their health care professionals. Unfortunately, many health care providers have not had the necessary training or experience to provide health care services for women with intellectual disabilities. Consequently, these women may have difficulty accessing services, either due to their refusal to be examined or to professionals' refusal to provide services (Gill, 1996). Kopac *et al.* (1996) found in their study examining attitudinal and health care system variables related to accessibility and availability of gynecological and reproductive services for women with intellectual disabilities, that some services were not provided by the service agencies, such as mammograms (9%), health education for sexual/reproductive knowledge (17%), STD counseling/treatment (45%) and prenatal care (79%).

Attitudes toward persons with intellectual disabilities

A common myth is that disability is primarily a health issue. However, people with disabilities no longer see themselves necessarily as patients. They are beginning to assert their desire to live like anyone else and obtain services and supports that they control. Women with disabilities have reported that health care professionals often lack knowledge and sensitivities about their disabilities and tend to focus more on their disabilities rather than their immediate health problems, hence treating them as a 'diagnosis' rather than as a person. An additional barrier relates to the health professionals' and the general public's inability to separate disability from illness; and the ability to perceive individuals with disabilities as healthy and able to benefit from health promotion activities. This disparity in defining health for persons with disabilities may create barriers to successful health promotion interventions for adults with intellectual disabilities.

Families of adults with intellectual disabilities have anecdotally reported a critical need for health care personnel who are knowledgeable about conditions prevalent among adults with intellectual disabilities and who can provide effective community-based services. Because health care providers often define disability as a 'deficiency' or an 'abnormality' that needs to be cured (or fixed), the focus of services often does not extend beyond the disability to address health promotion and self-care activities. Consequently, the services provided by professionals often are not the type of services that people with disabilities are seeking. This disparity may further alienate and marginalize people with disabilities from obtaining and engaging in health promoting services.

Carers

Carers' attitudes can influence the degree of exercise participation among adults with intellectual disabilities. A study of exercise determinants among adults with cerebral palsy found that when carers perceived more benefits of exercise, the adults with cerebral palsy were more likely to exercise (Heller, Ying, Rimmer, & Marks, in press). These findings suggest that in order to mobilize persons with disabilities into higher levels of

Access barriers

Access barriers to health information include the following:

- *Communication barriers* that can prevent women with intellectual disabilities and visual or hearing disabilities from understanding health-related information
- *Programmatic barriers* including inflexible appointments that fail to accommodate transportation difficulties, or a lack of staff to assist in the examination room
- *Physical barriers* including inaccessible examination tables (too high or low to transfer from a wheelchair), lack of accessible rest rooms, lack of signage regarding the accessible entrances, and lack of Braille signage in the facility
- *Educational barriers* including inappropriate presentation of teaching materials, such as the absence of sign interpreters, of large print formats for health education materials, and of materials that are appropriate for individuals' intellectual functioning and lifestyles

physical activity, carers must be informed and educated about the benefits of exercise for adults with disabilities.

Rimmer and Rubin (1996) noted that many direct service staff and family carers have little training in physical exercise and therefore do not know how to develop or modify fitness programs that are challenging, safe, injury-free and successful. Additionally, if carers are inactive and uninterested in fitness, the likelihood that the persons for whom they are providing care will engage in exercise is low. Studies have also demonstrated the importance of carers' involvement in exercise and weight reduction programs (Fox *et al.*, 1985).

Violence and stress

The United Nations Population Fund (2000) report states that discrimination and violence against women 'remain firmly rooted in cultures around the world', stopping women from reaching their full potential. Globally, girls and women are still routinely denied access to education and health care, including control over their reproductive activity, equal pay, and legal rights. At least one in three women has been beaten, coerced into sex or abused in some way. Studies since the early 1990s suggest that women with intellectual disabilities are four to ten times more likely than other women to be targets of sexual assault and other violence (Sobsey, 2000); and more than 75% of women with intellectual disabilities are victims of sexual abuse.

Women with intellectual disabilities may have a greater risk of violence and abuse because they are easier targets of rape and physical assault. Women who have multiple disabilities or have contact with multiple health care providers, attendants or carers are more likely to be assaulted and abused (Sobsey, 1994). Although these women need a supportive and safe environment more than anyone, lack of accessible transportation and communication effectively shuts them out of many community-based services. Mainstream services assisting abused women, such as women's shelters and rape crisis centers, are often not physically and attitudinally accessible (e.g. lack of TTY/TDD – Teletypes/Telecommunications Device for the Deaf – volume control phones for deaf/hard of hearing women, lack of attendant care services, and attitudinal barriers of staff related to the woman's ability to perform tasks) (Traustadottir, 1990). Shelters also may focus on supporting women who are victims of partner abuse and may neglect issues specific for women with disabilities who often experience emotional and sexual abuse from carers/attendants, neighbors, health care workers and service providers. A woman who reports assault from an attendant may risk losing essential services; and a woman who reports an assault by a spouse may lose financial support or stability. Health care providers often fail to ask women with disabilities if such abuse is occurring. Much of this abuse goes unreported, and if it is reported it is frequently discounted by health care providers and the legal system.

In addition to increased risk of violence, women with intellectual disabilities also have many stressors related to housing, money, transportation and expensive disability technology that are exhausting both physically and emotionally. Unfortunately, they often have few friendships and social networks to mitigate stressors (Chapter 1). These stressors can lead to conditions exacerbated by stress, such as inflammatory bowel disease, heart disease, peptic ulcers, musculoskeletal problems, anxiety and depression. Unfortunately, diagnostic overshadowing may occur in that health care providers attribute complaints and symptoms to the individual's disability and neglect related routine screening tests.

Behavioral risk factors

Behavioral risk factors consist of inadequate exercise, poor nutritional habits, cigarette smoking and living in a psychological state of helplessness, without options for major life choices and decisions. Behavior can directly influence health for women with intellectual disabilities, and it can have an indirect affect on health by influencing environmental factors. Among women with intellectual disabilities, health behaviors can maintain or enhance health status and quality of life, control or remove deleterious risk factors, and prevent the onset of chronic conditions.

Physical fitness and exercise

Maintaining a physically active lifestyle is an essential ingredient in preventing heart disease and increasing overall health and longevity. Additionally, exercise can also reduce the incidence of chronic conditions in persons with disabilities (loss of cardio-respiratory and muscular function, metabolic alterations and systemic dysfunctions), which may maintain or enhance quality of life. Unfortunately, women have rarely been included in exercise programs. Women with intellectual disabilities also have highly sedentary lifestyles, especially in industrialized countries. This is especially critical as mortality rates decrease and the likelihood of developing chronic conditions related to lifestyle increases.

Data from the US suggests that adults with intellectual disabilities living at home exercise less frequently compared to older adults without disabilities. This sedentary lifestyle makes them more susceptible to secondary health conditions such as cardiovascular disease, obesity, osteoporosis, hypertension, Type II diabetes and depression. In addition to the negative effects on health, the high levels of obesity and the low levels of physical activity reported among adults with intellectual disabilities can create barriers to successful employment, participation in leisure activities and performance of daily living activities.

Nutrition and diet

Dietary factors are associated with four of the ten leading causes of death: coronary heart disease, some types of cancer, stroke, and Type II diabetes mellitus (National Center for Health Statistics, 1997). Dietary factors are also associated with osteoporosis and obesity. Good dietary habits must be combined with physical activity to maintain a healthy weight range.

The literature on cholesterol levels and blood pressure among women with intellectual disabilities is limited and inconsistent. Women living in community residential settings have similar cardiovascular risk profiles to those of individuals without intellectual disabilities (Rimmer *et al.*, 1994). However, residential setting may mitigate these findings as seen in a study which found that women who lived with a family member had higher levels of cholesterol and lower levels of cardiovascular fitness than the general population (Rimmer *et al.*, 1995).

Additional risk factors

Other health behaviors, such as smoking, alcohol use, medication management and stress management, in addition to exercise and diet, have been documented to affect health in the general elderly population, but have rarely been studied among women with intellectual disabilities. However, clinical experience has shown that the higher a person's cognitive functioning and the more autonomous the living arrangement, the greater the risk of substance abuse (O'Brien, 1994). Many women with intellectual disabilities have had little if any opportunity to receive appropriately planned sex education. This increases risk for acquiring sexually transmitted diseases, unplanned pregnancies and inappropriate sexual expression. Women may also be restricted from opportunities to discuss relationship issues and physical sexual activity and preferences (Morse & Roth, 1994).

Biological risk factors

Risk factors related to biological factors can include genetic predisposition, age and gender. Although health promotion activities are directed toward factors that are changeable, consideration must be given to the biological risk factors that are not changeable. Biological risk factors include genetic predisposition, age, gender, race or ethnicity and climate. While these factors do not lend themselves to direct intervention, they must be taken into account when identifying high-risk population groups. Biological risk factors play a role in several leading causes of mortality, including heart disease, cancer, stroke, diabetes and cirrhosis.

Several genetic syndromes are associated with a variety of health-related conditions. Persons with Down syndrome are predisposed to certain types of health conditions, such as congenital heart disease (34%), hypotomia (100%), hearing concerns (70%), ocular concerns (15%–50%), cervical spine concerns (10%), thyroid disease, obesity, seizures (5%–10%), premature onset of Alzheimer disease (Rubin & Crocker, 1989), and hypotension (Beange et al., 1995). Many adults with Down syndrome residing in community settings have elevated risk factors for CVD, such as hypercholesterolemia, hypertriglyceridemia, elevated fasting insulin levels, abdominal obesity and a high prevalence of undiagnosed non-insulin dependent diabetes mellitus (Draheim et al., 2000). Persons with fragile-X syndrome have an increased incidence of heart disease and mitral valve prolapse (Loehr et al., 1986).

Women with intellectual disabilities may also be predisposed to physical conditions such as constipation and inadequate consumption of nutrients related to their disabilities (Steadham, 1994). Reduced intestinal motility can lead to constipation, which is associated with decreased muscle tone, anticonvulsive medication or insufficient intake of fiber and fluids. Women may also have problems swallowing due to decreased muscle tone, gastrointestinal concerns, or an inability to taste or smell. This may lead to problems with eating and insufficient calorie intake.

Key aspects of health promotion programs

Health is both an individual and a social responsibility. Implementing successful health promotion programs requires consideration of factors that support or prevent women with intellectual disabilities from initiating and maintaining health-promoting behaviors. Because personal health practices are just one of the determinants of health, health promotion programs must address environmental, cultural and social constraints that impact individuals and families.

Health promotion programs can incorporate practical interventions to control and prevent many chronic diseases. Key aspects of health promotion programs include:

- Preventive health care such as proper screenings and access to medical care
- Education and training for adults with intellectual disabilities
- Health promotion programs that focus on increasing positive health behaviors (proper nutrition, exercise and avoidance of high risk behaviors) for adults with intellectual disabilities.

Preventive health screening

Health prevention consists of activities directed toward decreasing the probability of acquiring a specific health condition, or increasing the early diagnosis of a particular condition. For women with intellectual disabilities, reducing the incidence of cancer means addressing behavioral and environmental factors that increase cancer risk, and making screening services available and accessible for early detection of cancer. Many of the complications associated with diabetes could be prevented with early detection, improved delivery of care and better education on diabetes self-management. Proven preventive measures to reduce dental decay include water fluoridation, dental sealants and smoking prevention and cessation programs. Yet they are often unavailable to those who need them most. Although prevailing myths have portrayed arthritis as an inevitable part of aging that can only be endured, effective interventions are available to prevent or reduce arthritis-related pain. Treatable depression among women with intellectual disabilities often goes undiagnosed and untreated. These women should receive routine mental health screenings.

Research on the general population and on women with physical disabilities provides some explanation for the lack of health screenings among women with intellectual disabilities. First, studies demonstrate that adherence to preventive screening guidelines is related to low income, low educational level, lack of a regular health care provider, seeing a male physician, lack of health insurance coverage, difficulty in arranging the examination, and lack of understanding the purpose of the procedure (Nosek & Howland, 1997). More women would be screened for breast and cervical cancer if their doctors recommended it. Second, among low-income black women, negative attitudes about mammography affect appointment-keeping (Crump *et al.*, 2000). Lastly, lack of adapted equipment may prevent women with musculoskeletal disabilities from receiving preventive health screening.

Education and training

To promote healthy behaviors and preventive health care among older women with intellectual disabilities, health education is needed for these women and for health professionals. These women may lack basic knowledge about their bodies and about health and aging. Moreover, they may be unaware of how their current lifestyles and behaviors can have an effect on their overall health and well-being. A major challenge in the coming years is to find ways to encourage health promoting behaviors among women with intellectual disabilities. Health behavior education needs to include preventive and promotive health care. Preventive health care topics include sexually transmitted diseases/HIV, heart disease and stroke, occupational safety, substance abuse, tobacco use, stress reduction and injury/violence prevention. Health promotive topics may include nutrition, food safety, physical activity and fitness, oral health, health communication and family planning.

Health care providers need to develop culturally appropriate educational materials for women with intellectual disabilities. Additionally, models that explain factors related to long-term adherence to health promoting activities among women with intellectual disabilities are needed. Due to these women's need for support from others in their daily lives, the role of carers in facilitating participation in health behaviors needs to be further assessed so that appropriate interventions can be developed. In order to foster a sense of control over their health, education on health promotion activities and appropriate environmental supports must be provided.

Health promotion programs that are directed at lifestyle change must address the realities of home, work and community environments. Community-based programs versus individual approaches to health education have several benefits. In a community-based program, the strength of the intervention is greater due to the opportunity for diffusion and change of the social norms. Community programs are based in the 'real world'. Lastly, programs in the community can be delivered to larger groups at a lower cost, and an environment of social support can be developed for risk-lowering and health promoting behaviors.

Examples of health promotion programs

Community-based health promotion programs need to incorporate several key principles:

- A successful program needs to build from a base of community ownership and partnership
- Programs need to target specific behaviors, such as nutrition and exercise
- Interventions need to incorporate sound theoretical frameworks as a basis for program plans
- Consideration must be given to what types of interventions work best given specific populations and circumstances.

Health promotion interventions can take place in a variety of settings including occupational settings, residential settings or community-based recreational programs.

The University of Illinois at Chicago's Center on Health Promotion Research for People with Disabilities, Rehabilitation Research and Training Center on Aging with Developmental Disabilities, and the Roybal Center on Health Maintenance have jointly developed a health promotion program for middle-age and older adults with intellectual disabilities. The program includes three components:

(1)   A center–based fitness intervention
(2)   A health education component
(3)   Education component for carers.

The 12-week center-based exercise program includes an hour a day of physical activity, three days a week. The exercise component consists of aerobic activity, muscle strength and endurance, and flexibility. The exercise modalities vary according to the preferences of the participant. Cardiorespiratory fitness activities include walking, stationary cycling, Nu-step recumbent stepping, arm ergometry, and low impact aerobics. For muscle strength and endurance, participants perform calisthenics and also use small equipment such as hand weights and elastic tubing. Free transportation to the center is provided to participants if needed. Motivational techniques are used to keep the participants interested in the program. Participants receive certificates, awards, personalized videos and workbooks upon completion of the program.

The education program for adults with intellectual disabilities, 'Exercise and nutrition health education curriculum for adults with developmental disabilities' (Heller *et al.*, 2001) is guided by two major theories of how persons change health practices. Prochaska & DiClemente's transtheoretical model states that changes in health behaviors occur in five stages:

(1) *Pre-contemplation* (no awareness of a need to change)
(2) *Contemplation* (awareness of the need to change)
(3) *Preparation* (making plans to change)
(4) *Action* (modifying behavior)
(5) *Maintenance* (incorporating change into routine).

(Prochaska *et al.*, 1994)

Bandura's social cognitive theory posits that behavior change is a function of outcome expectations associated with the behavior change, the tasks required to achieve those goals, and self-efficacy expectations for achieving the goals (Bandura, 1986).

The health education component is designed to:

(1) Help the participant understand the benefits of health promotion behaviors generally and for themselves personally (outcome expectations)
(2) Develop health promotion goals and action plans based on personal preferences
(3) Increase participants' self-efficacy in making choices and in attaining personal goals.

The trainers foster social contact among the participants by encouraging exercise and leisure activities outside of the center. At the end of the training, participants receive the personal written plan they developed, which includes their exercise goals and the steps they need to take to attain them.

The carer education program seeks to motivate primary support persons (family member or residential provider) to help participants set health promotion goals, develop action plans and attain their goals. It also includes specific information about the benefits of exercise, the specific exercise program tailored to the needs of the person, and ways to monitor physical activity jointly with the individual. This monitoring activity is intended to reinforce perceptions of exercise efficacy. The education program is held for two hours every other week (six sessions) over the same time that the individuals with intellectual disabilities receive their education and exercise intervention. Three of the education sessions are held jointly with the individual with intellectual disabilities.

To date, this project has assessed 62 participants of whom 22 have completed the exercise and education program. The project has developed a battery of new instruments to assess social-cognitive aspects of exercise adherence for adults with cognitive impairments. These instruments have been found to be reliable and should be useful to others interested in studying exercise adherence in this population. Preliminary results of the program demonstrate an increase in participant knowledge and exercise perception, life satisfaction, perceived social-environmental support for

Case study: Emily

Emily is a 38-year-old single woman who came to the exercise and nutrition health education program after hearing about it from her job coach. Prior to enrollment in the program, physician clearance was obtained. During the screening process, her height was noted to be 5 ft 1 in and her weight was 157 pounds. Her body mass index (BMI) ratio was 30. For her height, Emily's ideal weight should be between 106 pounds and 132 pounds. Emily said that she was excited to be coming to the exercise program. However, she confessed that she loves to eat chocolate candy bars and chips everyday at work, along with a half-liter of caffeinated, non-diet soda. She also reported that she did not like to exercise because it was 'too hard.' Emily was enrolled in the 12-week exercise and nutrition program.

The health education classes met three days a week for one hour. The sessions consisted of activities directed at helping Emily to understand her attitudes toward health, exercise and food; to find exercises that she enjoyed; and to gain the necessary skills and knowledge about exercises and healthy eating. Program facilitators also worked with Emily to identify personal goals for her exercise and nutrition plan. She stated that she wanted to lose weight (25 pounds), exercise three times a week, and eat fewer sweets while at work.

During the program, Emily received peer support in trying out various aerobic exercise activities, including dancing to videotapes. She enjoyed leading the group in exercise activities, along with trying new recipes. By the end of the 12 weeks, Emily had lost 5 pounds and was drinking diet soda at work. She was also eating fewer candy bars and was eating a few apples instead. Lastly, Emily decided to join a walking group at work three days a week.

exercise, and self-confidence in their ability to perform exercise activities (Heller *et al.*, 2000). Also, when carers perceived greater benefits of exercise and when there were fewer access barriers to exercise facilities and equipment, adults with intellectual disabilities were likely to exercise more frequently. In the health education classes, gender differences were noted with respect to men's and women's interests in participating in specific types of exercise activities. Men often preferred exercising to Tae Bo and martial arts type videos, whereas, women enjoyed doing aerobic exercises that involved dancing to a music CD or video.

Another health promotion program in the US is a curriculum on abuse titled *Taking charge: Responding to abuse, neglect, and financial exploitation* (Fitzsimons, 2000). This curriculum and workshop provides knowledge, skills and resources about abuse, neglect and financial exploitation, to people with disabilities, family members and advocates with the goal of empowering them to enforce their rights and the rights of persons with intellectual disabilities.

Researchers in the UK have developed a health promotion screening program for screening women with intellectual disabilities for breast and cervical cancer (Hollins *et al.*, 2000). A practice guide *Looking after my breasts* (Hollins & Perez, 2000), which is designed for women with intellectual disabilities, includes picture books without words to inform women and their carers about breast and cervical screening. The guide is disseminated within primary health care, women's health centers and specialist community health services for adults with intellectual disabilities.

Conclusion

Women with intellectual disabilities have unique health issues across their life span. Despite the documented significance of health promotion activities to maintain health or decrease or remove risk factors, individuals with intellectual disabilities, for the most part, have not been included in health promotion programs. However, the provision of health promotion activities for women with intellectual disabilities may also contribute to healthier and more productive lives. Women with intellectual disabilities will more fully achieve community integration when they are not constrained by poor health and can command the necessary power to change conditions affecting their health status. The provision of health education and environmental supports, along with personal choice and social and environmental support, will help women gain a sense of control over their health and the determinants of their health.

According to the WHO *Global Strategy for Health for All by the Year 2000*, health science and technology have reached a point where their contributions to further improve health standards can only make a real impact if people themselves become full partners in health protection and promotion. Although guidance and assistance in facilitating dialogue may be required for some individuals, many adults with intellectual disabilities are able to actively participate in health education programs and now have the right to actively participate with their peers who have no disabilities, in health-related activities including health promotion. However, future health promotion programs must account for the barriers to health care services to provide successful health education. Barriers include physical access, lack of health insurance coverage, pre-existing conditions, geographic unavailability of health services, lack of transportation, and negative attitudes toward disabled people among health care providers. For example, women may not be able to exercise due to the cost of the program, they may lack knowledge about where to exercise, they may not have access to exercise equipment at home or work, and they may not have carer support. Considering socio-environmental factors, including the type of residential setting, poverty conditions, support from carers and opportunities for choice, will foster successful participation in health promotion programs. Health care professionals and other carers in the community, many of whom are having more contact with adults with disabilities, will also need to acquire a greater understanding of health promotion activities that are appropriate for people with disabilities.

Acknowledgement

Preparation of this chapter was supported in part by the Rehabilitation Research and Training Center on Aging with Developmental Disabilities. Department of Disability and Human Development, University of Illinois at Chicago through the US Department of Education National Institute on Disability and Rehabilitation Research, Grant No. II133B980046 and the Roybal Center on Health Maintenance through a grant from the National Institute on Aging, Grant No. AG15890-12.

References

Bandura, A. (1986) *Social Foundations of Thought and Action: A Social Cognitive Theory.* Prentice Hall, Englewood Cliffs, NJ.

Beange, H., McElduff, A. & Baker, W. (1995) Medical disorders of adults with mental retardation: a population study. *American Journal on Mental Retardation,* **99** (6), 595–604.

Crump, S.R., Mayberry, R.M., Taylor, B.D., Barefield, K.P. & Thomas, P.E. (2000) *Journal of the National Medical Association*, **92** (5), 237–246.

Draheim, C.C., Williams, D.P., McCubbin, J.A., Jacks, J.N. & Oliver, J.C. (2000) Comparison of physiological coronary artery disease risk factors for adults with mental retardation and Down syndrome. *Medicine and Science in Sports and Exercise*, **32** (5), S261.

Fitzsimons, N. (2000) *Taking Charge: Responding to Abuse, Neglect, and Financial Exploitation*. Department of Disability and Human Development, University of Illinois at Chicago.

Fox, R.A., Rosenberg, R. & Rotatori, A.F. (1985) Parent involvement in a treatment program for obese retarded adults. *Journal of Behavior Therapy & Experimental Psychiatry*, **16** (1), 45–48.

Fujiura, G.T., Fitzsimons, N., Marks, B. & Chicoine, B. (1997) Predictors of BMI among adults with Down syndrome: the social context of health promotion. *Research in Developmental Disabilities*, **18** (4), 261–274.

Gill, C.J. (1996) Becoming visible: personal health experiences of women with disabilities. In: *Women with Physical Disabilities: Achieving and Maintaining Health and Well Being* (eds D.M. Krotoski, M.A. Nosek & M.A. Turk), pp. 5–15. Paul H. Brookes, Baltimore.

Heller, T., Rimmer, J. & Hsieh, K. (2000) *Exercise adherence among older adults with mental retardation: exercise knowledge, fitness, and life satisfaction outcomes*. Paper presentation at the Gerontological Society of America Annual Meeting, Washington, DC.

Heller, T., Marks, B. & Ailey, S. (2001) *Exercise and Nutrition Health Education Curriculum for Adults with Developmental Disabilities*. Rehabilitation Research and Training Center on Aging with Developmental Disabilities, University of Illinois at Chicago.

Heller, T., Hsieh, K. & Rimmer, J. (in press) Barriers and supports for exercise participation among adults with Down syndrome. *Journal of Gerontological Social Work*.

Heller, T., Ying, G., Rimmer, J.H. & Marks, B.A. (in press) Determinants of exercise in adults with cerebral palsy. *Public Health Nursing*.

Hollins, S. & Perez, W. (2000) *Looking after my Breasts*. Royal College of Psychiatry, London.

Hollins, S., Downer, J., Perez, W., Gray, S. & Chaseldine, J. (2000) Screening women for breast and cervical cancer. *Journal of Intellectual Disabilities Research*, **44**, 322–323.

Janicki, M.P., Dalton, A.J., Henderson, C.M. & Davidson, P.W. (1999) Mortality and morbidity among older adults with intellectual disability: health services considerations. *Disability and Rehabilitation*, **21** (5/6), 284–294.

Kopac, C.A., Fritz, J. & Holt, R. (1996) *Availability and Accessibility of Gynecological and Reproductive Services for Women with Developmental Disabilities*. American Network of Community Options and Resources (ANCOR), Washington, DC.

Lennox, N.G. & Kerr, M.P. (1997) Primary health care and people with an intellectual disability: the evidence base. *Journal of Intellectual Disability Research*, **41** (5), 365–372.

Loehr, J.P., Synhorst, D.P., Wolfe, R.R. & Hagerman, R.J. (1986) Aortic root dilatation and mitral valve prolapse in the Fragile X syndrome. *American Journal of Medical Genetics*, **23**, 189–194.

Morse, J.S. & Roth, S.P. (1994) Sexuality. In: *A Life-Span Approach to Nursing Care for Individuals with Developmental Disabilities* (eds S.P. Roth & J.S. Morse), pp. 281–295. Paul H. Brookes, Baltimore.

National Center for Health Statistics (1996) *Health, United States, 1995*. Public Health Services, Hyattsville, MD.

National Center for Health Statistics (1997) Centers for Disease Control and Prevention. Report of final mortality statistics 1995. *Monthly Vital Statistics Report*, **45** (11), Supplement 2.

National Organization on Disability (1998) *Survey of Americans with Disabilities*, Study No. 828373. Louis Harris & Associates Inc., Washington, DC.

Nosek, M.A. & Howland, C.A. (1997) Breast and cervical cancer screening among women with physical disabilities. *Archives of Physical Medicine & Rehabilitation*, **78** (12, Supplement 5), S39–44.

O'Brien, D.R. (1994) Health maintenance and promotion in adults. In: *A Life-span Approach to Nursing Care for Individuals with Developmental Disabilities*. (eds S.P. Roth & J.S. Morse), pp. 171–192. Paul H. Brookes, Baltimore.

Prochaska, J.O., Velicer, W.F., Rossie, J.S., Goldstein, M.G., Marcus, B.H., Rakowski, W., Viore, C., Harlow, L.L., Redding, C.A., Rosenbloom, D. & Rossie, S.R. (1994) Stages of change and decisional balance for 12 problem behaviors. *Health Psychology*, **13**, 38–46.

Rimmer, J.H. & Rubin, S. (1996) *Exercise, health, activity patterns, and barriers to exercise in adults with physical disabilities*. NIH Paralympic Congress Proceedings, Atlanta.

Rimmer, J.H., Braddock, D. & Fujiura, G. (1994) Cardiovascular risk factor levels in adults with mental retardation. *American Journal of Mental Retardation*, **98** (4), 510–518.

Rimmer, J.H., Braddock, D. & Marks, B.A. (1995) Health characteristics and behaviors of adults with mental retardation residing in three living arrangements. *Research in Developmental Disabilities*, **16**, 489–499.

Rimmer, J.H., Rubin S.S. & Braddock, D. (2000) Barriers to exercise in African American women with physical disabilities. *Archives of Physical Medicine and Rehabilitation*, **81**, 182–188.

Rubin, I.L. & Crocker, A.C. (1989) *Developmental Disabilities: Delivery of Medical Care for Children and Adults*. Lea & Febiger, Philadelphia.

Sobsey, D. (1994) *Violence and abuse in the lives of people with disabilities: the end of silent acceptance?* Paul H. Brookes, Baltimore.

Sobsey, D. (2000) Faces of violence against women with developmental disabilities. *Impact*, **13** (3), 23–25.

Steadham, C.I. (1994) Health maintenance and promotion. In: *A Life-span Approach to Nursing Care for Individuals with Developmental Disabilities* (eds S.P. Roth & J.S. Morse), pp. 147–169. Paul H. Brookes, Baltimore.

Stiefel, D.J., Truelove, E.L., Persson, R.S., Chin, M.M. & Mandel, L.S. (1993) A comparison of oral health in spinal cord injury and other disability groups. *Special Care in Dentistry*, **13** (6), 229–235.

Traustadottir, R. (1990) *Women with Disabilities: The Double Discrimination.* Center on Human Policy, Syracuse, NY.

United Nations Population Fund (2000) The State of World Population 2000: Lives Together, Worlds Apart Men and Women in a Time of Change. Retrieved from the World Wide Web 19 January, 2001: http://www.unfpa.org/swp/2000/english/press_kit/summary.html.

Vignehsa, H., Soh, G., Lo, G.L. & Chellappah, N.K. (1991) Dental health of disabled children in Singapore. *Australian Dental Journal*, **36** (2), 151–156.

WHO (1988) *Health Promotion for Working Populations: Report of a WHO Expert Committee.* Technical Report Series 765, World Health Organization, Geneva.

12 Building Health Supports for Women

Mary McCarron and Kathryn Pekala Service

Introduction

The WHO's global strategy for women's health emphasizes the right of all women, including those with intellectual disabilities (ID), to the best attainable standard of health along with the right to access adequate health care services (Walsh *et al.*, 2000). All minority groups, for example people with ID, often present with above average health care requirements (Moss & Turner, 1996). An increasingly competitive health care market reinforces the need to ensure that adequate safeguards are in place to promote equal access for individuals at risk. Despite the apparent need for a policy framework to address the specific health care needs of women in the general population (Department of Health, 1995), efforts to empower women with ID with practical assistance and support to access optimum levels of health care are lagging (Lunsky & Reiss, 1998).

In a study of health care needs of people with ID in the community, Thornton (1996) concluded that practitioners working within primary health care teams had little awareness of the health needs of adults with ID. This was partially attributed to lack of confidence and inadequate knowledge and previous experience, combined with a shortfall in human and financial resources. Opportunities in education specifically on treating women with ID are now expanding in the general medical community (Bradshaw *et al.*, 1996).

This chapter expresses a lifespan perspective on health care issues that are of unique concern to women, with an emphasis on women with intellectual disabilities. It focuses on those components of primary care which are central to health and well-being, such as nutrition and exercise, sexuality and self-image, reproductive health including health screens and examinations, and fertility and menstruation, along with specific aging issues such as menopause, osteoporosis and uro-gynecology problems. The promotion of opportunities and the means to assist women with ID to achieve optimum health care across these health care areas will be explored.

Background

Nurses have a long and rich tradition of supporting individuals without discrimination, including those with ID, as they navigate the uneven terrain of health. Guided by standards of practice for nurses who specialize in working with people with ID, the nursing profession focuses primarily on interventions that maximize the psychosocial, physical, affective, cognitive and developmental strengths of individuals and their families (Aggen, 1995). Nurses who provide primary care for individuals with ID experience a high degree of interdependent planning and collaboration with other members of the multidisciplinary teams (Aggen, 1995). They have also developed their role from providers to partners with individuals and their support networks.

The history of nursing has been referred to as an episode in the history of women. Issues of women have influenced the progress of nursing. There has long been a social dimension to nursing work (Donahue, 1985) and nurses have responsibly cared for vulnerable and stigmatized populations. For these reasons, women with ID historically have had a high level of direct and trusting contact with nurses. This continues to be the case.

A study on health issues of 26 women with ID (Sonpal-Valias, 2000) concluded that women with ID and other adult women had similar health needs. Furthermore their general understanding with respect to health-related issues mirrored that of women without ID. They may however require additional supports and individualized interventions to address these needs effectively. Communication difficulties between persons with ID and members of the primary health care team often have a negative impact on individuals' ability to access appropriate health care services (Kerr *et al*, 1997; Stanley, 1998). Because of their 24-hour contact and frequently long-term relationship with persons with ID, nurses may develop an intuitive understanding and skill in assisting women to feel comfortable with all aspects of care. Social relationships are an important determinant of health, especially for women with ID (Sonpal-Valias, 2000). Staff support is key for many women with ID to access health-related or other services (Kopac *et al.*, 1998). Thus, the partnership between a woman with ID and her health care provider may extend beyond this dyad to encompass other professionals or advocates who are instrumental in building support for women in this group.

Nutrition and exercise

Proper nutrition and exercise can increase health and longevity. Many losses in function have been attributed in error to the aging process when they occur because of poor nutrition, overeating, lack of exercise and resultant deconditioning of muscle strength and other physical abilities. As people age, their caloric requirements decrease, but the food must still be dense in nutrients. While popular with the general population in the western culture, interest and research in these areas for women with intellectual disabilities is growing. Nutrition and exercise screenings and assessments are initial activities that provide a baseline. From this, interventions can be developed to maintain or improve the women's functional status, reduce preventable diseases including secondary conditions – for which people with ID are at a higher risk – reduce the costs of health care, and overall enhance the well-being and quality of life for these women. Diet and exercise reviews are considered by many experts to be an integral part of the yearly physical assessment. Comprehensive discussion of the specifics of nutritional and exercise screens and assessments are available (Mughal, 2000).

Eating and food have been acknowledged to reflect tradition and culture, rewards and punishment. These latter factors have been pertinent in the western culture in working with people with ID. Behavior modification programs have traditionally utilized food as a positive re-inforcer (O'Brien, 1994). Yet knowledge alone is not a significant predictor of adherence to health or medical advice. While it is important to educate people about nutrition and exercise, other factors also influence acceptance and enjoyment of food (Mughal, 2000). For women with ID as for other women, these include poverty, socioeconomic class, the influence of the media, ease with and independence in preparing convenience foods, even pleasing their support persons or modeling themselves after staff. Community activities are often centered on activities that focus on eating. Women with certain disorders such as cerebral palsy are prone to chewing and swallowing difficulties, food aspiration and gastro-esophageal reflux disease. Dental problems are quite prevalent with people with ID. Studies have reported a high proportion of cancers of the gastrointestinal tract in persons with ID (Cooke, 1997). Other nutritional disorders that may be of significance for women with intellectual disabilities include undernutrition, constipation, malabsorption, iron deficiency anemia, pica (Lennox & Beange, 1999), rumination (O'Brien 1994), and drug and nutrient interactions (Mughal 2000).

Individuals who have certain syndromes, such as Down syndrome (Rubin *et al.*, 1998) and Prader-Willi syndrome, have been shown to have higher incidence of obesity. Other disorders, such as Turner's syndrome, show physical features such as short stature that predispose individuals to obesity. Many medications that are often utilized by people with ID also have weight gain as side effects, especially psychotropic medication. In general, among adults with ID, obesity (Lennox & Beange 1999) and cholesterol levels (Walsh *et al.*, 2000) are higher. Environment, too, plays a role. Women who live at home may have higher levels of cholesterol and obesity and lower cardiovascular fitness than the general population, which puts them at higher risk for cardiac problems (Rimmer *et al.*, 1995). There are often problems with obtaining an accurate weight of women who use wheelchairs. The role of exercise on health, such as cardio-vascular fitness, mirrors that for women without ID (Ridenour & Norton, 1997). It appears that factors contributing to low fitness levels are remarkably similar to those applying to the general population (Heller *et al.*, 2000). Among these are cost, being tired or bored, problems with equipment, and lack of support. Of note, women with certain syndromes such as Down syndrome should be screened for pre-existing medical conditions such as cardiac disease and atlantoaxial subluxation. Just as for the general population, before starting exercise programs older women should have stress tests, especially if they have any positive cardiac dis-ease history (O'Brien, 1994).

Good nutritional and exercise habits are lifelong investments. Many women without intellectual disabilities experience difficulties with the abstract concepts of nutrition and exercise and 'cause and effect' upon health, especially when temporal relationships and time are considered. Interventions that nurses have found useful include many of the techni-ques that women in general use. Structured and regular nutritional counseling for the woman and her support network by nurses or regis-tered dieticians has been shown to be helpful. These professionals can also answer questions as to the confusing barrage of nutritional mes-sages from a variety of sources including the media, commercial oper-ations and friends and family (Mughal, 2000). Although education on nutrition and exercise tailored to individual learning styles is para-mount, other factors that influence motivation need equal con-sideration.

Staff and family can function as role models or support reinforcements. The use of non-edible items, such as personal 'one to one' interactions, in behavioral modification programs is recommended. Teaching and modeling in food selection help to reinforce healthy eating habits, espe-cially in highlighting nutritious yet convenient alternatives that women with intellectual disabilities can learn to prepare, assisting in meal preparation, and reinforcing the quality and number of servings (Ridenour & Norton, 1997). Further, structured and regularly scheduled exercise times can nurture the development of habitual behavior. Special Olympics have proved to be an effective means by which exercise can be enjoyed. Involvement in Special Olympics has been shown to promote cardiovascular endurance (Wright & Cowden, 1990) and improve self-esteem and social competence (Dykens & Cohen 1996). It is generally acknowledged that exercise is easier to maintain when there is a positive social component (National Institute on Aging, 2001).

In conclusion, as with anyone, interventions must be individualized both according to the woman's preferences and to her health status. Community-based responses that are appropriate for others in the general population may need modification. Alternatives need to be continually explored and tried. We all share the need for mutual support and understanding when it comes to maintaining good nutrition, regular exercise and lifestyle choices that will enable us to 'grow old gracefully'.

Health screens and examinations

Many governmental agencies and medical organizations have standards for health screening and promotion. It is acknowledged by many of the health care providers who work with people with intellectual disabilities that screening tests and exams should be performed according to the same indications and contraindications as for the general population (Evenhuis et al., 2000; Lennox & Beange 1999). A study on gynecological services for women with ID reported that 40% of the women surveyed had not received health education regarding gynecological care. Barriers to accessing services included financial difficulties, fear of examinations and difficulties in accessing health care professionals to provide such services (Kopac et al., 1998). Access to preventative health care varies by country (Walsh et al., 2000).

Basic preventative and gynecological screening for women with disabilities is frequently overshadowed by more obvious physical or neurological problems, which may require more immediate focus. Thus, screening for diabetes, hypertension, hyperlipidemia and thyroid imbalances, all of which are common concerns for women, may be neglected (Kirschner et al., 1998). This is frequently compounded by the difficulty of detecting disease in people who cannot self-report symptoms. The diagnosis of some diseases such as cancer may not take place until the disease has reached an advanced stage and opportunities for treatment may become more limited (Cooke, 1997). The knowledge that many syndromes have specific age-related risk factors can lead to enhanced prevention or early diagnosis of potentially impairing conditions (Evenhuis et al., 2000). As women age, there is a higher risk of cardiovascular problems that may be overlooked.

Many women have difficulty obtaining comprehensive, accessible and dignified physical examinations. For women with cerebral palsy, spina bifida and other physical disabilities, there have been reported difficulties obtaining gynecological care (Welner et al., 1999). There may be physical, attitudinal, knowledge, and financial barriers (Kirschner *et al.*, 1998). Physical barriers may limit access for many women with ID. Other access issues include transportation, access to buildings and examination rooms, limited number of willing or trained providers, allowing more time to examine a person with a disability, and money. In the US, for example, there are time constraints imposed by managed care and there may be limitations to certain insurance policies. Adaptive equipment greatly enhances access, such as table adjusts for height and head positioning, hand rails, boots and straps, hoyer lifts, transfer boards, even warmed and pediatric speculums, and liberal application of lidocaine gel to the perineal area. There are a number of alternative positions – the knee-chest or diamond-shaped positions – for the pelvic examination such as for the person with cerebral palsy who may have severe flexion contractures (Welner *et al.*, 1999).

Many women with ID may have difficulty cooperating with gynecological and other physical examinations. This may be due to a number of factors such as cognitive impairment, negative past experiences with the medical system and previous history of sexual abuse. There is an inclination for women to receive sedation or even general anesthesia based upon historical difficulties with examinations, known behavior problems and level of cognitive impairment. These factors may be indicators for health care providers to modify the approach while minimizing the use of sedation (Pulcini *et al.*, 1999).

There are a number of nursing models of care that are guided by the concept of partnership (Pulcini *et al.*, 1999). These models strive to empower the woman by incorporating education of the woman and her support networks, desensitizing techniques and special approaches to the physical examination. Desired goals are improved self-care and knowledge about the exam. Some practical suggestions include offering choices of provider or even time of day for the examination; education using videos (e.g. the video and workbook, *Let's Talk About Health: What Every Woman Should Know*, Heaton, 1996); anatomic models, and actual exam equipment; role playing and peer support; and allowing adequate time in a relaxed environment and adequate opportunities for reinforcement garnered from the literature (Pulcini *et al.*, 1999). Focus groups have even been used (Fraser & Fraser, 2001) with suggestions of training moderators and interpreters for group success. For very frightened women, individual and personalized desensitization and education processes have been found to be helpful.

An important part of this assessment is that of taking the woman's history in interview. Depending on the woman's circumstances, there may be volumes of information or very little information that may generate more questions than answers. Many women rely on their support networks, both natural and paid, to supply information to and from the health care provider. There may not only be questions as to the quantity, but also the quality, of the information based on the third party informant. Likewise, because of the third person the focus may be shifted from the woman, with some providers addressing the support person and not the woman (Service, in press).

Breast health

Breast cancer is the single most common cause of death among women aged 40–50. The incidence of breast cancer for those aged 50 is 2:1000 (McPherson *et al.*, 1994) and being older than 50 years is the strongest risk factor (Machia, 2001). Breast health for women with disabilities is usually discussed within the general context of gynecological health (Welner *et al.*, 1999). Risk factors for breast cancer include age, personal history, family history, age of menarche lower than 11 years, and nulliparity. These last three factors may be especially significant for women with ID as early history may not be available and many women with ID may be childless. There is a need for increased awareness to identify women at risk, as women at higher risk will need closer and earlier surveillance, and possibly preventative options (Machia, 2001).

In a more recent study (Davies & Duff, 2001), it was reported that only one-third of women with ID who lived in community settings regularly had breast examinations and that a similar proportion were scheduled for mammograms. As with other screens, the frequency and need for mammography is the same for all women. Mammograms may be problematic due to the woman's inability to lean her body forward in a certain way or even raise her arms. Some equipment requires that the woman needs to stand. Newer systems are being developed to accommodate the woman. Self-breast exams may not be performed regularly for many reasons, including physical limitations such as contractures of the shoulders and elbows, dexterity and cognitive limitations. Breast exams by staff may be limited due to tactile defensiveness of the woman, and even care staff's fear of abuse allegations or misinterpretations by the woman. As with other aspects of the gynecological exam, concerns may be present as many women with ID have been taught not to let others touch their 'private parts', such as breast and genitals (Ridenour & Norton, 1997). Some care staff view breast exams as an activity only to be done by nurses.

There are opportunities for nurses and other primary health care providers to support women with ID and their carers in breast health awareness. These opportunities include knowledge to access and expectations in existing generic services, education in the necessary skills, and assistance to those who are unable to self-exam regularly (Davies & Duff, 2001).

Sexuality and self-image

Research indicates that health care professionals often regard women with ID as asexual, which is reflected in the paucity of knowledge on the changing health care needs of these women across the lifespan (Sulpizi, 1996). Women with ID have the same sexual needs, rights and responsibilities as other women. While it is beyond the scope of this chapter to review details of sexuality issues (see Chapter 6 for this) including societal and cultural attitudes, these women and their support networks deserve education and knowledge in areas of sexually transmitted diseases, contraception, safe sexual practices and parenting. This should be implemented according to their capacities to understand and to complete tasks (e.g. with limitations of fine motor skills) acknowledging the profound cultural differences in sensitivity as to content, and of the support networks (Walsh *et al.*, 2000).

There are interventions such as videos (*Let's Talk About Health: What Every Woman Should Know*, Heaton 1996), and other teaching materials. We have found that peer support groups for these women are beneficial, especially with regard to discussion and understanding of the power discrepancies that are felt by women in general (Walsh *et al.*, 2000). In addition, women with intellectual disabilities face challenges with issues of self-esteem, self-concept and body image, for instance as the result of the physical characteristics of syndromes. For example, women who have Turner's syndrome have reported low self-worth and dissatisfaction with their lives. In order to provide appropriate education and counseling for the woman and her support network, nurses and other health care providers need to have knowledge about the health needs and factors that affect coping (Kagen-Krieger, 2001). Likewise, there needs to be acknowledgement that low self-esteem can contribute to increased difficulties with negotiations around sexual activity for these women (Walsh *et al.*, 2000).

Women with ID very often require considerable support and education in respect of issues such as appropriate social and sexual relationships, fertility and pregnancy, and menstrual self-care. In the past hysterectomy was often perceived by carers as the most appropriate approach for the management of fertility and menstruation challenges (Passer *et al.*, 1984). Ethical issues combined with the risk to the individual of major surgery have focused attention on less invasive approaches in the management of these issues. It is now generally accepted that appropriate education with regard to issues of sexuality and menstrual self-care, tailored to the individual's unique learning style, can be effectively utilized in the management of fertility and menstruation difficulties (Sulpizi, 1996; Prevatt, 1998). Low dose oral contraceptives may also be the preferred choice for some women with ID and/or their carers. The long-term effects from more radical contraceptive methods in women with ID warrant investigation (Gill & Brown, 2000).

While contraceptive methods may help in pregnancy prevention they do not protect women with ID from sexually transmitted diseases, or the physical and psychological trauma of sexual abuse. Women with ID are vulnerable to physical or sexual abuse due to their inability often to defend themselves, or lack of knowledge with respect to what constitutes abuse (Walsh *et al.*, 2000). Due to communication difficulties many women with ID may not be able to report symptoms of abuse or discomfort associated with infections or trauma. They are thus reliant on nurses and other health care professionals to be alert for subtle symptoms such as foul or bloody discharges, trauma or laceration of the hymen (Furman, 1989). Other emotional symptoms such as anxiety, restfulness, fearfulness, apathy and withdrawal may also be relevant. In conclusion, in common with women in general, women with ID have the right to appropriate education, advice and support on all matters affecting their own bodies and general health.

Menstrual matters

Regardless of the presence of ID, puberty in females stimulates a variety of physical and emotional changes such as breast development, body hair growth and commencement of menses, along with mood and emotional changes. Women with ID appear comparable to peers in the general population with respect to age of onset and regularity of menstruation (Schupf *et al.*, 1997; Walsh *et al.*, 2000). Similar to the general population, premenstrual syndrome symptoms and dysmenorrhea are also common in women with ID. Symptoms are often manifested through behavioral problems, decreased mood and tearfulness, self-abusive behavior, and occasionally an increase in seizure activity. One of the most fundamental difficulties affecting individuals with ID is their inability to express their feelings adequately. From the authors' clinical experience, women with ID may not be able to describe pain or discomfort often associated with the menstrual cycle and thus depend on carers to assist in identifying causes of anxiety and distress.

Studies have shown that cyclical behavioral changes occur in 18% of women with intellectual disabilities and various treatments can improve behavior in 40–60% of women (Quint *et al.*, 1999). Careful consideration with respect to diet, fluid intake and exercise can help reduce discomfort. Medical management may involve the use of analgesics, low-dose oral contraceptives or mild diuretics (Sulpizi, 1996). There is an urgent need for research, which explores the relationship between challenging behavior and the menstrual cycle in women with ID. This will enable a more accurate assessment and analysis of behavioral problems, and thus permit the introduction of appropriate preventative and treatment measures.

Depending on the level of ID, women very often require considerable support and education in respect of issues surrounding menstruation, such as recording of menstrual history and attending to menstrual hygiene need; the latter may be amenable to behavior modification (Sulpizi, 1996). Assessment and identification of care requirements is heavily dependent on having an accurate health history and up-to-date information. Accurate menstrual profile must include date/month/year, duration of bleeding, description of flow and premenstrual or postmenstrual symptoms, along with noting any increase in concurrent medical problems such as seizure activity. Accurate information on menstrual history and cessation of menstrual periods is necessary to assist aid in determining the role of menopause in the risk of age-related medical conditions in women with ID, and particularly women with Down syndrome.

Prolonged use of psychotropic and anti-seizure medication, which is often evidenced in this population, may precipitate menstrual dysfunction and infertility, along with age-related disorders associated with estrogen deficiency such as osteoporosis (Gill & Brown, 2000).

Menopause: physical and psychological care needs

There is a paucity of information with respect to the issue of menopause in women with ID (McCarthy, 2000). In the general population an increasing body of research has focused on a variety of estrogen-related health conditions such as heart disease, depression, breast cancer and dementia following menopause (Harlow & Ephross, 1995). This research is not replicated in the field of ID, and the relevance of menstrual history in contributing to understanding health-related conditions in women with ID, has received limited attention.

Estrogen is known to have an important influence on the brain structures involved in Alzheimer's disease. Evidence suggests that it promotes the growth of cholinergic neurones (Tang *et al.*, 1996), acts as an antioxidant (Niki & Nakano, 1990) and suppresses levels of Apolipoprotein E, all of which are known to have an important influence in the pathogenesis of Alzheimer's disease.

Evidence of premature aging and the precocious development of Alzheimer's disease in persons with Down syndrome (Evenhuis *et al.*, 2000) has increased awareness and stimulated research on the potential relevance of the menstrual history of women with Down syndrome to health-related conditions (Schupf *et al.*, 1997; Cosgrave *et al.*, 1999; Seltzer *et al.*, 2001). Earlier age of menopause has repeatedly been reported in women with Down syndrome (Cosgrave *et al.*, 1999; Schupf *et al.*, 1997). Seltzer *et al.* (2001) suggest that women with Down syndrome have a median age of menopause that is 4–5 years earlier than women in the general population, with estimates ranging from 45.8 years to 47.1 years depending on method of analysis employed. This compares to a reported median age of menopause for women in the general population of 51.2 years (Brambilla & McKinlay, 1989). Cosgrave *et al.* (1999) reported a mean age of menopause in 42 women with Down syndrome at 44.7 years, and a significant relationship between the age of onset of menopause and age of onset of dementia for 12 post-menopausal subjects was also reported. These findings suggest that women with DS in particular are at an increased risk for postmenopausal health related disorders.

This has a number of implications with regard to the estrogen-related health conditions for these women and their care providers. Hormone replacement therapy (HRT) has been shown to be effective as a protective against Alzheimer's disease in the general population (Kawas *et al.* 1997; Tang *et al.*, 1996). But it has not been studied systematically for its associated benefits in reducing the risk of osteoporosis and heart disease among women with ID. Women with ID do not receive the same degree of preventative and therapeutic interventions as women in the general population (Walsh *et al.*, 2000). Hence, nurses who support women with ID need to be alert and proactively advocate with their colleagues in the general medical community for the same standard of care.

Women with ID may lack understanding of the physical and emotional changes that often occur to a greater or lesser degree during the menopausal period, such as headaches, mood changes and irritability, reduced energy and drive, hot flushes and various psychological factors. To date there is little research on how the menopause affects women with ID, or on their level of understanding or awareness with regard to these matters (McCarthy, 2000).

Nurses need to work with women who may be entering the menopause, and their carers whose attitudes often influence these women (Martin *et al.*, 2001), so as to identify treatment options available to women without ID. As with all treatments, they must be individualized to the women based on a number of factors, including understanding the difference between short-term symptom relief and long-term preventative effects because of the different risks and benefits of each type of treatment

Case study: Beatrice

Beatrice is a 42 year-old woman with Down syndrome. She lacks the ability to communicate verbally and generally makes her needs known through pointing and visual gaze. For a year Beatrice had frequent fluctuating episodes of behavioral changes such as irritability, apathy, screaming and shouting along with self-injurious behaviors such as banging her head and hitting herself. The unpredictability of these behavioral outbursts presented a major challenge to carers and was a frequent source of stress and anxiety to other members in the group home. Clinical assessment ruled out any major physical health-related problems and Alzheimer's disease was ruled out at this time. Thorough assessment and recording of these behaviors using a detailed functional analysis and closer examination of her menstrual cycle indicated a positive association between the symptoms of premenstrual tension and episodes of these behaviors. Further hormonal studies revealed that Beatrice was starting the perimenopausal period. Education, counseling and a combination of mild analgesics, HRT, and natural remedies were utilized and assisted to success-fully minimize the distress which Beatrice was obviously experiencing during the premenstrual period. This thoughtful and comprehensive assessment elimi-nated the requirements of more restrictive treatments such as psychotropic medications and enabled Beatrice and her network to experience a better quality of life.

(Martin *et al.,* 2001). The lack of knowledge both of the health care pro-vider and the woman and her network, and poor communication, can result in incorrect or suboptimal decisions.

Osteoporosis

There is increasing evidence of high incidence of osteoporosis for indi-viduals with ID. There are a number of risk factors including immobility, small body size, poor diets, low vitamin D levels (Lennox & Beange, 1999), and the prolonged use of psychotrophic and anticonvulsant medications that lead to reduced estrogen levels. Consequently, women who have certain conditions such as cerebral palsy and epilepsy (Jancar & Jancar, 1998) are especially prone to the development of osteoporosis. There are suggestions that this may occur at earlier ages, which can lead to an increased possibility of fractures (Gill & Brown, 2000). Recent research indicated that when compared to males, women with ID are more predisposed to fractures (Jancar & Jancar, 1998) as women are near a critical fracture threshold that is related to a decreased bone mass and accelerated peri and postmenopausal states (van Schrojenstein Lantman-de Valk, 1998).

For women with ID, general prevention activities and management of osteoporosis should be the same as for other women. With the prevalence of so many risk factors, the possibility of osteoporosis should be carefully thought about in the early health exams and screens for young women with ID. The severity of osteoporosis should be established by bone density tests, and underlying diseases that may be responsible for the fragility should be treated and risk factors removed, if possible. Drug therapies such as calcium supplementation (800–1000 mgm daily of elemental calcium for premenopausal women and 1500 mgm for post-menopausal women), Vitamin D (600–800 IU daily), hormone replacement therapy, biphosphonates, or calcitriol or ergocalciferol, should be strongly considered (Lennox & Beange, 1999). Use of these latter medications with younger women with such risk factors as small size and immobility should be considered carefully. We also need to educate support networks as to instituting measures to prevent falls, such as environmental modifications that are widely available in the general gerontological literature. Because of frequent and close personal contact when providing care, carers need to be educated as to safe and considerate 'hands-on' provision of care for vulnerable individuals.

Uro-gynecology

It is well known that urinary incontinence is a very common problem for older women with a prevalence rate twice as high among women than with men. Although there are a number of aging changes in the urinary system, incontinence is not a part of the normal aging process. The development of incontinence in women with ID should not be peremptorily attributed as a normal phenomenon of aging. In the population without ID about one third of women who live in the community over the age of 60 experience some degree of urinary incontinence. Whether this is replicated in women with ID has received little attention and there is a need for an increased awareness with respect to the issues of incontinence in this population. Without proper baseline information, women with ID are at risk of inadequate assessment. As is known, there are a number of different causes for urinary incontinence such as stress incontinence and urge incontinence due to detrusor instability (Lennox & Beange, 1999). Different types require different treatments, which emphasizes the necessity of a careful and thorough assessment.

Similar to their peers in the general population, women with ID may also be embarrassed and reluctant to report or discuss this problem despite the considerable distress experienced. For women with ID, there may be difficulties in obtaining an assessment, as was noted in the earlier section on health screens. Treatments include a combination of medication including estrogen, bladder training, avoidance of dietary irritants and pelvic floor strengthening. As Lennox & Beange (1999) note, interventions such as education of the person and carers, behavioral strategies, use of appropriate aids or appliances, even surgery, need to be tailored to the person's needs and abilities. While uro-gynecology clinics are becoming a more visible feature of the health care landscape, the capability of these services to respond effectively to the needs of women with ID requires investigation. This is an opportunity for the concept of partnership to grow to include the nurses who work with women with ID, seeking collaboration with the nurse advisors who specialize in incontinence issues.

Conclusion

Specialist support is required to assist and enable practitioners working in primary health care teams to meet the health care requirements of people with ID. Women with ID very often require assistance to understand the range of health care options available to them that historically were not offered or available. Nurses working in this field need to be proactive in identifying specialist health services required by women with ID, and act as an advocate, supporter and educator to members of the primary health care team ensuring timely and appropriate access. Nurses need to become more actively involved in researching and developing innovative ways in which the health care needs of women with ID can be more effectively accessed and addressed. As scientists continue to investigate the biological and physiological aspects of women health, other empirical work is urgently required which focuses on advancing our understanding and finding solutions to the experiences and challenges currently encountered by women with ID.

Nurses have a pivotal role in empowering and supporting women with ID to become actively involved in all discussions relevant to their safety, sexuality and health care needs. Educational programs to be meaningful and effective must include the opinions, aspirations and perceived needs of the women themselves and/or their carers. In this way a preventative health education program can be more effectively designed and individualized, encompassing both the woman's preferences and needs.

References

Aggen, R.L. (1995) *Standards of developmental disabilities nursing practice.* Developmental Disabilities Nurses Association, Eugene.

Bradshaw, K.D., Elkins, T.E. & Quint, E.H. (1996) *The Patient with Mental Retardation: Issues in Gynecologic Care*. University of Texas Southwestern Medical Center, Dallas.

Brambilla, D.J. & McKinlay, S.M. (1989) A prospective study of factors affecting age at menopause. *Acta Obstetrica Gynecologia Scandinavia*, **53**, 69–72.

Cooke, L.B. (1997) Cancer and learning disability. *Journal of Intellectual Disability Research*, **41** (4), 312–316.

Cosgrave, M.P., Tyrrell, J., McCarron, M., Gill, M. & Lawler, B.A. (1999) Age at onset of dementia and age of menopause in women with Down's syndrome. *Journal of Intellectual Disability Research*, **43** (6), 461–465.

Davies, N. & Duff, M. (2001) Breast cancer screening for older women with learning disability living in community group homes. *Journal of Intellectual Disability Research*, **45** (3), 253–257.

Department of Health (1995) *Developing a Policy for Women's Health: A Discussion Document*. Dublin Stationery Office, Dublin.

Donahue, M.P. (1985) *Nursing: The Finest Art*. The C. V. Mosby Company, St. Louis.

Dykens, E.M. & Cohen, D.J. (1996) Effects of Special Olympics International on social competence in persons with mental retardation. *Journal of the American Academy of Child and Adolescent Psychiatry*, **35**, 2.

Evenhuis, H., Henderson, C.M., Beange, H., Lennox, N. & Chicoine, B. (2000) *Healthy Aging – Adults with Intellectual Disabilities: Physical Health Issues*. World Health Organization, Geneva.

Fraser, M. & Fraser, A. (2001) Are people with learning disabilities able to contribute to focus groups on health promotion? *Journal of Advanced Nursing*, **33** (2), 225–233.

Furman, L.M. (1989) Institutionalized disabled adolescents: gynecologic care: the pediatrician's role. *Clinical Pediatrics*, **28** (4), 163–170.

Gill, C.J. & Brown, A.A. (2000) Overview of health issues of older women with intellectual disabilities. In: *Aging and Developmental Disability: Current Research, Programming and Practice Implications* (eds J. Hammel & S.M. Nochajski), pp. 23–36. The Haworth Press, Inc., Binghamton.

Harlow, S.D. & Ephross, S.A. (1995) Epidemiology of menstruation and its relevance to women's health. *Epidemiologic Reviews*, **17**, 265–286.

Heaton, C. (1996) *Let's talk about health: What every woman should know* (workbook and video). Available from the ARC of New Jersey, North Brunswick, NJ, USA.

Heller, T., Hsieh, K. & Rimmer, J. (2000) Barriers and supports for exercise adherence among adults with Down syndrome. *11th World Congress of the International Association for the Scientific Study of Intellectual Disabilities Abstracts*, **44**, 312–313.

Jancar, J. & Jancar, M.P. (1998) Age-related fractures in people with intellectual disability and epilepsy. *Journal of Intellectual Disability Research*, **42** (5), 429–433.

Kagan-Krieger, S. (2001) Factors that affect coping with Turner syndrome. *Journal of Nursing Scholarship*, **33** (1), 43–45.

Kawas, C., Resnick, S., Morrison, A., Brookmeyer, R., Corrada, M., Zonderman, A., Bacal, C., Donnell Lingle, D. & Metter, E. (1997) A prospective study of estrogen replacement therapy and the risk of developing Alzheimer's disease. *Neurology*, **48**, 1517–1521.

Kerr, M., Richards, D. & Glover, G. (1997) Primary care for people with a learning disability: a group practice survey. *Journal of Applied Research in Intellectual Disability*, **9**, 347–352.

Kirschner, K.L., Gill, C.J., Reis, J.P. & Welner, S. (1998) Health issues for women with disabilities. In: *Rehabilitation Medicine: Principles and Practice* (eds J.A. DeLisa & B.M. Gans), pp. 1695–1716. Lippincott-Raven Publishers, Philadelphia.

Kopac, C.A., Fritz, J. & Holt, R.A. (1998) Gynecologic and reproductive services for women with developmental disabilities. *Clinical Excellence for Nurse Practitioners*, **2** (2), 88–95.

Lennox, N. & Beange, H. (1999) Adult health care. In: *Management Guidelines: People with Developmental and Intellectual Disabilities* (eds N. Lennox & J. Diggens), pp. 47–60. Therapeutic Guidelines Limited, Melbourne.

Lunsky, Y. & Reiss, S. (1998) Health needs of women with mental retardation and developmental disabilities. *American Psychologist*, **53**, 319.

Machia, J. (2001) Breast cancer: risk, prevention, and tamoxifen. *American Journal of Nursing*, **101** (4), 26–36.

Martin, D.M., Cassidy, G., Ahmad, F. & Martin, M.S. (2001) Women with learning disabilities and the menopause. *Journal of Learning Disabilities*, **5** (2), 121–132.

McCarthy, M. (2000) 'Change of life': the menopause and women with intellectual disabilities. *11th World Congress of the International Association for the Scientific Study of Intellectual Disabilities Abstracts*, **44**, 384.

McPherson, K., Steel, C.M. & Dixon, J.M. (1994) Breast cancer: epidemiology, risk factors and genetics, ABC of breast diseases. *British Medical Journal*, **309**, 1054–1057.

Moss, S. & Turner, S. (1996) The health needs of adults with learning disabilities and the health of the nation strategy. *Journal of Intellectual Disability Research*, **40**, 438–450.

Mughal, D.T. (2000) Health promotion and disease prevention. In: *Community Supports for Aging Adults with Lifelong Disabilities* (eds M.P. Janicki & E.F. Ansello), pp. 193–227. Paul H. Brookes, Baltimore.

National Institute on Aging (2001) *Exercise: A Guide from the National Institute on Aging* (NIH Publication No. 01-4258), US Government Printing Office, Washington, DC.

Niki, E. & Nakano, M. (1990) Estrogens as antioxidants. *Methods in Enzymology*, **186**, 330–333.

O'Brien, D.R. (1994) Health maintenance and promotion in adults. In: *A Lifespan Approach to Nursing Care for Individuals with Developmental Disabilities* (eds S.P. Roth & J.S. Morse), pp. 171–192. Paul H. Brookes, Baltimore.

Passer, A., Ruah, J., Chamberlain, A., McGrath, M. & Burket, R. (1984) Issues in fertility control for mentally retarded female adolescents: 11. Parental attitudes towards sterilization. *Pediatrics*, **73**, 451–454.

Prevatt, B. (1998) Gynecologic care for women with mental retardation. *Journal of Obstetric, Gynecologic, & Neonatal Nursing*, **7** (3), 2516.

Pulcini, J., Taylor, M.O. & Patelis, T. (1999) The relationship between characteristics of women with mental retardation and outcomes of the gynecologic examination. *Clinical Excellence for Nurse Practitioners*, **3** (4), 221–229.

Quint, E.H., Elkins, T.E., Sorg, C.A. & Kope, S. (1999) The treatment of cyclical behavioral changes in women with mental disabilities. *Journal of Pediatric & Adolescent Gynecology*, **12** (3), 139–142.

Ridenour, N. & Norton, D. (1997) Community-based persons with mental retardation: Opportunities for health promotion. *Nurse Practitioner Forum – Current Topics and Communications*, **6** (1), 19–23.

Rimmer, J.H., Braddock, D. & Marks, B. (1995) Health characteristics and behavior of adults with mental retardation residing in three living arrangements. *Research in Developmental Disabilities*, **16** (6), 489–499.

Rubin, S.S., Rimmer, J.H., Chicoine, B., Braddock, D. & McGuire, D.E. (1998) Overweight prevalence in persons with Down syndrome. *Mental Retardation*, **36** (3), 175–181.

van Schronjenstein Lantman-deValk, H. (1998) *Health Problems in People with Intellectual Disability*. Unigraphic, Maastricht.

Schupf, N., Zigman, W., Kapell, D., Lee, J.H., Kline, J. & Levin, B. (1997) Early menopause in women with Down syndrome. *Journal of Intellectual Disability Research*, **41**, 264–267.

Seltzer, G.B., Schupf, N. & Wu, H.S. (2001) A prospective study of menopause in women with Down syndrome. *Journal of Intellectual Disability Research*, **45** (1), 1–7.

Service, K.P. (In press) *Health Assessment of the Adult and Older Adult with Developmental Disabilities* (Computer software). Indiana University, Bloomington, IN.

Sonpal-Valias, N. (2000) *Midlife Issues of Women with Developmental Disabilities*. Paper presented at Building Bridges Conference, Victoria, BC, Canada, April.

Stanley, R. (1998) The primary health care provision for people with learning disabilities: a survey of GPs. *Journal of Learning Disabilities for Nursing, Health, and Social Care*, **2** (1), 23–30.

Sulpizi, L.K. (1996) Issues in sexuality and gynecologic care of women with developmental disabilities. *Journal of Obstetric, Gynecologic, and Neonatal Nursing*, **25** (7), 609–614.

Tang, M., Jacobs, D., Stern, Y., Marder, K., Schofield, P., Gurland, B., Andrews, H. & Mayeuz, R. (1996) Effect of oestrogen during menopause on risk and age of onset of Alzheimer's disease. *Lancet*, **348**, 429–432.

Thornton, C. (1996) A focus group inquiry into the perceptions of primary health care reams and the provision of health care for adults with a learning disability living in the community. *Journal of Advanced Nursing*, **23** (6), 1168–1176.

Walsh, P.N., Heller, T., Schupf, N. & van Schrojenstein Lantman-de Valk, H. (2000) *Healthy Aging – Adults with Intellectual Disabilities: Women's Health Issues*. World Health Organization, Geneva.

Welner, S.L., Foley, C.C., Nosek, M.A. & Holmes, A. (1999) Practical considerations in the performance of physical examinations on women with disabilities. *Obstetrical and Gynecological Survey*, **54** (7), 457–462.

Wright, J. & Cowden, J.E. (1990) Changes in self-concept and cardiovascular endurance of mentally retarded youths in a Special Olympics swim training program. In: *Special Olympics International. Inc. Research Monographs*. Joseph P. Kennedy Jr. Foundation, Washington, DC.

13 Approaches for Health Education and Policies in Health and Social Care

Margaret Flynn and Sheila Hollins

Introduction

The health of people with intellectual disabilities is at a critical juncture early in the new millennium. Since the mid–1990s, we have acquired an uncomfortable awareness of the ways in which the health of people with intellectual disabilities are compromised (e.g. Hollins *et al.*, 1998; Pearson *et al.*, 1998; Keywood *et al.*, 1999; Department of Health 1998a, b, 1999a, b). At a time of unprecedented change in the medico-legal environment, in instantaneous communications, in technology and in the mechanisms of health care delivery and health care financing, the poor health status of citizens with intellectual disabilities cannot be doubted.

However, now is not an easy time to create a new culture of health care for people with intellectual disabilities. Globally, an economic/political process for delivering sufficiency, security and peaceful co-existence remains to be determined. In the UK, there has been considerable institutional investment in areas such as education, medicine, health care and welfare. While the level of investment may have created a contrary impression, these institutions seem ill-equipped to respond effectively to the needs of disadvantaged populations. The institutions are dogged by scarce resources, reorganizational upheaval, divergent demands and the shifting duties and responsibilities specified in new policies, guidance and legislation.

A basic thesis of this chapter is that the fundamental reason for our failure to generate inclusive health policies stems from a continued refusal to see more similarities than differences in the health needs of people with intellectual disabilities. Even though we may adopt the discourse of rights, equality, equivalence, autonomy and non-discrimination, there is a familiar parallel in this failure: although we know we are all members of a single species, we behave as if separate nations accommodated separate species. In turn, we are tempted to overlook the co-existence and even the humanity of members of other nations.

Drawing from our experiences of sitting at the Department of Health's policy tables in the UK, we offer in this chapter an insight into the framing and implementation of health policies oriented to promote the health of people with intellectual disabilities. We focus on the design and development of four documents and some accompanying materials published between 1998 and 2000 (i.e. *The Healthy Way* for people with intellectual disabilities, Department of Health, 1998a; *Signposts for Success* for the commissioners and providers of services for people with intellectual disabilities, Department of Health, 1998b; *Once a Day* for primary health care teams, Department of Health, 1999b; and *Good Practice in Breast and Cervical Screening for Women with Learning Disabilities* for cancer services and services for people with intellectual disabilities, National Health Service Cancer Screening Programmes, 2000a). Using these documents, we examine the principal themes and the guidance and educative approaches of these publications. We consider these texts as discontinuous footnotes to England's *Valuing People: A New Strategy for Learning Disability for the 21st Century* (Department of Health, 2001).

A chronicle of developing ideas

The design and publication of *The Healthy Way – How to Stay Healthy – A Guide for People with Learning Disabilities* expressed a sea change. ('Learning disabilities' is a term used in the UK for 'intellectual disabilities'.) The Department of Health invited people with intellectual disabilities to contribute to the design of a booklet about their health and their health care. Some 500 people suggested experiences, memories, concerns and ideas using cartoons and 'word bubbles'. The text is accompanied by an audio cassette, using the voices of a man and woman with intellectual disabilities, and a board game suggested by a group of people with intellectual disabilities in Sefton, Merseyside. Starting in a waiting room, players have to throw a dice and score six to start 'The Healthy Way' – reflecting the views of the designers of this game that 'learning about health should be enjoyable' (Flynn, 1999: 17).

The text introduces such learning/discussion points as: 'You said ... we need to know about our bodies ... our bodies are not rude ... [and] we need help with our feelings.' Examples of the concerns expressed include: 'You said ... sometimes it is difficult to say things to other people ... it is sometimes frightening to go to the dentist ... [and] we want help when we go to hospital.'

Crucially, the guide asserts, 'We can teach health workers too' and the linked cartoon illustrates a woman teaching a doctor and nurse who are sitting behind school desks. Importantly also, the guide includes cartoons of a naked man and woman to address the concern of some contributors to the guide that they did not know how their bodies were different from those of the opposite sex.

Paul Boateng, the Parliamentary Under-Secretary of State for Health, wrote an introduction which was followed by a compelling 'message' from Anya Souza, a woman with Down syndrome. Paul Boateng affirmed, 'We want to work with you to make things better and we have made this guide to help you.'

The publications *Signposts for Success in Commissioning and Providing Health Services for People with Learning Disabilities* and *Once a Day – One or More People with Learning Disabilities are likely to be in Contact with your Primary Healthcare Team, How can you help them?*, are both badged as 'good practice' by the Department of Health. The purpose of *Signposts for Success* is expressed as: 'To promote good practice by clarifying the role of the NHS in providing services to people with learning disabilities within the community,' and the purpose of *Once a Day* is: 'To promote good practice in enabling people with learning disabilities to access and receive good quality services from primary health care teams.'

Both contain forewords by the Parliamentary Under-Secretary of State. Significantly, using an identical opening sentence, both forewords assert the unfairness of people's poor health care experiences:

'The National Health Service was founded on the principle that good quality health services should be available to all. Unfortunately, despite a great deal of progress, some groups and individuals are not getting a fair deal – and that applies to many people with learning disabilities.

The Government is already taking steps to tackle the root causes of ill health and health inequalities. This should help people with learning disabilities as it should help others. One of the commitments that we have made is to turn social exclusion into social inclusion. We also intend to deal with the specific issues that face people with learning disabilities and to improve their access to the NHS.'

(Department of Health, 1998a: i)

Signposts for Success outlines how 'good practice' should manifest in 'all services ... all health services ... general health services ... specialist health services ... [and] in service redevelopment' (Department of Health, 1998b: iii). It affirms the policy guidelines of 1992 and reproduces these in an appendix. It has an explicit value base and a key refrain is 'partnership and co-operation'. *Signposts for Success* affirms the importance of staff training and competencies and the crucial role of specialist services. Importantly also, it trails some of the NHS's wider reform agenda.

Once a Day outlines the difficulties that people with intellectual disabilities experience in health services. It states the frequently expressed concern of primary health care teams that they are poorly equipped to work with patients with intellectual disabilities, not least because they do not see enough patients to develop expertise. Also, *Once a Day* introduces the concerns of people's relatives and support personnel that the health of people with intellectual disabilities occasions insufficient interest and urgency.

The two texts have similar design features. They were both informed by conferences for people with intellectual disabilities and professionals, and focus groups hosted by the Department of Health. They are enlivened by quotations from people with intellectual disabilities, their relatives and health and social care personnel. In terms of content, both texts include ideas for action, information summaries and sources of information in respect of people's low self-reporting of their health problems, poor 'consent to treatment' practices and the importance of lifelong and competent support services.

There are three insistent and cross-cutting themes of *Signposts for Success* and *Once a Day*:

- There is a gap between the aspirations of people with intellectual disabilities and all that the 'good practice' texts commend, and what most people currently experience.
- Primary care has a key role in the health of people with intellectual disabilities.
- The involvement of primary care teams with local specialist services is helpful, most particularly in the role of the latter as advisors and facilitators of better generic health care, and especially if that interface demonstrates the influence of people with intellectual disabilities.

The publication *Good Practice in Breast and Cervical Screening for Women with Learning Disabilities* arose from a request by the National Screening Committee, 'to ensure that women with learning disabilities have the same rights of access as all other women to the NHS Breast Screening Program (NHSBSP) and the NHS Cervical Screening Program' (NHSCSP) (National Health Service Cancer Screening Programmes (2000a: 1). The good practice guide is aimed at staff who support women with intellectual disabilities, including members of primary care teams and staff who provide breast and cervical screening, and community learning disability teams. It asserts the importance of prescreening preparation, the provision of accessible information and the importance of understanding changes in our bodies.

The book outlines the stages in determining women's suitability for the two forms of screening and establishing their consent to these. It cross-references *Signposts for Success* and *Once a Day* and alerts staff in breast screening units and smear takers to the ways in which barriers to screening may be lowered or removed. The text contains sample letters and ideas for responding to questions that are typically asked. It also contains a listing of materials for readers who may wish to read beyond the materials featured in the references.

Two illustrated leaflets, *50 or over? Breast Screening is for you* (National Health Service Cancer Screening Programmes, 2000b) and *Having a Smear Test* (National Health Service Cancer Screening Programmes, 2000c) are designed to inform women with intellectual disabilities about screening programs. Two associated picture books in the Books Beyond Words series, published by St George's Hospital Medical School and the Royal College of Psychiatrists – *Looking after my Breasts* (Hollins & Perez, 2000) and *Keeping Healthy 'Down Below'*, (Hollins & Downer, 2000) – were designed to make communication about women's screening easier. They describe in sequence the events of receiving an invitation letter for screening, deciding whether to attend, preparing for the screening appointment, attending, getting the results and being recalled for further tests. Designed by women with intellectual disabilities, each contains a supporting text and information. It is noteworthy that 17 of the 27 people in the working party producing *Good Practice in Breast and Cervical Screening for Women with Learning Disabilities* were not part of the intellectual disabilities specialism. Their origins were in, for example, public health, nurse training, family planning, radiology, health policy, breast cancer care and General Practice. Further, the working party included two women with intellectual disabilities who co-authored the two picture books and played a significant part in identifying the information needs of other women. The publications were widely distributed to primary care teams, breast and cervical screening programs and community learning disability teams.

Some inconsistencies

No review of *The Healthy Way, Signposts for Success, Once a Day* and *Good Practice in Breast and Cervical Screening* would be complete without reference to some perplexing inconsistencies and shortcomings. Problems with distribution plagued the first three publications, not helped by inadequate print runs and the absence of dissemination plans. The Department of Health was silent on how partnerships with local health promotion practitioners are achieved, and the multiple contexts and settings for health promotion; silent too on the how and where of targeting *The Healthy Way* and its congruence/incongruence with the national curriculum as interpreted by special schools (Office for Standards in Education (OFSTED), 1995); and health programs in colleges, day and accommodation and support services were not considered. Further, program deliverers were not identified, ways of taking account of people's prior knowledge (Ausubel *et al.*, 1978) were omitted, and no means of monitoring of progress in using the materials were proposed.

Of the 'good practice' materials, these are voluntary, with inevitable consequences. Such materials cannot assume that the value of change is acknowledged, that they are not giving more work to overcrowded work programs, or that they are welcomed by an energetic community of practice. Nor can 'good practice' materials assume that the reiteration of 'leadership', 'partnership' and 'co-operation' resonate with existing beliefs and practice. In short, 'good practice' is unequal to breaking into distinctive ways of decision-making and operating. It appears a low-impact leverage point for intervention. The failure to engage with primary health care team professionals in the design and development of *Once a Day* was critical. In part, this is associated with a long standing, if mis-placed reimbursement motive for undertaking health checks in primary care (Martin, 2001), even though disconnected health checks cannot, per se, transform people's health status.

It is striking that the *Good Practice* materials hold back from offering any macro-analysis of the deficiencies in earlier policies and models of health care, the cultures within these, their associated power structures of uni-professional groups and the reach and influence of these. They are silent also in reflecting on the societal contexts in which different approaches became established and unchallenged as 'custom and practice'. Sig-nificantly, the *Good Practice* materials do not have direct links to profes-sional development and learning outcomes. Such disconnectedness, in contrast to *Good Practice in Breast and Cervical Screening for Women with Learning Disabilities*, does a disservice to the richness of hard-earned, experiential knowledge (Schon, 1983).

Valuing People: A New Strategy for Learning Disability for the 21st Century (Department of Health, 2001) states of NHS provision:

> 'Because mainstream health services have been slow in developing the capacity and skills to meet the needs of people with learning dis-abilities, some NHS specialist learning disability services have sought to provide all encompassing services on their own. As a result, the wider NHS has failed to consider the needs of people with learning disabilities. This is the most important issue which the NHS needs to address for people with learning disabilities.'

> (para. 6.3: 60)

Nine 'key actions' are identified to realize the:

> 'Government Objective: To enable people with learning disabilities to access a health service designed around their individual needs, with fast and convenient care delivered to a consistently high standard and with additional support where necessary.'

> (Department of Health, 2001: 59).

They are:

> 'Action to reduce health inequalities … to challenge discrimination …
> Health facilitators identified by Spring 2003. All…to be registered with a
> GP by 2004. All … to have Health Action Plans by June 2005. NHS to
> ensure that all mainstream hospital services are accessible…
> Development of local specialist services for people with severe chal-
> lenging behavior… Mental Health NSF [National Service Framework]
> will bring new benefits to people with learning disability. New role for
> specialist … services, making most effective use of their expertise.'
>
>   (Department of Health, 2001: 61)

All of this is to be achieved on a shoestring.

It is difficult to align these actions with the mantras of 'rights', 'independence', 'choice' and 'inclusion' enshrined within 'Valuing People', or
indeed with the compelling directions proposed by *The Healthy Way,
Signposts for Success, Once a Day* and *Good Practice in Breast and Cervical
Screening.* Primary care is unavailable to people with intellectual disabilities still living in the fiction of long-stay 'hospitals' that are not proper
hospitals. For the majority of people who live with their families, who do
not access primary care or secondary care as often as their health needs
would determine, there is no change. Their relatives will continue to
accompany them, to mediate and provide the help they need.

There are an estimated 11 000 intellectual disability nurses who, it is
believed, will assume the role of health facilitators for the 1.2 million
people with intellectual disabilities, and will take a lead on people's
health action plans (which have no parallels in the NHS – they are
planned only for people with intellectual disabilities). Clearly, there are
constraints surrounding 'solutions' that are anchored in the health
specialism of intellectual disability and are compromised by the legacies
of aligning people's health care with the disciplines of psychiatry and
intellectual disability nursing.

Foundations and ideas for progress

Curriculum change and reform are part of the landscape of education,
including medical and nurse education (Pideaux, 1999; Nowicki, 1996).
Models of co-teaching, combining the skills of clinical practitioners and
academics, foster reflection on the responsiveness of teaching to experience, custom and practice (Orlander *et al.*, 2000). Our experience of co-
teaching with two women with intellectual disabilities (employed as
training advisors) in St George's Hospital Medical School, arose from a

desire to provide undergraduate nurses and doctors with the learning environment that promotes collaboration and the connection between theory and practical experience (British Medical Association, 1995). Although learning from patients is fundamental to the education of nurses and doctors, traditionally patients have a passive role (e.g. Crotty *et al.*, 2000).

Having drawn back from the presentation of materials in lecture format, to a unidisciplinary audience, we tilt our work towards active learning, which is fundamental to 'learning communities' and has a particular resonance in medical education in St George's (Starratt, 1996; Hollins, 1998; Retallick *et al.*, 1999). That is, the learning agenda is continually related to the exploration of questions important to our lives; it is accepted that knowledge is partial and fallible and that the enrichment of knowledge arises from sharing meanings and interpretations. In St George's, drama work with a theatre company of people with intellectual disabilities; collaboration with specialist health care professionals; linking the lessons of visiting people's homes and places of occupation, involving storytelling and making sense of people's contrasting worlds; and examinations involving people with intellectual disabilities, have motivated us to view such initiatives as a microcosm of associated learning communities. We recognize that as a developing learning community, we have to be producers of knowledge about our own practices, which includes addressing challenges in competing for curriculum spaces. Further, we have to engage with other medical school communities in order to explore new possibilities for ongoing education and professional development.

Good Practice in Breast and Cervical Screening for Women with Learning Disabilities was launched by Yvette Cooper, the Parliamentary Secretary for Public Health. Unlike *The Healthy Way*, *Signposts for Success*, and *Once a Day*, this text and the associated materials arose from a request by the Cancer Screening Program itself. The use of these 'accessible' materials will be triggered by screening invitations targeted at women with intellectual disabilities. Significantly, the response of the National Screening Committee to the finished materials was to recognize their relevance to women for whom English is not a first language (Box, 1998) and for women with literacy problems.

There are some small-scale, compelling local initiatives led by personnel from primary care and services for people with intellectual disabilities (Flynn & Kitt, in preparation). These are characterized by learning with and from people with intellectual disabilities and their families, networks of collaborative peers (including those shaping the national curriculum in special schools) and a conspicuous public health perspective. Investment from the anticipated reconfiguration of health services for people with intellectual disabilities will be essential. However, unless such strongly needed investment is tied to specific outcomes, as with the English National Service Frameworks, we will continue to fail people with intellectual disabilities. Achieving comprehensive health care is a long-term project in which we have an obligation to create anxiety in 'the mainstream NHS' about lopsided interpretations of equality and discrimination, and our roles in sustaining these.

The production of printed information for patients is a key component of many health education activities. However, the use of such publications is highly variable, supply issues prevail (Williams & McIntosh, 1996; Dixon Woods, 1998) and their target audience is assumed to be literate.

We have to rethink the specialism of intellectual disability if its impermeability and the isolation of its materials are to be challenged. Snappy solutions are hard to come by. If we are to begin progress beyond 'best practice' to a more inclusive NHS, we need mainstream policy-makers in the Department of Health to be champions of inclusion (not just specialists in intellectual disability as at present). Other resources are also needed to combat the lethargy of excluding systems and endemic discrimination, and to animate senior clinicians in Primary Care Trusts to enable 'the mainstream NHS' to meet its obligations to people with intellectual disabilities and other vulnerable patients. Our experiences indicate that the onus to make links with 'the mainstream NHS' cannot reside solely with specialist personnel. This has to be a two-way process.

Health education for women with intellectual disabilities cannot be considered in isolation from the educational needs of health and social care professionals. The creation of NHS Workforce Confederations (Department of Health, 2000) may offer the best chance to 'promote a better understanding of the needs of people with learning disabilities amongst the wider workforce' (Department of Health, 2001) and greater 'health consciousness' in service provision. The subject is of wide and increasing importance. It is unlikely that 'health consciousness' will result without participatory development activities and partnering (Kerr, 1996). If the co-option of words such as 'partnership', 'participation' and 'development' are not accompanied by examples and ideas relating to understanding and practice they become debased by ambiguity. Having an intellectual disability is powerfully determinative of being offered the means to survive beyond infancy, if the stigmata of a syndrome are present (Royal Brompton Hospital, 2001), and of health status from childhood to adulthood, through to the manner of dying (Brown et al., 2000). We must not concede the inevitability of these disadvantages. We have the means and an obligation to do better.

References

Ausubel, D.P., Novak, J.S. & Hanesian, H. (1978) *Educational Psychology: A Cognitive View*. Holt, Rinehart and Winston, New York.

Box, V. (1998) Cervical screening: the knowledge and opinions of black and minority ethnic women and of health advocates in East London. *Health Education Journal*, **57**, 3–15.

British Medical Association (1995) *Report of Working Party on Medical Education*. BMA, London.

Brown, H., Flynn, M. & Burns, S. (2000) The service needs of people with learning disabilities who are dying. *Psychology Research*, **10** (2), 39–48.

Crotty, M., Finucane, P. & Ahern, M. (2000) Teaching medical students about disability and rehabilitation: methods and student feedback. *Medical Education*, **34**, 659–664.

Department of Health (1998a) *The Healthy Way – How to Stay Healthy – A Guide for People with Learning Disabilities*. Department of Health, Wetherby, UK.

Department of Health (1998b) *Signposts for Success in Commissioning and Providing Health Services for People with Learning Disabilities*. NHS Executive, London.

Department of Health (1999a) *Facing the Facts – Services for People with Learning Disabilities: A Policy Impact Study of Social Care and Health Services*. Department of Health, London.

Department of Health (1999b) *Once a Day – One or More People with Learning Disabilities are likely to be in Contact with your Primary Healthcare Team. How can you help them?* NHS Executive, London.

Department of Health (2000) *A Health Service of all the Talents: Developing the NHS Workforce*. Consultation Document on the Review of Workforce Planning (CWP) 21325, NHS, London.

Department of Health (2001) *Valuing People: A New Strategy for Learning Disability for the 21st Century*. A white paper. Cm5086, The Stationery Office, London.

Dixon Woods, M. (1998) Dissemination of printed information for patients: a qualitative study of general practices. *Health Education Journal*, **57**, 16–30.

Flynn, M. (1999) Involving users at all levels. In: *Making a World of Difference: Developing Primary Health Care* (eds K. Billingham, M. Flynn & J. Weinstein), pp. 14–21. Royal College of General Practitioners, London.

Flynn, M. & Kitt, L. (in preparation) *Developing the Primary Care Agenda for and with People with Learning Disabilities*. St George's Hospital Medical School and the National Development Team, Manchester.

Hollins, S. (1998) Teaching the doctors. *Soundtrack: Health Special Edition*. National Development Team, Manchester.

Hollins, S. & Downer, J. (2000) *Keeping Healthy 'Down Below'*. St George's Hospital Medical School and the Royal College of Psychiatrists, Gaskell, London.

Hollins, S. & Perez, W. (2000) *Looking After My Breasts*. St. George's Hospital Medical School and the Royal College of Psychiatrists, Gaskell, London.

Hollins, S., Attard, M.T., von Fraunhofer, N., McGuigan, S. & Sedgewick, P. (1998) Mortality in people with learning disability: risks, causes, and death certification findings in London. *Developmental Medicine and Child Neurology*, **40**, 50–56.

Kerr, M. (1996) *Partnering and Health Development – The Kathmandu Connection.* University of Calgary Press, Calgary.

Keywood, K., Fovargue, S. & Flynn, M. (1999) *Best Practice? Health Care Decision-making by, with and for Adults with Learning Disabilities.* National Development Team and the Institute of Medicine Law and Bioethics, Manchester.

Martin, G. (2001) 'Valuing People' – a new strategy for learning disability for the 21st century: how may it impinge on primary care? *British Journal of General Practitioners*, **51**, (471), 788–790.

National Health Service Cancer Screening Programmes (2000a) *Good Practice in Breast and Cervical Screening for Women with Learning Disabilities.* NHS Cancer Screening Programmes, NHSBSC Publication No. 46/ NHSCSP Publication No. 13, Sheffield.

National Health Service Cancer Screening Programmes (2000b) *50 or Over? Breast Screening is for you.* NHS Cancer Screening Programmes, Sheffield.

National Health Service Cancer Screening Programmes (2000c) *Having a Smear Test.* NHS Cancer Screening Programmes, Sheffield.

Nowicki, C.R. (1996) 21 Predictions for the future of hospital staff development. *Journal of Continuing Education for Nurses*, **27**, 259–266.

OFSTED (1995) *Nursery and Primary Schools, Special Schools and Secondary Schools.* The Stationery Office, London.

Orlander, J.D., Gupta, M., Fincke, B.G., Manning, M.E. & Hershman, W. (2000) Co-teaching: a faculty development strategy. *Medical Education*, **34**, 257–265.

Pearson, M., Flynn, M., Maughan, J. & Russell, P. (1998) *Positive Health in Transition: A Guide to Effective and Reflective Transition Planning for Young People with Learning Disabilities.* National Development Team, Manchester.

Pideaux, D. (1999) Writing about curriculum change: beyond the local and particular. *Medical Education*, **33**, 004–005.

Retallick, J., Cocklin, B. & Coombe, K. (eds) (1999) *Learning Communities in Education: Issues, Strategies and Contexts.* Routledge Research in Education. Routledge, London.

Royal Brompton Hospital (2001) *The Report of the Independent Inquiries into Paediatric Cardiac Services at the Royal Brompton Hospital and Harefield Hospital London.* Royal Brompton Hospital, London.

Schon, D.A. (1983) *The Reflective Practitioner: How Professionals Think in Action.* Basic Books, USA.

Starratt, R.J. (1996) *Transforming Educational Administration: Meaning, Community and Excellence.* McGraw Hill, New York.

Williams, S. & McIntosh, J. (1996) Problems in implementing evidence based health promotion material in general practice. *Health Education Journal*, **55**, 24–30.

14 Men's Health: 'The Female of the Species is More Healthy than the Male'

Mike Kerr

Introduction

Individuals with intellectual disabilities experience a considerable disadvantage in health status as compared with the general population. They have greater mortality, more significant health conditions and a poorer general standard of health care. The reasons for this are varied including:

■ Higher morbidity
■ Conditions associated with genetic abnormalities
■ Poor health promotion
■ Difficulties in the recognition and treatment of illness.

Men, put simply, die younger than women do and from a different range of conditions. It is this inequality which justifies the placement of this chapter in a book dedicated to women's health. It may appear that the male with an intellectual disability experiences, in health terms, a form of double jeopardy; for he will have poorer health than women from his disability and from his gender.

This chapter will, firstly, explore the evidence that exists relating to the health needs and differential in health outcomes between men and women. Secondly, I will discuss a plan for good quality health care provision for the man with an intellectual disability.

The differential health status of the male

Ample data exists from the male population as a whole identifying a significantly reduced life span, an increase in certain morbidities and a range of male specific health problems (Kirby *et al.*, 1999).

Mortality

Considerable evidence exists as to the reduced life expectancy in men. In the general population men live, on average, for approximately five years less then women. Within the UK, for example, this means a reduction from 79.2 years for women to 73.9 for men. There is also a differential in cause of death. Cardiovascular deaths remain the largest cause of death, with cancer second. The etiology of this difference is unknown but it may be that women are to some degree *biologically protected* by their estrogen status or by a reduction in *health risk behavior*. Men are particularly prone to excessive health risk behavior with an increase in obesity, smoking and alcohol consumption. These behavioral differences may also influence the fact that lung cancer accounts for 10% of all male deaths. Lastly, a proportion of deaths are sex specific, such as the 4% of deaths caused by prostate cancer.

Does the hypothesis of poorer biological protection and increased health risk behavior explain the picture in males with intellectual disabilities? Several studies have confirmed that people with an intellectual disability have a decreased life span (Lawrenson *et al.*, 1997), with an increased likelihood of death of seven times the general population in the age band 20–39 years.

Studies have also explored differences within the population with intellectual disabilities. In particular, a sex difference has been observed in non-Down syndrome individuals over the age of 35 years (Strauss & Eyman, 1996). Strauss and Kastner (1996), in a further study, also showed that while male mortality was similar to female mortality at age 40, it was nearly 50% higher by age 65. In a study of deaths among adults of 40 years or older (Janicki *et al.*, 1999), the average age at death for women was 66.7 years and for men 63.3 years.

Greater morbidity

In the general population a differential distribution of morbidity can be seen in the male as compared with the female. Some of these, as already mentioned, are male specific such as prostate cancer. Prostatic cancer and prostate disease produce a considerable amount of morbidity in the male. Prostate cancer is the second most common cause of death (with lung cancer the most common). It is also estimated that 43% of men over the age of 65 years will suffer from the symptoms of benign hypertrophy of the prostate. These include two broad areas of symptoms: obstructive with poor flow and incomplete bladder emptying, and irritative with increased frequency, passing of urine at night and urgency. Testicular cancer will affect up to one man in 500 by the age of 50 years. This risk increases in mal-descended testes – a particular issue among men with intellectual disabilities. While great treatment advances have been made, these are linked to early diagnosis and thus stress the importance of self-examination and health promotion.

Other morbidities appear linked to some aspects of male health risk behavior. These include death by trauma and violence and death related to HIV infection. The remainder, however, are conditions that appear in both sexes. These latter conditions include a broad range of cardio-vascular diseases such as angina and hypertension. The male is also at a higher risk of some forms of emotional ill-health, in particular suicide. In comparison with the general population, the population with an intel-lectual disability has higher morbidity and unrecognized disease (e.g. Beange *et al.*, 1995). Unfortunately, little of the published morbidity data differentiates between the sexes.

Why the difference? The male picture

It appears that a part of this greater mortality and morbidity in males is related to biological differences. This can be seen in the case of the male cancers and in aspects of increased cardiovascular ill-health. Within the population with intellectual disability the same is true and in fact more specific biological factors may play a role in those conditions linked to the X-chromosome. Our understanding of the physical and behavioral cor-relates of such conditions will expand, as has been seen in the fragile-X syndrome (Hirst *et al.*, 1992).

More controversy exists over the relative importance of male health risk behavior in the adult with intellectual disability. The picture in the general population, while a little stereotyped, points out the crucial role of health promotion in male health. The male is pictured as having unhealthy lifestyle and dietary habits leading to obesity, increased alcohol intake and increased smoking. The impulsive nature of the man leads him to reckless behavior, unprotected sexual activity, injury or suicide. However, it is difficult to match this stereotype to the male with intel-lectually disability. It is worth exploring more closely the risk areas.

Obesity and cardiovascular risk

Several surveys have investigated the prevalence of obesity among people with intellectual disabilities. Rubin *et al.* (1998) investigated its prevalence in an American specialist clinic-based population. The authors compared their sample with generic American population estimates of the prevalence of being overweight, which is 33% for males and 36% for females. A prevalence of being overweight in the sample with Down syndrome was 45% for males and 56% for females. A British study (Prasher, 1995) similarly showed figures of 48% for males and 47% for females in a population with Down syndrome. A Finnish study explored the prevalence of overweight, as defined by body mass index (BMI), in a cohort of 20-year-olds with intellectual disability of all causation (Simila & Niskanen, 1991). Here much lower prevalences were found of 9.8% obesity and 7.1% seriously obese. Beange, in an Australian survey of attendees at a specialized health clinic for persons with intellectual disabilities, found a prevalence of obesity of 22%. A further study (Beange *et al.*, 1995) found a prevalence of obesity among persons with intellectual disabilities of 16.3% for males and 26.5% for females. This compared with general population estimates of 7.7% for males and 8.5% for females.

Rimmer *et al.* (1995) explored the area of cardiovascular risk factors through serum cholesterol measurement in a sample of 329 individuals with intellectual disabilities in the US. Three residences were investigated; a 16 bed facility with a high prevalence of profound disability, a group home, and family settings with proportionately greater prevalence of mild intellectual disability. The study showed similar risk profiles to the general population though with some variation across place of residence.

Alcohol use

There is little data to suggest that alcohol intake is as significant a public health issue for persons with intellectual disabilities as for the general population. A study from the US in 1986 (Edgerton, 1986) showed that individuals with a disability used alcohol less frequently than family members and showed little evidence of problem drinking behavior. A more recent Scotland-based study was performed by Lawrenson *et al.* (1994). This survey was performed on attendees at day facilities within the city of Dundee. The study showed that 68% of females with intellectual disabilities, as compared to 92.8% of female controls, drank alcohol; this compared with 83% and 98% for males. Furthermore, the average consumption in units of alcohol per week was low, with a mean for females of 2.1 and 3.1 for males.

Smoking

A small Australian study (Tracy & Hosken, 1997) showed a smoking prevalence of 39% of men and 33% of women, though overall consumption was low with over a half smoking fewer than 10 cigarettes per day. This compared with an underlying community prevalence of smoking at 25.6% men and 24.8% women.

In summary, the male with an intellectual disability has broadly similar health needs (see Table 14.1) to his female counterpart, with the main exception being an increased susceptibility to cardiovascular risk factors and a range of male specific conditions. In the next section I will discuss the evidence as to how best to meet these needs.

Table 14.1 Factors leading to poorer health status.

Individual-based	Service-based
Serious co-morbidity: swallowing, mobility, sensory difficulties and epilepsy. Behavioural or psychiatric co-morbidity inhibiting examination and investigation. Severe communication difficulties. Specific genetic abnormalities such as Down syndrome, fragile-X.	Inadequate housing and nutrition. Poor health promotion: in particular diet. Poor primary care reliant on self-report and opportunistic health provision. Poor health advocacy. Restricted access to evidence-based interventions e.g. novel anti-epileptic drugs.

Meeting the need – delivering health care to the male

The appropriate delivery of health care to males with an intellectual disability should recognize the health needs and address them across the life span. However, the ability to do this is tempered by our knowledge of the current health delivery to people with an intellectual disability. Research has consistently shown that individuals with an intellectual disability have a poorer standard of health. The case of JD (see case study) illustrates the problems that can arise for males with health problems who have an intellectual disability. In this section I will firstly discuss the reason for this poorer health care and secondly address appropriate interventions.

A poorer standard of health care?

Several researchers have explored the current health status of individuals with an intellectual disability (Beange *et al.*, 1995; Crocker, 1990). They find three key areas of poor health status:

(1) Untreated, yet treatable, medical conditions
(2) Untreated specific health issues related to the individual disability
(3) A lack of uptake of generic health promotion, such as blood pressure screening.

There are, of course, many factors that can lead to an individual having this poor level of health status. Broadly speaking these include features inherent to the disability and factors relating to the quality of care provision. Table 14.1 highlights the barriers to care provision.

Delivering health care to the male

When exploring how best to deliver care, two areas of health intervention appear to be the most relevant. The first focuses on techniques designed to ensure that health care is accessed, health promotion is given and needs are recognized. This addresses the issue of *screening*, or as it may be best referred to in the context of intellectual disability, *health checking*.

The second relates to the evidence that exists for *specific therapies* for those conditions discovered by screening or otherwise. The latter area is covered in published documents and readers are referred in particular to the Health Evidence Bulletin Wales Learning Disabilities (National Assembly for Wales, 2001), which critically analyses the worth of investing in certain interventions.

The male health check

The crucial issue for any man with an intellectual disability is that the health care is planned. It is unlikely that unplanned opportunistic health care, such as impromptu health screening in primary care, will adequately meet his needs (Jones & Kerr, 1996).

The case of 'JD' highlights a care plan for a male with an intellectual disability aiming to produce maximum health gain. Health checking allows for regular structured review of an individual. While having great face validity as a means to address the needs of individuals who access care poorly, the efficacy in terms of prolonged health outcome is still lacking. However, ample evidence exists of its ability to identify previously unrecognized health problems and deliver appropriate health promotion (Kerr *et al.*, 1996). Health checking must be backed up by accurate information on the individual. Males with intellectual disabilities will need health advocates to help explain and explore their symptoms.

Any male should have regular health checks. The majority of these will address general health measures, but particular attention will need to be given to cardiovascular risk, testicular examination and questioning for symptoms of prostatic disease.

Case study: 'JD'

'JD' was a 43-year-old man with Down syndrome who lived with his carer. His carer had become concerned that JD was not himself. His appetite was poor and he seemed irritable. He had little verbal language so found it hard to express his symptoms. He was brought to his primary care physician who could find no obvious cause for his problems. Both the physician and JD's carer were concerned that he might have Alzheimer's disease.

Some months passed and JD continued to deteriorate. He was sleeping poorly and was 'restless at night'. Staff at his day center were concerned over his excess sleepiness. The staff raised the possibility that JD might have an underactive thyroid; this was not the case.

His carer was finding his restless nights increasingly difficult to cope with and asked for further help. A community nurse who came to see him noticed that JD's nighttime restlessness involved repeated trips to the toilet.

The nurse organized a further visit to the family physician and attended with him. At the consultation she stressed to the physician her concerns that he may have a physical cause for his restlessness. The physician recommended a urine sample to identify possible infection. A urinary infection was identified and treated. This led to only a mild improvement in his symptoms. Still concerned, the nurse arranged a further consultation suggesting the possibility of prostate disease. JD returned to the family physician who on examination felt that he had an enlarged prostate. He was referred to the urologist who performed a resection of a benign prostate. Following this JD settled considerably, regaining the skills he had lost.

Conclusion

The male with intellectual disability has comparatively poorer health than a female, at least in terms of life expectancy. The reasons for this are not as clear-cut as in the general population where male health risk behavior explains considerable excess mortality. Certainly the male with intellectual disability experiences the specific male health problems of testicular and prostate disease. It would seem most likely that health promotion behaviors will result in the greatest gains. The male is particularly susceptible to the impact of obesity, a significant community problem in people with intellectual disabilities. In addition, difficulties in communicating ill-health make specific questioning for prostatic disease a priority. It is crucial that care pathways develop for men that recognize their special conditions and susceptibility across the life span.

References

Beange, H., McElduff, A. & Baker, W. (1995) Medical disorders of adults with mental retardation: a population study. *American Journal of Mental Retardation*, **99,** 595–604.

Crocker, A.C. (1990) Medical care in the community for adults with mental retardation. *American Journal of Public Health*, **80,** 1037–1038.

Edgerton, R. (1986) Alcohol and drug use by mentally retarded adults. *American Journal of Mental Deficiency*, **90,** 602–609.

Hirst, M., Suthers, G. & Davies, K. (1992) X-Linked mental retardation: the Fragile-X syndrome. *Hospital Update*, **18** (736), 42.

Janicki, M.P., Dalton, A., Henderson, M. & Davidson, P. (1999) Mortality and morbidity among older adults with intellectual disability: health services considerations. *Disability and Rehabilitation*, **21**, 284–294.

Jones, G. & Kerr, M. (1996) A randomised controlled trial of opportunistic health screening in primary care for people with learning disability – preliminary results. *Congress Abstracts: 10th World Congress of the International Association for the Scientific Study of Intellectual Disabilities*, Helsinki, 8–13 July 1996.

Kerr, M., Fraser, W., Felce, D. & Hewitt, R. (1996) A randomised controlled trial of general practice based yearly health checks for people with a learning disability. *Congress Abstracts: 10th World Congress of the International Association for the Scientific Study of Intellectual Disabilities*, Helsinki, 8–13 July.

Kirby, R.S., Kirby, M.G. & Farah, R.N. (1999) *Men's Health*. Isis Medical Media, Oxford.

Lawrenson, H., Lindsay, W. & Walker P. (1994) The pattern of alcohol consumption within a sample of mentally handicapped people in Tayside. *Mental Handicap Research*, **8**, 54–59.

Lawrenson, R., Rohde, J., Bott, C., Hambleton, I. & Farmer R. (1997) Trends in the need for services for people with learning disabilities: implications for primary care. *Health Trends*, **29**, 37–41.

National Assembly for Wales (2001) *Health Evidence Bulletin Wales: Learning Disability (Intellectual Disability)*. National Assembly for Wales, Cardiff.

Prasher, V.P. (1995) Overweight and obesity amongst Down's syndrome adults. *Journal of Intellectual Disability Research*, **39**, 437–441.

Rimmer, J.H., Braddock, D. and Fujiura, G. (1995) Cardiovascular risk factor levels in adults with mental retardation. *American Journal on Mental Retardation*, **98**, 510–518.

Rubin, S., Rimmer, J., Chicoine, B., Braddock, D., & McGuire D.E. (1998) Overweight prevalence in persons with Down syndrome. *Mental Retardation*, **36**, 175–181.

Simila, A. & Niskanen, P. (1991) Underweight and overweight cases among the mentally retarded. *Journal of Mentally Deficiency Research*, **35**, 160–164.

Strauss, D. & Eyman, R. (1996) Mortality of people with mental retardation in California with and without Down syndrome, 1986–1991. *American Journal of Mental Retardation*, **100** (6), 643–653.

Strauss, D. & Kastner, T. (1996) Comparative mortality of people with mental retardation in institutions and the community. *American Journal of Mental Retardation*, **101**, 26–40.

Tracy, J. & Hosken, R. (1997) The importance of smoking education and preventative health strategies for people with intellectual disability. *Journal of Intellectual Disability Research*, **41**, 416–421.

Epilogue

Health is a matter of right, not privilege. People with intellectual disabilities in every country should enjoy equal opportunities for good health. These principles express nothing less than self-determination, the right of an individual to shape the life she or he wishes to lead. To make effective decisions about their own health, women need information specific to their needs at each stage of the life span.

Today's trends point to a bright albeit challenging future for women with intellectual disabilities. Greater longevity will be coupled with greater presence in everyday life – if social and health systems in each country implement policies of social inclusion and non-discrimination. As women live longer, they will become more visible as family members, neighbors and co-workers. A wealth of social roles signals more diversified opportunities, more freedoms, more normalized aspirations. The fact that some women may not already be prepared for richer personal and social lives should lead to creative approaches to lifelong learning rather than fresh threats to their autonomy.

The next generation of women with intellectual disabilities will write their own history. More will be equipped with educational and employment achievements. They will more frequently express hopes and dreams similar to those of their peers. As their voices emerge and strengthen, women will increasingly shape the supports they need to live healthy lives. Fewer will bear the marks of segregated, institutional living – removal from gender, from family, from culture. But new sources of risk for abuse and mistreatment may arise. Vigilance and monitoring on the part of women and their advocates will be crucial in striking a balance between risk and autonomy. Professional workers should be able to rely on opportunities for continued professional development throughout their careers to ensure that their skills are responsive and refreshed.

As health interventions move away from prevention to promotion, greater attention will focus on the interplay of the individual and the environment. A contextual approach takes into account the cultural, social and economic factors helping to determine health, as well as strategies for encouraging individuals to learn effective health behaviours. Family members, professional workers, health professionals and policy-makers too, must learn to meet women's distinctive health needs. Concerted, specific action founded on scientific evidence will help to create change at systems level.

Other volumes in this series explore the factors conducive to healthy aging – physical and biobehavioral – for men and women with intellectual disabilities. This book ends as it began with a call to recognize that health is a state of living, not a commodity, and that promoting health for all is a shared investment to be welcomed, not begrudged.

Index